THE ANNOTATED
I CAUGHT CRIPPEN

EX-CHIEF INSPECTOR WALTER DEW

THE ANNOTATED
I CAUGHT CRIPPEN

MEMOIRS

OF

EX-CHIEF INSPECTOR

WALTER DEW, C. I. D.

OF SCOTLAND YARD

EDITED WITH
AN INTRODUCTION AND NOTES

BY

NICHOLAS CONNELL

MANGO BOOKS

LONDON

MANGO BOOKS
18 Soho Square, London W1D 3QL
www.mangobooks.co.uk

First published 2018

ISBN: 978-1-911273-31-8 (hardback)
ISBN: 978-1-911273-32-5 (ebook)

THE ANNOTATED
I CAUGHT CRIPPEN

CONTENTS

———

I CAUGHT CRIPPEN : MEMOIRS OF

EX-CHIEF INSPECTOR WALTER DEW, C.I.D. OF SCOTLAND YARD

ACKNOWLEDGEMENTS

W HEN I first wrote about Walter Dew in *Walter Dew: the Man Who Caught Crippen*, I remarked that the text of Dew's book *I Caught Crippen* was a word-for-word reprint of an earlier newspaper series. This hasty conclusion came after checking several dozen random paragraphs of the book against the series that had appeared in *Thomson's Weekly News*. Some years later, I needed to obtain a missing page from my copies from the bound volumes of the English edition of *Thomson's* held at the British Library. The cheaper and quicker option was to make the copy from the microfilm of the Scottish edition of *Thomson's*. Upon seeing this, it was noticeable that the two newspaper editions were slightly different, and upon a closer comparison with the book text it became clear that a word-for-word examination was required to see what else Walter Dew had to say about his most famous cases. To quote the late crime historian Jonathan Goodman, who had a great interest in the Crippen case: "I must write about the case again, contradicting some of what I wrote before."[1]

I would like to thank Adam Wood at Mango Books for taking on this project. Also, Lynne Burton, Viveen Chin, Stewart Evans, David Green, Jon Ogan, the late Richard Whittington-Egan and David Worrow sr. for their valuable contributions. Mark Ripper and Lindsay Siviter kindly proof-read the final manuscript and made numerous excellent suggestions on how to improve the book, for which I am very grateful. Walter Dew's granddaughters, the late Kathleen Arthur and the late Heather Odgers, supplied me with useful and interesting information, much of it obtained from recordings of family reminiscences made by their elder cousin Noel who knew Walter Dew for years.

---

1   Goodman, *Masterpieces of Murder* (2005), p. 4.

The British Library, Cambridge University Library, Hertfordshire Archives and Local Studies, Islington Local History Centre, the National Archives, Tower Hamlets Local History Library, the University of Glasgow Archives Service and Worthing Library provided their usual sterling service during the research.

*

Nicholas Connell has written extensively on Walter Dew and Dr. Crippen, including *Walter Dew: The Man Who Caught Crippen* and *Doctor Crippen: The Infamous London Cellar Murder of 1910*. He is also the co-author (with Stewart P. Evans) of *The Man Who Hunted Jack the Ripper: Edmund Reid-Victorian Detective*.

NOTES ON THE TEXT

———

THE main text is a transcription of the book *I Caught Crippen* by Walter Dew, published in 1938 by Blackie & Son. The contents of the book had previously been serialised in *Thomson's Weekly News*, which published both an English and Scottish edition. The two newspaper editions consulted were the bound copies of *Thomson's Weekly News* held at the British Library. Any notable differences between the text of the book and the newspapers are recorded in the footnotes.

When both editions of *Thomson's Weekly News* contained the same change from the book it is noted as *TWN*. If a change only appeared in the English edition of *Thomson's* it is noted as *ETWN* and if the Scottish edition of *Thomson's* contained a unique change it is noted as *STWN*.

Minor changes in punctuation and capitalisation between the book and newspaper versions have not been noted. Nor have obvious typographical errors in the newspaper version, although typographical errors in the book are highlighted to show that they are not mistakes in my transcription of *I Caught Crippen*. Such errors in any substantial work are almost unavoidable, and I take full responsibility for any of my own that made it into the final proofs. Other trivial changes in the texts—for example, "taking a chance" being replaced by "taking the chance", "walking on the deck" instead of "walking on deck", and "would expect" instead of "could expect"—have not been recorded in the footnotes.

I Caught Crippen was not a conventional autobiography and the biographical details about Walter Dew were scattered throughout the work. Rather than write a concise biography of Dew in the introduction of this work, the biographical details in the text have been expanded in the footnotes to avoid repetition.

All the transcriptions throughout the book use the punctuation and grammar from the original publications, which accounts for some inconsistencies that appear.

In the third part of Dew's book, *From Pitch and Toss to Murder*, some additional details about the cases were obtained from www.oldbaileyonline.org and the criminal registers that are now searchable at www.findmypast.co.uk. All other sources consulted are cited in the footnotes and bibliography.

Abbreviations

ETWN–English edition of *Thomson's Weekly News*.

ICC–*I Caught Crippen* by Walter Dew.

NBT–Notable British Trials, *The Trial of Hawley Harvey Crippen*, ed. Filson Young.

PRO–Public Record Office documents held at the National Archives.

STWN–Scottish edition of *Thomson's Weekly News*.

TWN–*Thomson's Weekly News*.

UGAS–University of Glasgow Archives Service.

INTRODUCTION

———

SINCE its publication in 1938, *I Caught Crippen*, by retired Detective Chief Inspector Walter Dew, has been an important source of information for crime historians. Dew was a young detective constable in the East End of London during the unsolved Jack the Ripper murders of 1888. His final case in 1910, as a Scotland Yard detective chief inspector, was the trans-Atlantic chase and capture of Dr. Crippen who murdered his wife in North London. Dew's accounts of these cases were the lengthiest ever written by a police officer involved in their investigations. A third section of the book covered a variety of other crimes which Dew solved during his twenty-eight-year career with the Metropolitan Police. Today the book is a scarce and valuable collector's item, copies of which sell for hundreds of pounds and more still with a dust jacket.

Walter Dew joined the Metropolitan Police in 1882 after working as a railway porter. He served all over London, beginning as a uniformed police constable in the Paddington Division where he spent five years. Then he was transferred to the notorious Whitechapel Division for eighteen months. To his relief, he was transferred back to Paddington in December 1888, where he was promoted to the rank of sergeant in 1889 and remained until 1894. A transfer to Scotland Yard and promotion to inspector followed. In 1900 he became the head of C.I.D. at the Hammersmith Division and three years later went to the Bow Street Division. Dew's final transfer was back to Scotland Yard in 1906, where he spent the remainder of his career as a detective chief inspector, investigating crimes throughout the country.

When Dew retired from the police in 1910, aged forty-seven, he ran "Dew's Detective Agency" for around eighteen years.[1] Towards

---

1   Initially he worked from home at 16 Allfarthing Lane, Wandsworth. When he acquired an

the end of his time as a private detective he began to write and in 1926 had an article published in the *Daily Express* about his capture of Dr. Crippen.[2] This was followed by several articles in national newspapers in which he gave his opinion on the high-profile police investigations of the day.[3]

What was Dew's motive for putting pen to paper? The *Daily Express* article was the winning entry in a writing competition with a £100 prize, so financial gain may have been the incentive in that instance. Dew would also have been paid for his other journalism, but he was in receipt of a police pension, valued in 1910 at £238 5*s*. 8*d*. a year[4] and had received monetary rewards as a police officer. Furthermore, he had won large sums in damages in a series of libel victories in 1911 against nine newspapers that had made bogus claims about his conduct in the Crippen investigation.[5] Dew does not appear to have lived extravagantly in his retirement, his main hobby being gardening,[6] but his circumstances had changed after moving to a small cottage in Worthing on the south coast in 1928.

That year the widowed Dew married Florence Idle, the widow of a store assistant. In doing so, he became the stepfather to her two children, Iris and Leslie. Iris had formerly worked as a shorthand typist, but was struck down with *encephalitis lethargica*, more commonly known as "sleepy sickness."[7] A worldwide epidemic had occurred in the 1910s and 1920s, affecting millions of people, with over one million dying from the condition. Many survivors

---

office, Dew placed an advert for the agency: "Mr. Walter Dew. Pensioned Chief Inspector, C.I. Dept. World-wide reputation and experience. Inquiries of every description and the most delicate character undertaken. Secrecy assured.–50, Buckingham Palace-road, London, S.W. Telephone 7067 Victoria." (*The Sunday Times*, 19 July 1914). His business was listed at Buckingham Palace Road until 1922 and at 25 Ebury Street from 1923–29 in London telephone directories.

2   See Appendix 1

3   *Ibid.*

4   PRO, MEPO 21/39.

5   For details see Connell, *Walter Dew: the Man Who Caught Crippen* (2006), pp. 210-218. Dew may have used some of this money to buy "The Nook" in Perivale Lane, Greenford, Middlesex, for which he paid 200 guineas cash in 1911. (Goodman, *The Crippen File*, p. 90). The house had eight rooms and more than half-an-acre of grounds. (*The Daily Telegraph*, 16 August 1962).

6   A photograph of Dew in his garden appeared in a newspaper in 1913 under the headline "CRIMINAL TRACKER AS GARDENER." (*ETWN*, 30 August 1913).

7   Not to be confused with sleeping sickness, caused by the bite of an infected tsetse fly.

lost all ability to move or speak, despite being conscious. Iris may have known she had caught the disease shortly before she wrote her will in 1923. When some of Dew's family visited him in 1931 they described her as a "complete invalid."[8] Perhaps Dew needed more money to help to care for Iris until her death at the age of forty-eight in 1946. However, there may have been more to Dew's writing than it being just an additional source of income.

Referring to the Crippen case, Dew himself declared that the reason for writing his memoirs was to "leave behind an authoritative record of the biggest case I was privileged to handle while an officer at the Yard."[9] It would also have put his name back in the public eye. Dew might have found it difficult to adjust from being the most celebrated and written about detective in the world after arresting Crippen to becoming a private detective, working discreetly[10] and without the acknowledgement and praise from magistrates, judges and senior police officers to which he had become accustomed.[11] Perhaps it was a desire to be remembered for his great achievement, being the man who caught Dr. Crippen, a fact he managed to include in most of his articles.

However, Florence Dew's description of Walter contradicts this conjecture. She said that her husband had been publicity shy and always reluctant to write for newspapers when they approached him. He was: "A philosopher", and he "despised money." Dew never spoke to Florence about his work and "was such a modest man that it was not until we had been here [Worthing] for some considerable time that the news got around that he was the famous ex-Chief Inspector Dew who caught Crippen. He was entirely devoted to his

---

8   Email from Kathleen Arthur to author, 28 August 2005. Iris may have recovered slightly as her death certificate described the *encephalitis lethargica* as "Past" and gave the primary cause of death as "Cerebral Degeneration." Despite her condition, Iris still appeared on the Worthing electoral register from 1929-1945.

9   *ICC*, p. 7.

10   Dew's name did get into a newspaper in 1919 when he was employed by Lieutenant Donald Musselwhite who suspected his wife Muriel of adultery. Dew had been keeping Muriel under observation and discovered she was having an affair with Major Harold Barnes. Dew and Musselwhite confronted the pair *in flagrante delicto* at the Grand Hotel, Dawlish. Dew had to prevent his client attacking Barnes and the story of the incident and subsequent divorce appeared in *The Times*, 2 December 1919.

11   These acknowledgements were a source of pride for Dew who frequently referred to them in his book.

home and did not mix in any of the social life of the town or join clubs. His pastimes were gardening—he had a wonderful garden which was his pride and joy—reading and walking."[12]

THE NEWSPAPER MEMOIRS

Whatever the reasons were for Dew writing his reminiscences, they were originally published in the Saturday tabloid newspaper *Thomson's Weekly News* (which sometimes went under the name of *The Weekly News*). By 1934 D.C. Thomson, who had published the title since 1855, had offices in Dundee, London, Glasgow and Manchester. Their numerous publications enjoyed a weekly circulation of over three and a half million copies.[13]

Thomson's Weekly News was published in both an English and Scottish edition. Their pages were filled with stories of crime, show business, society gossip, sports results, letters to an agony aunt, fiction serials and popular song lyrics. It was never without a sensational non-fiction series, often featuring confessions from a variety of colourful people; deserters from the French Foreign Legion, film stars, spiritualist mediums, retired criminals, aristocrats who had fallen on hard times, tales of rags to riches and riches to rags, white slavery and opium dens. Another mainstay of the paper was serials about infamous historical crimes and retired detectives' memoirs.[14] Walter Dew's story would have satisfied two of *Thomson's* criteria; thrilling tales of detection and the exploits of notorious criminals. In Dew's favour, he had investigated the two biggest names of all: Dr. Crippen and Jack the Ripper.

Dew's memoirs were divided into three parts and published over a three-year period. First there was *The Whole Truth About the Crippen Case*, published over seven weeks from 15 September—27

---

12   *Worthing and District Review*, January 1948. Although Florence claimed that Dew's identity was not known in Worthing for years it had been revealed in a local newspaper that Dew was "now a Worthing resident, with a house in Beaumont-road" the year after he moved there. (*Littlehampton Gazette*, 16 June 1929).

13   *The Newspaper Press Directory* (1935), p. 197.

14   Although published on a different day, *Thomson's* was a good example of what George Orwell described in his 1939 novel *Coming Up For Air*: "But the editors of the Sunday papers had grasped that people don't really mind whether their murders are up to date and when there was no new murder on hand they'd hash up an old one, sometimes going as far back as Dr. Palmer and Mrs. Manning."

October 1934. *My Hunt For Jack the Ripper* followed as a nine-part series published between 19 January–16 March 1935. The final instalment was *From Pitch and Toss to Murder*,[15] a selection of Dew's other cases, published over eight weeks. In the English edition of *Thomson's* they appeared from 4 July–22 August 1936. The Scottish edition ran the series a week earlier.

It is not known whether Dew approached the newspaper with a view to publishing his reminiscences or if they asked him first,[16] but it would appear that Dew had originally only planned to write about Crippen and the success of that led to *Thomson's* asking for more.[17] The Jack the Ripper series was announced as "ANOTHER breath-taking series of revelations by the man who caught Dr Crippen",[18] and the following year *From Pitch and Toss to Murder* was advertised with "EX-CHIEF Inspector Walter Dew is again to write for "Thomson's Weekly News""[19] suggesting that they had been written separately.

There were differences between the English and Scottish newspaper page layouts and sub-headings. Words were changed here and there while sentences and paragraphs sometimes appeared in one but not the other. However, these changes may have been made by a sub-editor to make the articles fit on the page, rather than by Dew himself.[20]

I CAUGHT CRIPPEN THE BOOK

Dew secured a book publishing deal for his complete memoirs with Blackie & Son Ltd. of London and Glasgow, with Christy

---

15   Pitch and Toss being a game involving throwing pennies at a wall, with the coin landing nearest winning.

16   Unfortunately, the archives of D.C. Thomson are uncatalogued and unavailable for public consultation. (email from Barry Sullivan, D.C. Thomson archivist, to author, 6 November 2015).

17   If Dew's memoirs had all been written at once *Thomson's* could probably have published them all in one go. They had published extremely lengthy series before, including one by Crippen's mistress Ethel Le Neve that ran for twenty-three weeks in 1920–21.

18   *STWN*, 12 January 1935.

19   *ETWN*, 27 June 1936.

20   *Thomson's* had no qualms about altering the text of *The Whole Truth About the Crippen Case* when they quoted from it in Dew's obituary. Dew was described as the "Ace detective of his time" in the article. (*STWN*, 20 December 1947).

& Moore Ltd. of London acting as his literary agent.[21] On 12 January 1938 Dew signed a contract for the book which was to be called *I Caught Crippen–Memoirs of Ex-Chief Inspector Walter Dew of Scotland Yard*. When published, the title changed slightly to *I Caught Crippen Memoirs of Ex-Chief Inspector Walter Dew, C.I.D. of Scotland Yard*. The terms of the contract stipulated a £100 payment to Dew on the day the book was published in advance of royalties.[22] Once that sum had been earned, Dew would receive a royalty payment of 12½% on the first 1,000 copies, 15% on the next 2,000 and 20% on any sales above that. If a cheaper edition was published at a later date that retailed for less than 50% of the price of the original hardback (12s. 6d.), then Dew would receive a 10% royalty.[23]

The publisher requested at least twelve illustrations be sent to them by 31 January, but the book contained only four photographs. These were a portrait photograph of the author, the exterior of Crippen's house (39 Hilldrop Crescent), Dew escorting Crippen off the *Megantic* ship at Liverpool and Crippen and his mistress Ethel Le Neve in the dock at Bow Street Magistrates' Court.[24] This was in stark contrast to the newspaper version which had been heavily illustrated with photographs of Dew throughout the years, drawings and photographs of characters from the Crippen case and six original sketches of incidents from the Jack the Ripper story.

Dew delivered the manuscript promptly, and on 30 March Blackie & Son sent a copy of the proofs to their solicitors, McClure Naismith Brodie & Co. of Glasgow, for them to check for any potential libellous content. They replied that they had noticed:

> one or two points which had occurred to us on our reading of the proof but we do not know that there is anything in them provided the statements made

---

21   They also represented George Orwell.

22   UGAS, ACCN 3633/2. Presumably Dew was the sole author of the work and it hadn't been partly ghost written by a *Thomson's* journalist as he was the only recipient of the advance and royalties.

23   *Ibid.* A cheaper edition was never published.

24   None of the photographs were new. Dew's portrait had been published several times in the *TWN* series. The Hilldrop Crescent photograph had appeared in *The Daily Graphic* (15 July 1910), and the other two photographs featured in many newspapers in 1910. The photographs were not credited, so it is not clear whether they were Dew's own copies or if he had obtained them from a press agency.

by the Author are true, which, of course we have no means of ascertaining. On the whole we would say that from our reading of the proof there would be no serious risk from the point of view of libel in publishing the Book as in the proof.[25]

Blackie & Son wanted more reassurance and asked the solicitor:

Regarding the point you raise as to the truth of the statements made by the author in this book we, like yourself, have no means of ascertaining whether they are true or not. We have no reason whatever to doubt the good faith of the author and, in addition, we have a contract with him in which he guarantees that the work contains nothing of a libellous character, as well as the usual indemnification clause.

It seems to us that he can give us no stronger guarantee than this, even were the point put to him again in the form of a letter.

With this in view, do you confirm that we shall be running no serious risk from the point of view of libel in publishing the book as in the proof?[26]

The solicitor replied:

We note that you, like ourselves, have no means of ascertaining whether the statements in the Book are true or not, but that you have no reason whatever to doubt the good faith of the author, and in addition have a contract with him in which he guarantees that the work contains nothing of a libellous or scandalous character as well as the usual indemnification. As we have already said we can, of course, give no guarantee, but our view remains that you, as Publishers, have taken all reasonable precautions, and there would not appear to be any serious risk from the point of view of libel in publishing the Book as in the proof which we read.[27]

Their fears allayed, Blackie & Son published *I Caught Crippen* on 19 May 1938. It contained many minor—and several more significant—changes to the text that had appeared in the newspaper serialisation. Some of these changes were just correcting typographical errors, or making new typographical mistakes that

25 UGAS, ACCN 3633/2. Dew was aware that the veracity of his work might be questioned. He told a journalist: "There is an old saying that truth is stranger than fiction. I can't help thinking that when some people read these stories, although I have minimised them, they will toss their heads and say they never happened." (*The Worthing Herald*, 10 June 1938).

26 *Ibid.*

27 *Ibid.*

only appeared in the book. There were differences in spelling, most obviously with the book replacing many uses of the letter "s" with "z", (for example, criticized instead of criticised), and "c" with "x", (such as connexion rather than connection). This was probably just the publisher's style, as were the variations in capitalisation and punctuation. Had Dew made the other more substantial changes himself, or had the publisher insisted on them? Perhaps some of the people mentioned in the newspaper series had read it and raised issues with Dew who amended the book accordingly.

I Caught Crippen included a new prologue that gave a brief history of Dew's early life. The Crippen section consisted of six chapters, while the newspaper series had been in seven parts. Dew's hunt for Jack the Ripper was told in nine chapters, each one reflecting a week of the newspaper serial. *From Pitch and Toss to Murder* had an additional chapter about one of Dew's old cases, which may have been written to meet a required word count, and a brief epilogue. The other eight chapters were the same as the eight-part newspaper series.

Dew explained the title for final section of the book:

> "From pitch and toss to manslaughter" is a saying sometimes used to illustrate the limits of crime.
>
> As far as my own career is concerned, it is more accurate to say "Pitch and toss to murder", for at one time and another I have arrested persons for every offence it is possible to commit under the criminal law.[28]

The tales Dew selected were not arranged in chronological or thematic order and only represented a tiny proportion of the cases he had dealt with. They included stories about manslaughter, blackmail, murder, fraud and coining.

Dew withheld the names of the people involved in the cases, or only identified them by an initial. He did give names in two cases; those of fraudster Henry Clifford and jewel thief Harry the Valet/ William Johnson, but these were their aliases and their real names were not revealed. This seems overly discreet as they had all been named in the newspapers which had reported the crimes. One hint

---

28   *ICC*, pp. 213-214. Coincidentally Dew also used the phrase in the book to describe how a boat he was on "pitched and tossed" on rough seas. (*Ibid.*, p. 203).

Dew gave to explain this was that he didn't write about a particular murder case, "lest it should give pain and annoyance to some of the relatives, or those associated with the cases."[29] Fortunately Dew left enough clues, such as his rank at the time and the location of the crimes, to now identify the individuals involved.

WALTER DEW'S MEMORY

It is difficult to know exactly how much of *I Caught Crippen* was written from memory, although Dew told a journalist that "most of it was."[30] He prided himself on having an excellent memory, declaring that [during the Whitechapel murders]: "One of my chief assets then–and, indeed, through the whole of my police career–was a splendid memory. I made notes, of course, sometimes lengthy ones as to what prisoners said on arrest, but it was rarely indeed that I made use of my notebook when giving evidence."[31] When *I Caught Crippen* was published, Dew's daughter Kate, who had married and moved to South Africa, was interviewed by the *Natal Daily News*. She described her father's memory as being "still faultless. I think it is remarkable that a man of 75 who has led a life so varied and exhausting should be able to recall so many details of his experiences."[32] Dew's wife Florence concurred: "He had a wonderful memory and did not have to refer to any of the notes he made of the Crippen case and other matters."[33]

At the start of his account of the Whitechapel murders Dew suggested that this part of the book was written from memory and excused any mistakes by saying: "In writing of the "Jack the Ripper

---

29   *Ibid.*, p. 241. Dew had no such reservations when writing about the Crippen case when he did name names. Perhaps this was because it was such a well-known story that to withhold the names would have been pointless.

30   *The Worthing Herald*, 10 June 1938.

31   *ICC*, p. 140.

32   *Natal Daily News*, 12 November 1938. The article stated that Kate had helped her father write the book. Dew had a copy of the article pasted into a scrapbook. In the margin he wrote: "Quite incorrect. No such assistance was ever given or asked for." He also revealed his political leanings by adding: "I was not aware that my daughter's husband was a member of the Labour party, of whom I am not in sympathy." (*I Caught Crippen* scrapbook. See footnote 48 for details). Dew read the Conservative supporting *Daily* and *Sunday Express* newspapers. He was also a Freemason, having joined the Dalhousie Lodge in Hounslow in 1891. (www.ancestry.co.uk).

33   *Worthing and District Review*, January 1948.

crimes", it must be remembered that they took place fifty years ago, and it may be that small errors as to dates and days may have crept in."[34] They had, so why hadn't Dew consulted sources on that case which could have eliminated these errors?[35]

Much of Dew's Ripper reminiscences could have been written from memory. On several occasions Dew indicated that they were. "If I remember rightly it was on a Saturday morning," wrote Dew about the murder of Ripper victim Annie Chapman.[36] It had been on a Saturday morning, and he was correct again when he recalled the time that the murder of Mary Kelly was reported: "If I remember rightly it was between ten and eleven o'clock in the morning."[37] He was also able to recall many other trivial facts such as the address and nightly charge of Ripper victim Mary Ann Nichols' lodging house.[38]

These examples, among others, suggest that Walter Dew possessed a good memory long into his retirement. But could Dew have remembered so much of, for example, the three alleged Jack the Ripper letters that he quoted (albeit with slight changes)–the Dear Boss and Portsmouth letters and the Saucy Jack postcard–without consulting a source?

Dew must have referred to the *Notable British Trials* (*NBT*) volume on the Crippen case which was published in 1920 and included Dew's name in the acknowledgements.[39] In *I Caught Crippen* Dew wrote nearly four pages of Crippen's initial statement to the police which had appeared in full in the *NBT*. That book must have been the source for Dew's truncated transcription, his trial quotes and the precise transcriptions of two of Crippen's letters that appeared in both *I Caught Crippen* and the *NBT*. But again there is evidence that Dew was relying on a good memory. When

---

34   *ICC*, p. 85

35   A lack of reliable published sources on the Whitechapel murders available at that time could
      have been the reason. However, there are similarities between parts of *My Hunt For Jack the
      Ripper* and *When the People Were in Terror*, a lengthy series about the Whitechapel murders by
      journalist Norman Hastings, published in *Thomson's* over eight weeks between September-
      November 1929.

36   *ICC*, p. 113.

37   *Ibid.*, p. 143.

38   *Ibid.*, pp. 107-108. But he did get her age wrong. Dew thought she was thirty-eight, but she
      was forty-three.

39   *NBT*, p. vii.

he quoted from a card he found on Crippen when he arrested him, Dew remembered that it read, "II (there were two I's)."[40] This is confirmed by a photograph of the card that appeared in a later book[41] and a transcription of the note in the case files,[42] but the *NBT* transcription only had one I.[43]

Another example of Dew's good memory featured in *From Pitch and Toss to Murder* when Dew recalled from an 1891 case that umbrella thief Mary Reynolds' height was recorded as 5 ft. 6 or 7 in the 1891 "persons wanted" list (admitting that there were other trivial details "which I have now forgotten.")[44] This was verified in a Scotland Yard Convict Supervision Office Illustrated Circular which gave her height as 5 ft. 6 in.[45]

However, the details about Archibald Johnstone's criminal background tally closely with press reports. In *I Caught Crippen* Dew wrote:

His name had certainly been registered as a student at one of the halls, but on the Vice-Chancellor discovering his true character his name had been expunged.

For a considerable time he had lived in Oxford, where he swindled many hotel-keepers.

One of his dirtiest tricks was to steal money and a gold watch from a governess, and then threaten to accuse her of immorality if she exposed him. He never paid his landladies, and on one occasion he had behaved indecently towards his landlady's daughter.

Only once had he found his way into the dock. Then he was acquitted on a charge of indecent assault.[46]

A contemporary newspaper account of Johnstone's trial reported:

he never paid his landladies for his board or lodging. At one of his lodgings he behaved with great indecency to a landlady's daughter... He

40   *ICC*, p. 46.
41   Browne & Tullett, *Bernard Spilsbury*.
42   PRO, CRIM 1/117, Exhibit number 12, has two Is. However, the transcription in PRO, DPP 1/13 (Ex.2) only has one.
43   *NBT*, p. 46.
44   *ICC*, p. 168.
45   Hertfordshire Archives and Local Studies, HPF/H/21.
46   *ICC*, p. 188.

was tried at the assize for an indecent assault, but acquitted. He duped a governess of a gold watch and some money, and when she asked for her property back he threatened to accuse her of all sorts of immorality. He had got his name entered at St. Mary's Hall as a student, but on his character being ascertained the Vice-Chancellor ordered his name to be expunged.[47]

These similarities suggest that Dew consulted old newspaper cuttings when writing parts of his book. In his retirement Dew employed a newspaper cuttings agency (The General Press Cutting Association in London) to send him any references that they found about him. He possessed a scrapbook of cuttings concerning *I Caught Crippen*.[48] Had Dew collected and kept articles about his earlier cases? He was a newspaper reader and made his first wife iron his newspapers before he read them.[49]

After so many years, there were inevitably times when Dew's memory failed him, such as remembering a victim of theft as a colonel instead of a captain,[50] and calling Alfred Crow Albert Crow.[51] There are also examples of more significant lapses in Dew's memory. He could not "definitely remember" if he had arrested fraudster Conrad Harms in 1909, but thought that he had along with Sergeant James Berrett at the hotel where Harms was staying. Neither Dew nor Berrett made the arrest. Harms had been staying at a hotel, but the arrest had not taken place there. Dew covered himself by saying that he genuinely could not remember and did not want to take the credit for somebody else's arrest.[52]

In his study of the Crippen case, *Supper With the Crippens*, David James Smith raised the possibility that Dew had taken credit

47   *Bristol Mercury*, 18 August 1886.
48   The scrapbook contains reviews of *I Caught Crippen* from newspapers around the world, and other articles from around the time of its publication. For years it was in the collection of crime historian Jonathan Goodman (1931-2008), and is now in the Jonathan Goodman papers at Kent State University Special Collections and Archives (Box 2/Folder 4). In a conversation with the author, Goodman expressed an opinion that Dew may have had more scrapbooks like it on different topics, but admitted that this was just a hunch and he had no proof. The antiquarian book dealer Eric Barton (1909-1997), recalled the scrapbook, which he had "bought for three shillings through the trade but sold again soon after." (*Great Newspapers Reprinted*, no. 8, London, 1972).
49   Email from Kathleen Arthur to author, 23 August 2005.
50   *ICC*, p. 238.
51   *Ibid.*, p. 98.
52   *Ibid.*, pp. 193-194.

From: jacqueline murphy via PayPal <service@paypal.co.uk>
Subject: **Payment received from jackie_murphy@hotmail.com**
Date: 27 January 2018 13:06:01 GMT
To: Adam Wood <paypal@mangobooks.co.uk>
Reply-To: jacqueline murphy <jackie_murphy@hotmail.com>

P PayPal

27 Jan 2018 13:05:51 GMT

Transaction ID: 7HY27174SU337813T

Dear Mango Books Limited,

You received a payment of £24.00 GBP from (jackie_murphy@hotmail.com).

To see all the transaction details, please log in to your PayPal account. It may take a few moments for this transaction to appear in your account.

Buyer information
jacqueline murphy
jackie_murphy@hotmail.com

Instructions from buyer
None provided

Delivery information:
jacqueline murphy
4 Challacombe House
Poundbury
Dorchester, Dorset
DT1 3SW
United Kingdom

Delivery method:
Not specified

Description	Unit price	Qty	Amount

(UK)

Postage and packaging: £4.00 GBP
Total: £24.00 GBP

Postage and packaging charges are estimated rates.
Postage and packaging is based on the fall back rates you provided.

Receipt No: 4066-5608-4095-0659

Please keep this number for future reference, as your customer doesn't have a PayPal Transaction ID for this payment.

? If you have any questions, use our Help Centre at: www.paypal.com/uk/help.

Thanks for using PayPal - the safer, easier way to pay and get paid.

Please do not reply to this email. This mailbox is not monitored and you will not receive a response. For assistance, log in to your PayPal account and click Help in the top right corner of any PayPal page. To change your Notifications preferences, log in to your You can choose to receive plain text emails instead of HTML emails. To change your Notifications preferences, log in to your PayPal account at www.paypal.co.uk, go to your Profile, and click My account settings.

for a colleague's work. It was widely believed that Inspector Dew discovered the remains of Cora Crippen at 39 Hilldrop Crescent when he pushed a poker between two bricks on the cellar floor which loosened them. Yet, as Smith correctly pointed out, Sergeant Arthur Mitchell, who was with Dew when the remains were discovered, wrote in a report: "I dug the poker between two of the bricks in the centre of the floor. I loosened and removed them, and Chief Inspector Dew then dug the floor up, and uncovered some pieces of human remains as described."[53]

There were several reports made by the detectives about the discovery of the remains. Dew wrote that "on probing about the brickwork of floor, we found that some of them could be more easily moved than others. I therefore removed the bricks."[54] In another report Dew gave joint credit: "We then got a small poker and tested various parts of the flooring of the basement and probed about the brickwork of the cellar, and in doing so the poker, which has a thin point, went in between two of the bricks, which became loosened and Sergeant Mitchell and I then removed several bricks."[55] In his inquest deposition Dew said: "I again went there and made further examination and got a small poker and probed about in the cellar. I found a place where the poker went in and removed portions of bricks."[56] Mitchell deposed: "I was always with him [Dew] on his visits and confirm Inspector Dew's evidence in every way as to those visits and I was present on 13th July when the remains were found."[57] He also wrote a report stating: "I was present when the Chief Inspector found the human remains."[58]

So when Dew took full credit for the discovery in *I Caught Crippen* and at Crippen's Old Bailey trial he may have remembered events correctly. The contemporary evidence is not consistent enough to say otherwise. It seems unlikely that Dew was deliberately trying to undermine Mitchell's contribution. Such behaviour would appear to be out of character, for throughout *I Caught Crippen*

---

53 Smith, *Supper With the Crippens* (2005), pp. 144-145. Mitchell's statement was made on 7 September 1910. (PRO, DPP 1/13).

54 PRO, DPP 1/13. Dew's application for a warrant against Crippen and Le Neve, 16 July 1910.

55 *Ibid.* Report written by Dew, 5 September 1910.

56 *Ibid.* Dew's statement made on 12 September 1910.

57 PRO, CRIM 1/117. Mitchell's statement made on 26 September 1910.

58 *Ibid.* Mitchell's statement made at Bow Street Magistrates' Court, 8 September 1910.

he frequently acknowledged and credited colleagues for their assistance.

However, *I Caught Crippen* contained one striking example of Dew taking credit for something he did not do. In 1903 he investigated a distressing case when Edith Kersley abandoned her infant daughter in a field, where she died of exposure. Dew wrote about talking to Kersley during house-to-house inquiries before taking her to the mortuary to identify the body of the girl whom he believed to be her daughter:

> As long as I live, I shall never forget that experience. This woman entered the mortuary with me, and, without betraying a trace of emotion, gazed on the peaceful face of the little victim.
>
> She took one of the cold little hands in hers as she said: "Poor little dear. It is not my child. I have never seen her before."[59]

Yet in the Old Bailey trial transcript it was Detective Sergeant William Hailstone who described speaking to Kersley at her home and taking her to the mortuary, where she denied the child was hers. He then informed Inspector Dew what had happened. Other mistakes, such as forgetting Kersley had twin daughters, made Dew's account of the case in *I Caught Crippen* feel like an amalgamation of what he and Hailstone had done.

In spite of this peculiar discrepancy, and even if Dew had used some printed sources to supplement his memory, *I Caught Crippen* is broadly accurate when checked against surviving contemporary sources, although often wrong on precise details and dates. *I Caught Crippen* was a book of its time and not written with the more stringent standards of accuracy expected from today's publications. It was not a scholarly reference work, but began life as a series in a tabloid newspaper which had to satisfy a readership who expected sensational tales of crime and detection. That being the case it is perhaps fortunate that it turned out as accurately as it did.[60]

In his book *Crippen: The Mild Murderer*, Tom Cullen was possibly correct when he wrote: "More nonsense has been written

---

59   *ICC*, p. 177.

60   *Thomson's* was not particularly concerned about the accuracy of their stories. Parts of Ethel Le Neve's memoirs which they published in 1920-21 and 1928 were pure fiction.

about Hawley Harvey Crippen than about any other murderer with the possible exception of Jack the Ripper."[61] However, Walter Dew's *I Caught Crippen* did not fall into that category. Overall the book contained much more good and useful information than dubious, exaggerated and self-justifying material.

THEMES OF THE BOOK

The leitmotif of *I Caught Crippen* was how hard Walter Dew and his colleagues worked. With almost tedious regularity he informed the reader of the long hours they put in at all hours of the day and night. This was probably because it was true and Dew's main memory of being a police officer was how much hard work it had involved. He wasn't looking for sympathy when he reminded readers that during the Whitechapel murders:

Ordinary crime not only continued unabated, but actually increased. Every day people were robbed and assaulted, and the knife was freely used.

One would have thought that in the circumstances, these lesser criminals would have joined the fight against the common enemy. Unfortunately for the hard-pressed police they did not do so.

We *were* hard pressed.[62]

Dew reiterated his point that the Ripper murders were "an added burden thrust upon a body of men already grievously overworked. Other crimes were being committed and other criminals had to be hunted."[63] Yet despite being worn out from overwork, Dew and his colleagues were always quick to react and take action whenever a crime needed solving.

Walter Dew clearly possessed a sympathetic nature. He often described victims of crime (and sometimes the criminals) as "poor" and was "always forcing myself to remember that an arrested person is innocent until proved guilty. I was human enough, too, to feel that the poor devil had enough to put up with without circumstances being made deliberately worse for them."[64] In 1910 he informed Chief Constable Trevor Bigham: "I have always made it a practice

61   Cullen, *Crippen: The Mild Murderer*, p. 23.
62   *ICC*, p. 125-126.
63   *Ibid.*, pp. 101-102.
64   *Ibid.*, p. 214.

to treat prisoners with courtesy & consideration no matter what their position in life."[65]

However, his sympathy only extended so far and was largely reserved for the victims of crime. When Rose Bailey was arrested in 1891 for stealing two shillings from her employer at the Portobello Tavern, Notting Hill, she burst into tears and begged Dew to let her off "for the sake of her mother." Dew replied "they all had mothers, and he had a wife and family, and he must charge her." Bailey was sentenced to six weeks' hard labour.[66] One night in 1906, Dew was on Waterloo Bridge at midnight when he saw a young woman crying. The concerned detective followed her and saw her climb the parapet. He was just able to seize her in time before she could jump into the River Thames and then promptly arrested her for attempting to commit suicide.[67]

Once found guilty, Dew thought the criminals deserved everything they got: "I had the pleasure of seeing scores of them sentenced to long terms of imprisonment and lashes with the cat. I say I saw this with pleasure, for had I not seen the suffering of many of their victims?"[68]

Dew might have written that he too had suffered. He was no stranger to physical violence and accepted it as "part of the price to be paid."[69] Dew recalled: "I have been assaulted over and over again, but this was almost without exception when I was arresting a violent prisoner."[70]

In 1884 a drunken Charles Edwards knocked Dew to the ground as he tried to take the reins of a horse away from him. They both rolled over on the ground until P.C. Nunn came to assist (being struck three times himself). The two officers had to carry Edwards to the police station face downwards.[71] Two years later Dew was punched to the ground by powerfully built brass finisher Henry Caster who he had caught begging. Dew got up and tried to seize Caster, but was punched between the eyes and knocked down again.

---

65   PRO, MEPO 3/198.
66   *The Standard* (London), 30 March 1891.
67   *The Daily News* (London), 12 May 1906.
68   *ICC*, p. 89.
69   *Ibid.*, p. 213.
70   *Ibid.*, p. 214.
71   *The Standard* (London), 21 March 1884. Edwards was fined £4 for the assault and 50s. for the damage he did to a cab.

Undeterred, Dew pursued and caught Caster, only to be knocked down a third time. A man came to assist Dew, but Caster threw him off and hurled Dew against a wall before flooring him a fourth time and kicking him when he was down. The one-sided struggle ended when a passing fireman intervened and Caster was arrested. Dew, with a visibly swollen face, saw Caster sentenced at the Marylebone Magistrates' Court to six months' hard labour.[72]

After a house was broken into and robbed in 1892 Dew and some colleagues went to The George beerhouse in Notting Hill to arrest three suspects. The men struggled violently while a crowd in the beerhouse attempted to rescue them from the police. Dew was thrown to the ground, kicked and dragged along some distance before the police managed to get their prisoners to the police station.[73]

One evening in August 1897 Dew saw Francis Bertrand and another man on the Victoria Embankment. He knew Bertrand was wanted for stealing £16 from the hotel he worked at. When Dew told Bertrand he was going to take him into custody he was set upon by the two men. Dew attempted to summon assistance by blowing his whistle, but Bertrand knocked it down his throat. Dew, who was in plain clothes, retrieved it and managed to throw the whistle into the crowd who had gathered to watch the brawl. He asked for somebody to blow it, but no one did. Bertrand then bit two of Dew's fingers "and generally behaved like a madman." Eventually somebody came to help the exhausted Dew who managed to drag Bertrand to Scotland Yard.[74]

There was danger lurking around every corner, even if it did not always result in a brawl. When Dew confronted Archibald Johnstone in 1886 he saw that:

A tall man was standing at a mirror with a razor in his hand. He turned round as I entered and though his face was half-hidden by a copious covering

---

72 *The Weston Mercury*, 27 February 1886. The report suggested that Dew was working in plain-clothes as he had to tell Caster that he was a police officer and was described as a detective.

73 *The West London Observer*, 1 October 1892.

74 *The Illustrated Police News*, 4 September 1897; *The Times*, 11 September 1897. Bertrand was sentenced to six months' hard labour for the theft with another three months for assaulting Dew.

of lather, I recognized him at once as the gentleman I had formerly seen in the Westbourne Grove district.

With an open razor in his hand, and his powerful athletic build–he was much bigger than I was–looked a formidable customer. If he cut up rough, I thought to myself, I am going to have a job. I had not even my truncheon with me.[75]

The jewel thief Harry the Valet "had the reputation of being a desperate character, capable of violence if driven into a tight corner. Knowing this, one of the other inspectors–I think it was Froest–brought along a revolver."[76] Fraudster Conrad Harms "certainly had a loaded automatic in his possession, and was a particularly ill-tempered and dangerous subject."[77] Dew even suspected that the mild-mannered Dr. Crippen "had a loaded revolver in his pocket, and that revolver would have been used upon Mitchell and myself had we made the find which Crippen feared."[78]

The references to violence and danger in *I Caught Crippen* were not just included to make the stories more dramatic; policing London really was hazardous. It is impressive that, despite the long hours and dangerous nature of his work, Dew only took two or three weeks off sick in over twenty-eight years, and these were due to influenza and minor complaints.[79]

Fiercely protective of his reputation, Walter Dew's sensitivity to personal criticism was evident throughout *I Caught Crippen*. He always defended himself against what he called "my irresponsible critics" who had no knowledge of police procedure.[80] Dew had no time for what he described as "Senseless criticism of so-called police inefficiency."[81] He staunchly defended Scotland Yard and the police in general, although there was one exception when he suggested they should have employed the assistance of the press during the Ripper investigation.[82]

---

75   *ICC*, p. 186.
76   *Ibid.*, p. 233.
77   *Ibid.*, p. 193.
78   *Ibid.*, p. 22.
79   *Police Review and Parade Gossip*, 30 December 1910.
80   *ICC*, p. 78.
81   *Ibid.*, p. 124.
82   *Ibid.*, p. 102.

CASES NOT INCLUDED IN THE BOOK

I Caught Crippen was not a traditional autobiography, nor was it a comprehensive review of Dew's career. Contemporary criminal court registers and newspapers show the huge variety of other crimes Dew investigated; shootings, attempted murder, bigamy, drunk and disorderly, forgery, abduction, housebreaking, embezzlement and, perhaps strangest of all, defrauding women by pretending to be recruiting a team of female cricketers to tour Australia.[83]

There were more murders besides those committed by Crippen and Jack the Ripper, "many others, brutal ones all of them."[84] Some of the cases Dew did not record in his memoirs included that of Henry Williams who cut the throat of his five-year-old daughter Margaret in 1902. Williams believed the girl's mother, Ellen Andrews, had low morals and had been unfaithful with a sailor. He told Detective Inspector Walter Dew of the Hammersmith Division: "I did kill my lovely daughter to save her from becoming a prostitute. It is not many men who would have had the heart to do it but I bleeding well did and now I shall hang for it. I did it to save my old woman from putting her in bed with other men." An Old Bailey jury found him guilty of murder, but recommended the judge show mercy "on account of the somewhat honourable motive he had of saving the little girl from a life of prostitution."

The judge spoke to Dew who had investigated the condemned man's background. Despite being a heavy drinker, it appeared that Williams had been sober when he murdered the girl. There was some evidence of hereditary insanity as two of his sisters had been patients in lunatic asylums. However, Dew ascertained that there were tangible reasons for their incarcerations; one had an unhappy love affair and was only there briefly and the other had been ill-treated by her husband.

Williams had twice been charged with drunken assaults on police officers. He had stood trial for stabbing a man (which was declared accidental for lack of clear evidence) and there were suggestions that he had links with housebreakers and coiners. When courting

---

83 *The Times*, 3 July 1894. For this imaginative fraud Alphonse Redfern received ten months' hard labour.

84 *ICC*, p. 241.

his wife he boasted he had never done a day's work in his life and never intended to. After four months of stepping out she resisted his advances and he responded by hitting her in the face, throwing her to the ground and raping her, saying that she would have to marry him now and that he would kill her mother if she told her they were getting married. Williams regularly beat his new wife, refused to do any work and suggested she become a prostitute to support him. He later left her and moved in with Ellen Andrews and her daughter, also named Ellen. They all slept in the same bed and in 1898 Williams was found guilty of raping the daughter who was aged fourteen. Andrews thought he had been doing so for two years, but as she had allowed her daughter to share the bed for all that time Williams was only bound over.

Upon learning this, the judge could now guess the meaning of Williams's words: "Do you think I can let my little Maggie sleep with another man as I did with her daughter?" When Williams had slept with Ellen Andrews and her daughter, he raped her. He feared that would happen to Margaret if Ellen lived with another man. There were no grounds for mercy. Henry Williams was executed on 11 November 1902.[85]

In 1903 Thomas Washington Gibbs argued with his fiancée, Bridget McQuaid, and cut her throat with a knife. He was taken to North Fulham police station where Detective Inspector Walter Dew charged him, while "his shirt was saturated with blood, and there was blood also on his trousers and braces." Gibbs was sentenced to death, but this was commuted to life imprisonment after the jury recommended mercy on account of his age (he was twenty-one) and previous good character. Gibbs proved to be a model prisoner and was released on licence in 1915.[86]

While a detective inspector at Bow Street in 1905, Walter Dew received information that a murder had taken place at 37 Compton Street. Attending the scene, he found the body of forty-four-year old Catherine Ballard "lying in a pool of blood. Her throat was cut." She had been killed by her daughter's former fiancé, Albert Bridgman. His motive was that she had called him a bastard and to him this cast an unacceptable aspersion upon his mother's character. When

85   PRO, HO 144/678/101552.
86   PRO, CRIM 1/86/3; CRIM 1/582/25; HO 144/983/110126.

charged by Dew at Hunter Street police station, the unrepentant labourer, still wearing bloodstained clothing, replied: "I am ready to swing when the time comes." Bridgman was executed on 26 April 1905.[87]

In 1908 Detective Chief Inspector Walter Dew of Scotland Yard was sent to Salisbury to investigate the murder of twelve-year-old Edwin Haskell whose throat had been cut while he lay in bed at home. His mother Flora was found guilty of his murder at the coroner's inquest and magistrates' court. The jury at her assize trial were unable to agree on a verdict and she was declared not guilty after a retrial. Dew "was absolutely satisfied that Mrs. Haskell herself had committed a pre-meditated, coldblooded murder." His colleague, Superintendent Frank Froest, said Dew "performed his duty with marked skill and ability" and thought it "more than surprising that the jury should have acquitted this woman."[88] Perhaps this was the case Dew referred to when he mentioned having been "sent to a distant town to investigate a most fiendish murder, which left a lasting impression on my mind."[89]

It is not surprising that, having spent the best part of three decades dealing with the worst type of crimes and criminals, Dew took it as a compliment when "a highly-connected woman" who liked to attend court cases said to him: "I like to talk to you, Mr. Dew, because you are one of the few men I know who has had to handle pitch who has not become besmirched."[90]

REACTIONS TO *I CAUGHT CRIPPEN*

Upon its release *I Caught Crippen* was advertised by the publisher as "a classic in criminology." It was widely reviewed.

---

87 PRO, CRIM 1/97/4.

88 PRO, MEPO 3/187. For a study of the Haskell case See Moody & Purvis, *If I Did It... I Don't Remember* (2008).

89 *ICC*, p. 241. One notorious murderer Dew did not meet, but investigated, was Samuel Herbert Dougal who was executed in 1903 for the murder of Camille Holland at Moat Farm, Clavering in Essex. In 1895 Dougal was in custody at Watlington, Oxfordshire, on a charge of larceny. The Oxfordshire Constabulary asked the Metropolitan Police if they had any information about Dougal from when he lived in London. Dew established where Dougal had lived but found he had "always behaved himself in a respectful and quiet manner, and nothing is proven to his prejudice." (PRO, MEPO 3/159B).

90 *Ibid.*, pp. 61-62.

Howard Gray wrote in *The Observer*: "Mr. Dew has an admirable style for the tales of crime he has to unfold–easy, natural, and completely free from catch-words or the strain of literary affectation." His account of the Whitechapel murders "is here powerfully recalled without any sensational word-painting."[91] The *Daily Mail* found the book "very readable,"[92] while *The Daily Telegraph*'s reviewer "enjoyed his book immensely" particularly *From Pitch and Toss to Murder*, because "Inspector Dew tells these stories amusingly and well."[93]

Time and Tide was very complimentary, writing: "These are not varnished reminiscences but plain, sober, accounts, and Mr. Dew is evident in his book as a kindly, hard-working officer." The *News Chronicle* called it "an absorbingly interesting book" and *The Scotsman* was similarly impressed: "This is a fascinating book for readers interested in criminology. His account of the celebrated case can be accepted as the authoritative version."[94] The book was reviewed as far afield as Australia, where the New South Wales *Daily Telegraph* called Dew, "a good detective, and he's a good story-teller... First class drama."[95]

Dew's local newspaper, *The Worthing Herald*, heaped flattery on the book which "makes more thrilling reading than half-a-dozen best-sellers, simply because it is an unvarnished tale of sensational happenings. The material for a hundred shockers is given in the straightforward and objective language of a man whose training has taught him a respect for fact.

Mr Dew's natural economy of words has given his work an effect which a novelist might envy."

The town's other paper, the *Worthing Gazette*, called it "a fascinating book: having once started to read it, amateur criminologists will find it hard to put it down. "I Caught Crippen" makes more vivid and more dramatic reading than much fiction."[96]

Not all reviews were so favourable. *The Sunday Times*

91 *The Observer*, 29 May 1938.
92 *Daily Mail*, 26 May 1938.
93 *The Daily Telegraph*, 27 May 1938.
94 UGAS, ACCN 3633/12. These reviews were cited in Blackie & Son's general literature catalogue for 1939-40.
95 Undated cutting in Walter Dew's *I Caught Crippen* scrapbook.
96 *The Worthing Herald*, 24 June 1938; *Worthing Gazette*, 15 June 1938.

acknowledged that Dew's "narrative kills a few legends about minor details, but adds little to our knowledge of one of the most baffling men who ever died at the end of a rope." Their reviewer was unimpressed by Dew's "support to another myth always inspired by sex murders–that Jack the Ripper had a mysterious attraction for women. Surely we need find no such romantic explanation for the readiness of hungry middle-aged drabs to walk down an alley in the dark."[97]

The *Western Mail* reviewer found *From Pitch and Toss to Murder* to be the most enjoyable part of the book. Its chapters were "sufficiently good to fill an ordinary book, and I thought he devoted too much space to the Crippen case and the Jack the Ripper crimes. The facts have been so oft told that they tend to lose interest. Mr. Dew could have spread himself more on the pathological side of the investigations, which were intensely interesting, and also on the small points of detection, such as the pyjama clue, which needed so much work on such a small, but vital piece of evidence."[98]

The book received further publicity in a one-page feature in *The Evening News* on the day it was published,[99] but despite being extensively reviewed and advertised *I Caught Crippen* was not a best seller. It was never reprinted and ended up being reduced in price.[100] Walter Dew died on 16 December 1947 and his will stipulated that his youngest daughter Dorothy should receive any further royalties from his written works. In April 1948 a note was added to this effect to Dew's author agreement with Blackie & Son, possibly suggesting that there were still unsold copies of the book at that date.[101]

Other than firing off a couple of angry letters to newspapers over what they had written about the Crippen case[102] it seems that

---

97   *The Sunday Times*, 19 June 1938.

98   *Western Mail*, 7 June 1938.

99   *The Evening News* (London), 19 May 1938.

100   The cover price of the book was 12s. 6d. The author's copy has an "offered at 10'6" sticker on the spine and crime historian Richard Whittington-Egan (1924-2016) bought his in 1938 for 1s. 6d. from Boots in Liverpool, although this was an ex-library copy from their lending library. However, it was described as "best-selling" in one of Dew's local newspapers. (*The Worthing Herald*, 8 June 1945).

101   UGAS, UGD 61/6/1/4. An alternative reason for this could be that her details were needed in case the book was ever reprinted.

102   See Appendix 1.

Dew was satisfied that his version of events had been told and he was content to spend more of his time gardening.

If it was Dew's wish to be remembered in posterity then he achieved it. Obituaries appeared in numerous newspapers.[103] Furthermore, he has an entry in the *Oxford Dictionary of National Biography* and has appeared as a character in novels and films.[104] Of course, there was a huge element of chance in Walter Dew's posthumous fame. If he had not been stationed at Whitechapel in 1888, or been away on the day that Cora Crippen's disappearance was reported at Scotland Yard, Dew may have ended up a being one of the many former Metropolitan Police detectives spending a well-earned, but largely anonymous, retirement on the coast. However, his involvement in two of the most famous murder cases in British history, and his willingness to write about his experiences, means that his name will be remembered and his words quoted for as long as books and articles continue to be written and documentaries made about Dr. Crippen, Jack the Ripper and the history of Scotland Yard.

---

103   See Appendix 2. In 1946 Dew wrote to his grandson Noel and told him that he had opened his newspaper one morning and seen his own obituary. He went to the *Daily Express'* office and told them that the obituary was premature. (email from Kathleen Arthur to author, 1 October 2005). This story was not found during a search of the *Daily Express* digital archive and *Sunday Express* microfilms. However, in 1945 Dew did go to the offices of *The Worthing Herald* and asked them to inform their readers that he was still alive and well after having seen himself described as "the late" Chief-Inspector Dew in an evening newspaper. (*The Worthing Herald*, 8 June 1945).

104   For a list of these see Connell, *Walter Dew: the Man Who Caught Crippen*, (2006), pp. 248-250. Waxwork effigies of Walter Dew and Crippen appeared fleetingly in the 1951 film *The Lavender Hill Mob*.

WALTER DEW CHRONOLOGY

———

1863	Born at Far Cotton, Northamptonshire.
1873	Moved to London.
1876	Left school and worked for a solicitor and then as a clerk.
1877	Joined L.N.W. Railway as a junior porter.
1882	Joined the Metropolitan Police.
1882	Stationed at X Division, Paddington.
1884	Death of father Walter.
1886	Married Kate Dew.
1887	Transferred to H Division, Whitechapel and became a member of the C.I.D.
1887	Birth of son Walter.
1888	Involved in the hunt for Jack the Ripper.
1888	Transferred to F Division, Paddington.
1889	Promoted to sergeant (3rd class).
1891	Birth and death of son Raymond.
1891	Birth of daughter Ethel.
1893	Birth of son Stanley.
1894	Transferred to Scotland Yard and promoted to sergeant (2nd Class).
1895	Birth of daughter Kate.
1896	Promoted to sergeant (1st class).
1898	Promoted to inspector (2nd class).
1900	Transferred to T Division, Hammersmith.
1903	Birth of daughter Dorothy.
1903	Promoted to inspector (1st class).
1903	Transferred to E Division, Bow Street.

1906	Transferred to Scotland Yard and promoted to chief inspector.
1910	Captured Dr. Crippen.
1910	Retired from the Metropolitan Police.
1910-1928	Worked as a private detective.
1911	Won substantial damages in a series of libel cases.
1914	Death of mother Eliza.
1915	Death of son Stanley.
1927	Death of wife Kate.
1928	Retired and moved to Worthing, West Sussex.
1928	Married Florence Idle.
1934	Publication of Crippen memoirs in *Thomson's Weekly News*.
1935	Publication of Jack the Ripper memoirs in *Thomson's Weekly News*.
1936	Publication of *From Pitch and Toss to Murder* in *Thomson's Weekly News*.
1938	Publication of autobiography *I Caught Crippen*.
1947	Died and buried at Worthing.

Walter Dew at his writing desk.
(Thomson's Weekly News)

Advertising poster for Dew's newspaper memoirs.
(David Worrow Sr.)

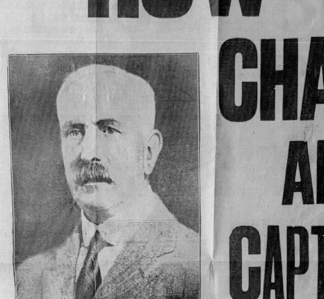

HOW I CHASED AND CAPTURED
DR. CRIPPEN
By Ex-Chief Inspector Dew
THOMSON'S WEEKLY NEWS

SCOTLAND YARD'S BIGGEST MURDER HUNT.

The Whole Truth
ABOUT THE
Crippen Case
by
EX-CHIEF INSPECTOR WALTER DEW

Ex-Chief-Inspector Dew.

Chief Inspector Dew is the man who chased and caught the notorious Dr Crippen and Miss Ethel Le Neve.

was in charge of the case from the time of the disappearance of Belle Elmore, Crippen's actress wife, up to Crippen's arrest and trial for murder.

For the first time ex-Chief Inspector Dew reveals the facts of the amazing murder mystery which thrilled the world twenty-four years ago. Every move in the case is laid bare.

This week the great detective told how the case was first brought to the notice of Scotland Yard by friends of Belle Elmore. They had been told by Crippen that she had died in California, but they were not satisfied.

Chief Inspector Dew visited Crippen and took from him a long statement which purported to explain his wife's disappearance.

It was quite late in the evening when Sergeant Mitchell and I, after examining 39 Hilldrop Crescent, said good-night to Crippen and Miss Le Neve.

It had been a gruelling day for both. We had been on the go early that morning.

I was dog tired, yet sleep I could not. My mind refused to rest. Events of the day kept cropping up.

Was that behind it all? There was something, I now felt sure. Crippen had a secret which he was strangely trying to hide. There could be no rest for me until I found out.

It has been stated in print that following the happenings of day my inclination was to go on with the inquiry on the ground that I was satisfied with the man's explanation.

I got some valuable information bearing on the flight from a dental mechanic employed by the firm. He told me that when he arrived at the office just before nine on the Saturday morning Dr Crippen, to his surprise, was already there.

He asked Crippen if there was any trouble. He replied, "Only a little scandal."

Crippen then did a strange thing. He sent the mechanic out to buy clothing for a "boy." The order was for a brown tweed suit, a brown felt hat, two shirts, two collars, a tie and a pair of boots.

"I look the parcel to the back room on the third floor," the man told me. "There was nobody there at the time. The room is shut up on Saturdays."

Quarry Had Gone.

The purpose of these purchases is now well known. Sometime during that Saturday morning Miss Ethel Le Neve, at the suggestion of Crippen, repaired to the back room and transformed herself into a "boy." Then when all was quiet, she joined Crippen and the pair of them slipped unobserved through one of the rear exits. That same day they travelled together to the Continent.

My quarry had gone, but the manner of his going pointed to guilt.

My view was that a completely innocent man with nothing to fear would have seen the thing through. A man of Crippen's calibre would certainly have done so. I had already seen enough of him to know that he was not the type to do anything foolishly rash.

Here was the first real clue.

His decision was a sudden one. Of that I felt convinced. A fair deduction seemed to be that he had been scared by the events of Friday.

The flight of Crippen and Miss Le Neve created a big sensation. The newspapers featured it. It was the talk of the country.

I came in for criticism. Certain people with a knowledge of police procedure and less of the law blamed me for allowing

Belle Elmore.

CRIPPEN HAD FLOWN. MISS LE NEVE WAS ALSO MISSING. PRETTY OBVIOUS THE COUPLE HAD GONE AWAY TOGETHER.

39 Hilldrop Crescent.

I got the big news from Dr ——, Crippen's partner in the dentistry business.

Dr —— was probably more surprised than I was. Only that morning he had received the following letter which told its own story:

"*Dear Dr ——, I now find that in order to escape trouble I shall be obliged to absent myself for a time. I believe that with the business as it is now going you will run on all right so far as money matters go . . . I shall write you later on more fully. With kind wishes for your success.—Yours sincerely, H. H. Crippen.*"

THERE WAS UP TO THIS TIME NO SHRED OF EVIDENCE AGAINST CRIPPEN UPON WHICH HE COULD

HAVE BEEN ARRESTED OR EVEN DETAINED. FUTILE TO TALK OF ARRESTING A MAN UNTIL YOU KNOW THERE HAS BEEN A CRIME.

No person can be charged with murder unless the body, or some portion of the body, or some very strong evidence that murder has been committed, is available.

The first thing I did was to cause a full description of Belle Elmore to be circulated right throughout the country.

Why not of Crippen and Miss Le Neve? That was still impossible. Although their running away pointed strongly to guilt in some form or another, we still lacked the evidence to bring any charge against them.

After talking over the new development with Superintendent Frank Froest, I took Mitchell with me and set out once more for Hilldrop Crescent. The house was now empty. The French maid had gone. I had got the key from the landlord.

I was eager to lose no time. Crippen's absence was in one way a great advantage. It gave me great scope. I now had the free run of the house. No Crippen at my elbow to hamper me and perhaps throw me off the scent.

If Crippen Had Stayed.

If Crippen had stood his ground and continued to live quietly at Hilldrop Crescent my difficulties would have been infinitely greater. Maybe the mystery would never have been solved, for with nothing more definite than suspicion to go upon it would have been exceedingly difficult to get the necessary sanction to make a thorough search.

The proof of the value to me of Crippen's blunder lies in the result. Within forty-eight hours of my receiving the news that he had gone I had found the remains of Belle Elmore in the coal cellar.

During this time Mitchell and I returned to the house again and again. We searched the building from top to bottom, combing every room and examining every nook and cranny of the gardens.

At first our quest seemed hopeless. The only evidence found bearing at all on Mrs Crippen's disappearance was the advertisement which Crippen had written out in my presence offering a reward of twenty-five dollars for information leading to the discovery of his wife.

There was one place in the house which had a peculiar fascination for me. This was the coal cellar. I have already described its location. It was at the end of a short dark passage leading from the kitchen to the back door.

It might well be asked why I concentrated so persistently on the coal cellar. I have asked myself the same question hundreds of times.

If, as I must confess, I was now beginning to suspect, Belle Elmore had been murdered, there was nothing at all to suggest that the crime had been committed at the house. Indeed, from the facts as then known and following the thorough searches I had made, it seemed more than probable that Crippen must have done away with her elsewhere.

Perhaps it was instinct. Anyway, that cellar stuck in my mind. Even in bed, what little I got of it during those hectic days, I couldn't keep my mind from wandering back to the cellar.

Mitchell and I had been making inquiries in the neighbourhood of Camden Town. We were both completely tagged out. Both of us had been on the go for two whole days and the greater parts of two nights.

My personal inclination was to go home and sleep for twenty-four hours. But that was impossible. It would remain impossible so long as the mystery of Mrs Crippen remained unsolved.

Let us go along to the house and have another go at the cellar, I said to my companion.

Armed with a poker. With this I worked away, too tired to say a word.

Presently a little thrill of excitement went through me. The sharp point of the poker had found its way between two of the bricks and one of them showed signs of lifting.

I toiled away more hopefully now, all sense of fatigue vanishing in the excitement of hope. The brick came out. Then another, and another. After this my work became easy.

Body Discovered.

Mitchell ran to get a spade from the garden. While I worked steadily for a few minutes. Then came evidence unmistakably unmistakable. The stench was unbearable, driving us both into the garden for fresh air.

I WAS NOW AS EXCITED AS I EVER ALLOWED MYSELF TO BE. I KNEW THAT I WAS ON THE EVE OF A GREAT DISCOVERY. WHAT WE HAD FOUND ALREADY COULD MEAN ONLY ONE THING, AND THAT WAS MORE THAN ENOUGH TO ACCOUNT FOR THE SUDDEN FLIGHT OF DR CRIPPEN. WHEN WE HAD SUFFICIENTLY RECOVERED WE RESUMED OUR TASK AND THIS TIME WE STUCK THE PUTRIFIED ATMOSPHERE LONG ENOUGH TO UNEARTH A LARGE PIECE OF WHAT I EASILY RECOGNISED TO BE HUMAN REMAINS.

Again we had to fly, and before re-entering the cellar a third time both Mitchell and I were fortified with a long drink of brandy which I sent for.

I knew that I had solved the mystery. What other explanation could there be of the presence in Dr Crippen's coal cellar of the parts of a human body?

I sent for the Assistant Commissioner, Sir Melville Macnaghten, and for Dr Thomas Marshall, divisional police surgeon for the Kentish Town district. I also sent for assistance in the further excavation of the cellar.

When the Assistant Commissioner and the doctor had arrived the work was resumed. The whole floor of the cellar was dug up.

We found only masses of human flesh. The head was missing. No bones were discovered. Identification seemed impossible.

Dr Crippen.

Continued on Page Four

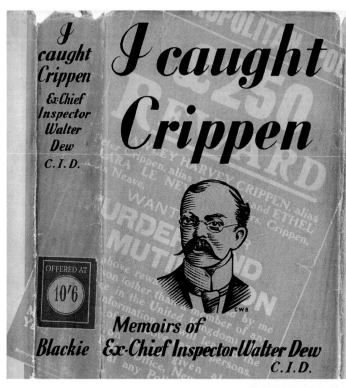

IN his long experience at Scotland yard, ex-Chief Inspector Walter Dew has met with every kind of crime, from Pitch and Toss to Murder. In telling of his most interesting cases he takes the reader behind the scenes and shows just how the C.I.D. man goes to work.

He is the man who caught Crippen. He was in charge of the case from the time of Belle Elmore's disappearance up to the time of Crippen's arrest and trial, the only man in a position to know all the facts of the case. In this book these facts are revealed; every move is laid bare. Then there was the most terrifying killer of all time— Jack the Ripper, the phantom-like fiend who stalked the streets of Whitechapel and terrorized the whole of the East End of London. Inspector Dew was the first policeman on the scene of one of these ghastly murders, and he tells how clue after clue was followed up and how near the police were to laying their hands on the probable murderer.

Shorter accounts of many other crimes—fraud, blackmail, coining, burglary—are included in this vivid account of Inspector Dew's life at Scotland Yard.

12s. 6d. net

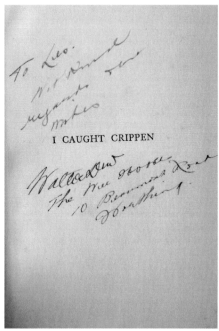

Autographed copy of I Caught Crippen.
(Stewart P. Evans)

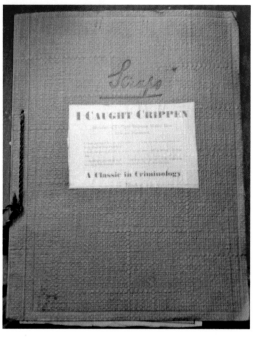

Dew's scrapbook of newspaper cuttings.
(Author's collection)

I CAUGHT CRIPPEN

MEMOIRS

OF

EX-CHIEF INSPECTOR

WALTER DEW, C. I. D.

OF SCOTLAND YARD

Dedicated

To the Memory of my son Stanley (Tom),[1]

23rd London Regiment,

Killed in action at Givenchy, May 1915

To my Daughters, Ethel, May, and Dorothy[2]

To F. for encouragement and help[3]

---

1 Walter Dew's youngest son (b. 1893). He worked as an insurance company clerk before the War. Dew's eldest son Walter (b. 1887), was not on the list of dedicatees, but was mentioned later on in the book. Another son Raymond (b. 1891), died aged seven months.

2 Dew's three daughters; Ethel (b. 1891), May (b. 1895 as Kate May), and Dorothy Bertha (b. 1903), known as "Dot".

3 This must be Dew's second wife Florence whom he married at Broadwater parish church, West Sussex, 10 December 1928. Florence "encouraged him to go forward with the project after offers had been made to him." She also read and corrected the galley proofs of the book. (*Worthing and District Review*, January 1948). Florence survived Dew by almost nineteen years, dying on 17 July 1966, aged ninety-one, at St. Leonard's Hospital, St. Leonards and St. Ives, Hampshire.

PROLOGUE[1]

A LTHOUGH I was born at a place called "Far Cotton" Northampton,[2] my father[3] belonged to an old yeoman family of Ledbury, in the charming county of Herefordshire, and my mother was a Norfolk woman,[4] whose one occupation in life seemed to be bringing up eleven children.[5]

When I was ten years old we migrated to London, and I candidly confess that, for some reason or other, I had an instinctive dread of the London policeman, which lasted more or less until I became one myself.

I detested school, and was an absolute dud there, and promptly left when I attained the ripe age of thirteen.

My first job was in a solicitor's office off Chancery Lane, and I frequently had to go to the old Law Courts at Westminster.

My master acted for the late Dr. Kenealy, a man who figured largely as a supporter of Arthur Orton, who called himself, and claimed to be "Roger Tichborne", and eventually received fourteen years' penal servitude in connexion with his fraudulent claims. I frequently met Dr. Kenealy, who then lived in Russell Square, and a most charming man he was.[6]

---

1   This prologue was not in the newspaper serialisation.
2   Dew was born on 7 April 1863 and baptised on 24 May at Hardingstone parish church.
3   Also named Walter Dew. He died in London on 2 April 1884, aged sixty-two, of renal disease.
4   Eliza Dew. She died on 21 September 1914 aged eighty-two. In all the census returns she gave her place of birth as Ireland.
5   Dew's siblings were George Walter (b. 1850), Elizabeth Mary (b. 1852), Lucy Sarah (b. 1855), George Richard (b. 1857), Eliza Helen (b. 1859), Roderick Harry (b. 1861), Ralph Walton (b. 1865), Alice Edith (b. 1867), Flora Adelaide (b. 1869) and Francis Arthur (b. 1872). Walter was the only one without a middle name.
6   Edward Kenealy (1819-1880), an Irish barrister and Arthur Orton (1834-1898), the "Tichborne Claimant." Orton fraudulently claimed to be the heir to the estate and title of Roger Tichborne, who had been declared lost at sea in 1854. Kenealy acted as his leading counsel from 1873 in a case that dragged on for years.

After a year I got fed up with the solicitor's office, and obtained a job as junior clerk at a great seedsman's in Holborn, where, after a few months, I got the "sack" for absenting myself for several hours, when, in my dinner hour, I saw the roof of the old Central Criminal Court on fire, I ran to the nearest fire station, gave the alarm, secured a ride on the manual, and boy-like, stayed watching the fire; little thinking that in years to come I was fated to give evidence there in many famous trials.

My real love was, however, the railway service, my father being an old London-and-North-Western guard, and I obtained service with that company, and for some years enjoyed every day of it.[7]

When I was nearly nineteen years old it was suggested to me that I should join the Metropolitan Police.

I scoffed at the idea, for I was just a slim sort of a youth, and never for one moment dreamed I was big enough, or could pass such a stringent medical examination as was required. However, I was prevailed upon to have a try, and in due time found myself at Great Scotland Yard to undergo a medical and educational examination.

My heart sank within me when I saw the great hefty fellows waiting for a like purpose, for I thought, what chance had I? However, this was where I began to get the first of many surprises, for I passed all right, and several of the biggest fellows got turned down.

Some days later I was summoned to attend again, and later was sworn in as a full-blown constable,[8] and directed to attend Wellington Barracks for drill the following morning, and told I should receive 15s. per week during the time I was learning my drill. This offered no difficulty to me as I had served in the volunteers.[9]

There was no Peel House or Hendon College in those days.[10] I am of the opinion that the young men of to-day would have had

7 Dew's ambition was to be a guard. (*Police Review and Parade Gossip*, 30 December 1910). He joined the L.N.W. Railway as a junior porter in June 1877 and was recorded as a railway porter in the 1881 census.

8 Dew was appointed on 12 June 1882 and given the warrant number 66711. (PRO, MEPO 4/354).

9 A volunteer military regiment. It is not known which volunteer regiment Dew was a member of.

10 "I'm glad there wasn't." Dew told an audience at a talk he gave in retirement. (*Worthing Gazette*, 19 April 1939).

a severe shock, as indeed I did, when several others and myself were directed to take up our lodgings at a coffee shop in Regency Street, Westminster, which I subsequently found was registered as a "Common Lodging House".

It is true it was kept by a pensioned constable, but I fear that made no difference to me, for on retiring for the night I found the visitors in my bed were many and plentiful, so much so that I and some of the others left, and procured fresh and nice rooms in the neighbourhood.

The next morning we were promptly hauled before the inspector at Wellington Barracks, and threatened with all sorts of pains and penalties for not sleeping (I ask you) at our lodgings, &c. When I made the complaint about the liveliness of the beds, I was promptly told I should be taken before the Commissioner, being told by one officer known as "Jumbo", that I should never make a good policeman.[11]

However, I was not taken before the Commissioner, and was told later in the day to return to my lodgings, where I should find matters improved; well they were, but there was still a certain amount of liveliness, and room for a vast improvement; but needs must when the devil drives.

I only mention these facts to compare yesterday with to-day, but I still don't know how some of my comrades lived on 15s. per week, for we had to pay just that amount at our refined apartments for board and lodging.

At the end of two weeks, with others, I was passed out of Wellington Barracks, and attended Scotland Yard to be fitted with uniform. I remember mine consisted of a thick pair of trousers, a tunic, no belt, and a helmet, without any front plate or ornament, and in this garb I walked to my lodgings in Regency Street to collect my belongings; to me it was a mile of purgatory.

In Strutton Ground I was surrounded with three or four husky coalmen, who amused themselves by asking each other, "what adjective regiment," I belonged to?

Doubtless it was funny for them, but it was sheer misery to me.

On returning to the Yard I, with four others, was placed in a

---

11   In another account Dew said that an inspector told him that "the best thing he could do was to resign, as he would never make a good policeman!" (*Worthing Gazette*, 19 April 1939).

four-wheeled cab by a somewhat pompous four-striped sergeant, and driven to the X or Paddington Green Police Station, where I was to be stationed, with a princely salary of 24s. per week,[12] which I received for a solid three years, and yet, believe me, after a few days I was quite happy and contented, as one of my companions, a Scotsman, must have been, for a few months afterwards he told me he had written home to say he was getting on all right, and was saving 15s. a week, and if it had not been for his adjective inside he would be saving a good deal more. What an optimist!

So commenced my career in the finest police force in the world. But I still retain happy memories of my railroad days.

---

12   Dew said that this was less than a dustman earned. For a time this was cut to 23s. 11d. Dew never knew the reason for the deduction. (*Worthing Gazette*, 19 April 1939).

New Scotland Yard.
(The Queen's London)

The young
Detective Constable Walter Dew.
(Thomson's Weekly News)

THE WHOLE TRUTH ABOUT
THE CRIPPEN CASE

THE WHOLE TRUTH ABOUT
THE CRIPPEN CASE[13]

I

MANY stories have been written about Dr. Crippen and his crime.

Some of them have approached the truth. Others have grossly misrepresented the facts.

As the Scotland Yard officer who handled the case from the beginning to the end, I am the only person who knows every detail of what happened, from the moment the disappearance of Belle Elmore was first reported to Scotland Yard until Crippen was condemned to death at the Old Bailey.

All these years, while others have been giving their versions from second-hand knowledge, I have remained silent.[14]

My reason for speaking now is that I feel that I should leave behind an authoritative record of the biggest case I was privileged to handle while an officer at the Yard.

It was the most intriguing murder mystery of the century.

---

13   *ETWN*, 15 September 1934, had the following introduction:

"Twenty-four years ago the world was thrilled by the chase and capture of the notorious Dr Crippen and Ethel Le Neve.

The doctor was wanted for the murder of his wife, Belle Elmore, a music-hall artiste. At his trial he was found guilty and hanged.

Ex-Chief Inspector Dew is the man who caught Dr Crippen. He was in charge of the case from the time of Belle Elmore's disappearance up to the time of Crippen's arrest and trial. He is the only man in a position to know all the facts of the case.

He reveals these facts in this series for the first time.

Every move is laid bare, and nothing more intense and thrilling has been published than the battle of wits between the shrewd police officer and one of the cleverest and most amazing personalities in the history of crime." The *STWN* introduction was very similar.

14   Although he had written a brief account of the case for the *Daily Express* in 1926. (See Appendix 1).

Think of the circumstances! The callous way in which the Doctor killed his actress wife, and the mutilation of her remains; the part played by Miss Ethel Le Neve, the "other woman" in the case; the flight of the couple with the girl dressed as a boy, and their dramatic arrest on the other side of the Atlantic.

There will never be another Crippen. There were two distinct sides to the man.

I have never entertained a doubt as to his guilt. He was, as he was proved at the Old Bailey, a callously calculating murderer.

Yet, detached from the crime, there was something almost likeable about the mild little fellow who squinted through thick-lensed spectacles, and whose sandy moustache was out of all proportion to his build.[15]

I certainly had no suspicion of the bigness of the case when the name of Crippen was first mentioned at Scotland Yard.[16]

Among the callers at the Yard on a day towards the end of June, 1910, were a Mr. and Mrs. Nash, who had just returned from America, where Mrs. Nash, under the stage name of Lil Hawthorne,[17] had completed a music hall tour.

They first saw Superintendent Frank Froest whom they knew personally.[18]

Presently a message was brought to me asking me to go along to the superintendent's room. Mr. and Mrs. Nash were still there,[19] I was introduced to the couple and the superintendent explained.

"They have called," he said, "to see me in connexion with the disappearance of a friend of theirs, a Mrs. Cora Crippen, a member of the Music Hall Artists' Guild,[20] and known on the stage as Belle

---

15   "and the sandy moustache out of all proportion to his build." in *ETWN*, 15 September 1934: "the mild little fellow with the sandy moustache out of all proportion to his build, who squinted through thick-lensed spectacles." in *STWN*, 15 September 1934.

16   "This is how it came about." added here in *STWN*, 15 September 1934.

17   "under the theatrical name of Lil Hawthorn" in *STWN*, 15 September 1934.

18   Frank Castle Froest (1857-1930), a long-time colleague of Dew's. He joined the Metropolitan Police in 1879 and retired in 1912. Dew was promoted to chief inspector at Scotland Yard in 1906 when Froest vacated that position upon his promotion to superintendent. Sometimes known as "the Prince of Detectives", Froest never smoked or drank when working on a big case and always dressed immaculately. Also known as the "Man with the Iron Hands", he could tear a pack of cards in half and break sixpences in two.

19   "Mr. and Mrs. Nash were still there" was not in *STWN*.

20   "Music Hall Artistes' Guild" in *STWN*, 15 September 1934. Its correct title was the Music Hall Ladies' Guild.

Elmore. She is the wife of a Dr. Crippen living out Holloway way.

"Mr. and Mrs. Nash are not satisfied with the story the husband has told. Perhaps you had better listen to the full story."

Mrs. Nash began by saying they were old friends of the Crippens, particularly of the wife. They had been associated with her professionally, and the two women had become greatly attached to one another.[21]

"When we got back from America a few days ago," Mrs. Nash went on, "we were told that Belle was dead.

"Our friends said she had gone suddenly to America without a word of good-bye to any of them, and five months ago a notice was out[22] in a theatrical paper announcing her death from pneumonia in California.[23]

"Naturally, we were upset. I went to see Dr. Crippen. He told me the same story, but there was something about him I didn't like. Very soon after his wife's death Dr. Crippen was openly going about with his typist, a girl called Ethel Le Neve. Some time ago they went to a dance together and the girl was actually wearing Belle's furs and jewellery.

"I do wish you could make some inquiries and find out just when and where Belle did die. We can't get details from Dr. Crippen."

What was really in the minds of Mr. and Mrs. Nash, what prompted them to seek the assistance of Superintendent Froest,[24] I cannot say, but it is quite certain that neither of them dreamt for a moment that there was anything very sinister behind the affair.

It is probable that they were actuated more than anything else by Crippen's lack of all decency in placing another woman so soon and so completely in the shoes of his dead wife.[25]

While Mr. and Mrs. Nash were still in the room, Froest turned to me and asked: "Well, Mr. Dew, that's the story. What do you make of it?"

Without a second's hesitation, I replied: "I think it would be just as well if I made a few inquiries into this personally."

Why did I not suggest that the inquiry should be handed over to

---

21   This sentence was not in *STWN*.
22   "a notice was put" in *TWN*, 15 September 1934.
23   This notice appeared in *The Era*, 26 March 1910.
24   "when they sought the assistance of Superintendent Froest" in *STWN*, 15 September 1934.
25   This sentence was not in *STWN*.

the uniformed branch or given to a subordinate?

Well, my experience as a police officer had taught me that it is better to be sure than sorry.

Supposing I had considered myself too big for such an apparently trivial job.

If I had turned the inquiry down all that could have happened was the transfer of the matter to the uniformed branch for the routine inquiries into an ordinary case of a missing person.

Then only in the event of some suspicious circumstances coming to light, would the case have been referred back to the Yard.

And even had this happened it is exceedingly unlikely that Crippen would have been trapped, for much invaluable time would have been lost.

That same day I went out alone and began my investigations into the mystery of Mrs. Crippen.

My first objective was to get into touch with people who knew most about the Crippens, and I decided that I couldn't do better than make a bee-line for the headquarters of the Music Hall Artists' Guild[26] in Albion House, New Oxford Street, the same building curiously enough in which Dr. Crippen had his offices.

I am not going to weary you with the details of all the preliminary work. I saw a lot of people and took a large number of statements. Among those I interviewed were Miss Melinda May, the secretary of the Guild;[27] Paul Martinetti, the famous music-hall star of those days, and his wife, and later Mrs. Eugene Stratton,[28] wife of the great comedian.

Most of the people I saw had heard[29] the story of Belle Elmore's death at first hand from Crippen, and had received the mourning cards he had had printed to send to his wife's friends.

Perhaps the most important discovery of all was that Mrs. Crippen had not been seen since the night of 10th January–five

---

26   "Music Hall Artistes' Guild" in *STWN*, 15 September 1934.

27   Melinda May gave evidence at Crippen's trial. She later moved to Great Yarmouth and became a recluse. When her money ran out she was admitted to the workhouse. There she became mentally unbalanced and believed she was being haunted by Dr. Crippen's ghost. She was admitted to a Norwich asylum as a pauper lunatic. (*ETWN*, 7 August 1926).

28   "as well as Mrs Eugene Stratton" in *TWN*, 15 September 1934. Her name was Annie Stratton.

29   "had had" in *STWN*, 15 September 1934.

months before–when Mr. and Mrs. Paul Martinetti were the guests of the Doctor and his wife at their home in Hilldrop Crescent.[30]

The Martinettis told me that Crippen and his wife had seemed on good terms at first, but later in the evening there had been some unpleasantness between them over quite a trifling matter. Quarrels between them, I gathered, were not infrequent.

But, taken as a whole, my inquiries had yielded little. I was no nearer solving the problem I had set myself.

I decided that the best thing I could do was to interview Crippen personally.

By this time I had called in, as an assistant, Detective-Sergeant Mitchell,[31] and he was with me at ten o'clock on the morning of 8th July, when, for the first time I knocked on the door of 39 Hilldrop Crescent.

The house was rather a large semi-detached dwelling of the old type standing well back from the road and partially screened from the street by overgrown trees.

After a minute or so a maid, who was obviously a foreigner, appeared.[32] I discovered later that she was French.

"Is Dr. Crippen at home?" I asked.

In broken English the maid asked us to step into the hall. Here there was another short wait before a young woman, whose age I guessed to be between twenty-five and thirty, came somewhat diffidently towards us. Miss Ethel Le Neve, I thought.

She was not pretty, but there was something quite attractive about her, and she was neatly and quietly dressed.[33]

One thing I spotted at once, she was wearing a diamond brooch which, from the description I had been given, I suspected had once been the property of Mrs. Cora Crippen.

"Is Dr. Crippen in?" I asked again.

"I am sorry, but he is not," the girl replied. "He is at business.

30   In fact it had been on 31 January.
31   Detective Sergeant Arthur Archibald Mitchell (1876-1929). He joined the Metropolitan Police in 1898 and retired in 1925 as a detective inspector. (PRO, MEPO 21/56).
32   Valentine Lecocq, who had been appointed on 11 June 1910. She thought Crippen and Le Neve were a married couple.
33   Le Neve later revealed her first impression of Walter Dew: "He was tall, well-dressed, and had nice eyes, but there was a very serious look in them." She thought the tone of his voice was "fatherly." (*ETWN*, 16 October 1920).

You will find him at Albion House, New Oxford Street."

And then, as a sort of afterthought, she said,[34] "I am his housekeeper, you know."

"So I assumed," I said. "You are Miss Le Neve, are you not?"

A faint flush rose to the girl's cheeks as she answered: "Yes, that's right."

"Unfortunate the doctor is out," I went on. "I want to see him rather urgently. I am Chief-Inspector Dew of Scotland Yard. Would it be asking too much for you to take us down to Albion House. I am anxious not to lose any time."

This I must confess, was a little subterfuge. I had quite another reason for asking Miss Le Neve to accompany us. If I had left her behind there was nothing to prevent her getting on the telephone to Dr. Crippen and warning him that I was on the way.

Miss Le Neve agreed to go with us[35] and excused herself while she ran upstairs to put on her things. A few minutes later we were all three seated in an omnibus bound for Tottenham Court Road.

We walked the short distance to Albion House, a big block of flats.[36]

Dr. Crippen's offices[37] I had discovered from Miss Le Neve were on the third floor. We had started to climb the stairs when the girl turned to me and said: "Please wait here, Mr. Dew. I will bring Dr. Crippen down to you."

I did not want this, but before I had a chance to stop her Miss Le Neve had darted up the stairs.

I am quite sure Miss Le Neve had no ulterior motive in forestalling us in this way. All she was thinking of was Dr. Crippen and his business. If police officers were to interview the doctor it was better, she doubtless thought, that the meeting should take place outside the offices in which he worked.

Only a few moments passed before she reappeared with an insignificant little man at her side.[38]

---

34 "she said" was not in *STWN*.

35 "Miss Le Neve seemed a little reluctant at first, but after momentary hesitation she agreed to go with us" in *STWN*, 15 September 1934.

36 "a big block of offices." in *TWN*, 15 September 1934.

37 "Crippen's offices" in *TWN*, 15 September 1934.

38 Crippen was 5 ft. 4 in. tall and weighed 142 lbs. on 23 November 1910, the day before his execution. (PRO, PCOM 8/30).

"This is Dr. Crippen," Miss Le Neve announced, and I found myself looking into the short-sighted eyes of the man who was already a murderer.

My thoughts have often gone back since to that first meeting between Crippen and myself on the stairs of Albion House. What a moment that must have been for him! The police had come. How much did they know? His mind must have been in a torment of anxiety. Yet he was as calm as I was.

I introduced myself formally.

"I am Chief-Inspector Dew, of Scotland Yard," I said. "This is a colleague of mine, Sergeant Mitchell. We have called to have a word with you about the death of your wife. Some of your wife's friends have been to us concerning the stories you have told them about her death, with which they are not satisfied. I have made exhaustive inquiries and I am not satisfied so I have come to see you to ask if you care to offer any explanation." He said, "I suppose I had better tell the truth." I said, "Yes, that would be better." He said, "The stories I have told about her death are untrue. As far as I know she is still alive." I said, "Any explanation you desire to make shall be written down in your own words and perhaps it would be more convenient if you told me all about yourself."

"Certainly, Mr. Dew. I will tell you all I know with the greatest of pleasure. You had better come into my office," said Crippen, and his voice was quiet and confident.

He took us into quite a pleasant little office on the third floor, and asked us to be seated.

Miss Le Neve left us, but she remained on the premises, and every now and then during the long hours that followed I saw her flitting to and fro with documents in her hands.[39]

---

39   *TWN*, 15 September 1934, had: "Some of your wife's friends are not quite satisfied with the explanation that has been given."

Still Crippen betrayed no fear.

"You had better come to my office Chief-Inspector," he replied, and his voice was quiet and confident.

He took us into quite a pleasant little office on the third floor and asked us to be seated.

Miss Le Neve left us, but she remained on the premises, and every now and then during the long hours that followed I saw her flitting to and fro with documents in her hands.

"My object in calling, doctor," I then explained, "is to ask whether you are prepared to make a voluntary statement with a view to clearing the whole matter up."

"Certainly, Mr Dew. I will tell you all I know with the greatest of pleasure," said Crippen.

We all sat down. Sergeant Mitchell, with pencil and paper ready, took his seat at the small table. I sat at his side, with Crippen immediately opposite me. I then began to put questions, and the doctor's answers were carefully taken down by Mitchell.

His replies came freely. There was no hesitation. From his manner one could only have assumed that he was a much maligned man eager only to clear the matter up by telling the whole truth.

I was impressed by the man's demeanour. It was impossible to be otherwise. Much can sometimes be learned by an experienced police officer during the making of such a statement.

From Dr. Hawley Harvey Crippen's manner on this, our first meeting, I learned nothing at all.

Looking back, it is quite plain to me that Crippen had anticipated my visit, or at any rate, the visit of a police officer. A clever man, he had thought out in the fullest detail the story he was going to tell.

It was an ingenious story. Half of it was true and half of it was false. His very frankness was misleading. By admitting things which in normal circumstances men like to hide from others, he hoped to convince me that he was telling the whole truth and had nothing to hide.

He was very open, for instance, about his relationship with Ethel Le Neve. He confessed that she had been living with him as his wife, that the association had begun long before Mrs. Crippen had disappeared, and admitted that while outwardly appearing to be on good terms, he and his wife had quarrelled frequently in the privacy of their home.

Sergeant Mitchell and I started to take the statement at noon. It was a big job. When lunch time came we had got little further than the introductory part of the story.

Having no intention of losing sight of the doctor, I invited him to join us at lunch. We went to a small Italian restaurant only a few yards from Albion House.

This was the only occasion on which Crippen had lunch in my company before his arrest. I mention this because, among the silly rumours which gained currency at the time was one which alleged that Crippen and I had frequently lunched together at the Holborn Restaurant. The suggestion behind this seemed to be that I had made quite a friend of the man. I had never set eyes on him before

I went to Albion House.[40]

There was not a word of truth in the suggestion. I was never in Crippen's company at the Holborn Restaurant in my life.[41]

At the Italian Restaurant to which we did go Crippen made a hearty meal. He ordered beefsteak[42] and ate it with the relish of a man who hadn't a care in the world.[43]

In all Crippen's statement took something like five hours to take, and he showed himself to be most willing to help. That of course he knew would be a point in his favour.

Crippen's whole statement was so long that it is impossible here to give more than the body of it.

First the doctor traced his early career. "I am forty-eight years of age," he said. "After being questioned by Chief-Inspector Dew as to the statement[44] made by me that my wife, known as Belle Elmore, is dead, I desire to make a voluntary statement to clear the whole matter up.

"I was born at Cold Water, Michigan, U.S.A., in the year 1862, my father being Myron Augustus Crippen, a dry-goods merchant. My mother's name was Andresse Crippen, née Skinner.

"I was educated at Cold Water,[45] Indiana and California, and then entered the university at Michigan until I was about twenty, and finished my education at the Hospital College at Cleveland, where I took the degree of M.D. . . .

"My first wife died, so far as I can remember, in 1890 or 1891.[46] We were living at Salt Lake City, where I was practising as an eye and ear specialist. . . ."

There were further details of Crippen's career and work before

---

40   This last sentence was not in *TWN*.

41   Dew's colleague Cecil Bishop claimed to have known Crippen socially, having often encountered him at the Holborn Restaurant where they both used to go for lunch, so perhaps this is where the confusion originated. (Bishop, *From Information Received*, p. 105). Bishop considered Dew a "a very shrewd detective." (*Ibid.*, p. 106). Another colleague, David Goodwillie, wrote that he knew Crippen and consulted him for dental treatment. However, he falsely claimed that he was with his "old friend" Walter Dew when Cora Crippen's remains were discovered. (*STWN*, 15 August 1925).

42   "a beef steak" in *ETWN*, 15 September 1934.

43   These two sentences were not in *STWN*.

44   "the statements" in *STWN*, 15 September 1934 and in *NBT* and PRO, CRIM 1/117.

45   "educated first at Cold Water" in *STWN*, 15 September 1934 and in the *NBT*.

46   Crippen's first wife Charlotte died on 24 January 1892. After Cora's death rumours began in the American press that Crippen had murdered her, but nothing came of these.

he reached the crucial part of the story, his first meeting with Belle Elmore. My eyes were fixed closely upon him when he mentioned his wife's name for the first time.

His face betrayed nothing. There was not so much as a flicker of an eyelid as he went on in that quiet voice of his to describe how, in 1893, while working with Dr. Jeffry, of Brooklyn, he first met Belle Elmore, who was one of Jeffry's patients.

"Her name at that time was Cora Turner. I forget where she was living, but she was living alone. She was only about seventeen years of age, and I, of course, was about thirty.

"She at this time was living under the protection of a New York manufacturer.[47] She had been living with him, but he had given up his house and had taken a room for her and was paying all expenses."

Just a faint trace of emotion crept into Crippen's voice as he spoke of his love for the woman who was another man's mistress.

"I took her to several places for some weeks," he told me, "as I was very fond of her. Then one day she told me this other man[48] wanted her to go away with him. I told her I could not stand that and would marry her straight away, and a few days later I married her at a minister's house in Jersey City."

It was not until some time after the marriage that he made the discovery that his wife's name was not Turner, but Kunigunde Mackamotzki, and that her father was a Russian Pole and her mother a German.

About 1899, he told me, his wife, who had a good voice, went from Philadelphia to New York for the purpose of having it trained, as she thought of going in for grand opera.

"I paid all her expenses, and occasionally visited her in New York, and then in about 1900 I came to England alone, where I was manager for Munyon's[49] . . . .

"It was in April that I came over. She joined me in August. She wrote and told me she was giving up her lessons in grand opera and was going in for music hall sketches. To this I objected, and told her

---

47   "under the protection of a stove manufacturer, of Water Street, New York." in *STWN*, 15 September 1934. Crippen named him as C. C. Lincoln in his statement.

48   "the manufacturer" in *STWN*, 15 September 1934.

49   Munyon's was a mail order homeopathic medicine business of dubious reputation.

to come over here. She came and we went to live in South Crescent.

"When she came to England she decided to give sketches on the music hall stage, and adopted the name of Mackamotzki. She gave a sketch at the old Marylebone Music Hall, but it was a failure, and she gave it up.

"I may say," he proceeded, "that when she came to England from America my wife's manner towards me had entirely changed, and she had cultivated a most ungovernable temper, and seemed to think I was not good enough for her, and boasted of the men of good position travelling on the boat who had made a fuss of her."

More followed in the same strain, especially when Crippen came to deal with the last five years of their lives together at 39 Hilldrop Crescent.

"Although we apparently lived very happily together, as a matter of fact there were frequent quarrels, when she got into the most violent tempers, and often threatened she would leave me, saying she had a man she could go to and would end it all. I have seen letters from a man[50] to her ended with 'love and kisses to Brown Eyes.'

"About four years ago, in consequence of these frequent outbursts I discontinued sleeping with her, and have never cohabited with her since.

"About two years ago she became honorary treasurer of the Music Hall Ladies' Guild, and was there every Wednesday.

"I never interfered with her movements in any way; she went in and out just as she liked, and did what she liked. It was of no interest to me."

Crippen was gradually leading up to his wife's disappearance, creating the atmosphere which, as he alleged, resulted in her running away.

The final incident, according to his story to me, came on a Monday night, "the day before I wrote the letter to the Guild resigning her position as treasurer. Mr. and Mrs. Paul Martinetti came to our place to dinner. After they had left, my wife abused me and said: 'This is the finish of it, I won't stand it any longer. I shall leave you to-morrow, and you will never hear of me again!'

50   Named as "Bruce (Miller)" in *STWN*, 15 September 1934. Miller was named in Crippen's statement and the *NBT*.

"I came to business the next morning, and when I went home between five and six p.m. I found she had gone.

"I sat down to think it over as to how to cover up her absence without any scandal.

"I think the same night, or the next morning (Wednesday) I wrote a letter to the Guild saying she had gone away, which I also told several people.

"I afterwards realized this would not be a sufficient explanation for her not coming back, and later on I told people she was ill with bronchitis and pneumonia, and afterwards I told them that she was dead from this ailment.

"I told them she died in California, but I have no recollection of telling anyone exactly where she died.

"I then put an advertisement in the *Era* that she was dead, as I thought this would prevent people asking a lot of questions.

"Whatever I have said to other people in regard to her death is absolutely wrong, and I am giving this as the explanation.

"So far as I know she did not die, but is still alive.

"When my wife went away I cannot say whether she took anything with her or not, but I believe there is a theatrical basket missing.

"She took some of her jewellery, I know, with her, but she left four rings behind–also a diamond brooch.

"It is true that I was at the Benevolent Fund dinner at the C——— Restaurant[51] with Miss Le Neve, and she wore the brooch my wife left behind. She has also worn my wife's furs.

"Miss Le Neve has been in my employ and known to me through being employed by firms I have worked for for the past eight years, and she is now living with me as my wife at Hilldrop Crescent. I have been intimate with her during the past three years, and have frequently stayed with her at hotels, but was never from home at nights.

"After I told people my wife was dead Miss Le Neve and I went to Dieppe for about five days, and stayed at a hotel in the names of Mr. and Mrs. Crippen.

"This is all I can tell you. . . ."

---

51   The Criterion Restaurant, which was named in *NBT* and PRO, CRIM 1/117.

It was six o'clock by the time the last word had been written. Crippen then read the long statement carefully through, and, having done so, initialled each page before signing his full signature at the end of the statement.

From Crippen's story I learned one vital thing. Beyond all question the man with whom I was dealing was an accomplished liar. It was in many ways a complete contradiction of the statements he had previously made. But you can't charge a man with being a liar.

My job was to find out if he was telling the truth now. Somehow I did not think he was. Anyhow[52] I was determined to probe the matter further by searching 39 Hilldrop Crescent.

At this stage I could only do this with Crippen's consent. There was not enough evidence against the man—indeed any evidence at all—on which I could have asked a magistrate for a search warrant.

I made up my mind to ask Crippen's permission, but before doing so sent for Miss Le Neve and asked if she would care to tell us all she knew about the affair.

She readily agreed to do so. The girl showed some signs of embarrassment when she came to the admissions about her relations with Crippen. But making due allowance for this, there was nothing in Miss Le Neve's manner which gave rise to anything in the nature of suspicions.

I have often marvelled at the complete control shown by Crippen. Miss Le Neve, eventually acquitted by the jury,[53] showed that she had nothing to hide.[54]

This is the brief summary of what Miss Le Neve told me.

"I am a single woman, twenty-seven years of age, and am a shorthand typist. Since the latter end of February I have been living at 39 Hilldrop Crescent with Dr. Crippen as his wife, I have been on intimate terms with Dr. Crippen for two or three years.

"In the early part of February I received a note from Dr. Crippen, saying Mrs. Crippen had gone to America. I know Mrs. Crippen.[55] She treated me as a friend.

---

52   "Anyway" in *TWN*, 15 September 1934.
53   "Miss Le Neve's eventual acquittal by the jury" in *TWN*, 15 September 1934.
54   "nothing criminal to hide." in *STWN*, 15 September 1934.
55   "I knew Mrs Crippen" in *TWN* and PRO, DPP 1/13.

"About a week after he had told me she had gone to America I went to Hilldrop Crescent to put the place straight, as there were no servants kept; but at night I went to my lodgings. I did this daily for about a fortnight. The place appeared to be quite all right and quite as usual. He took me to the Benevolent Fund Dinner, and leant me a brooch to wear. Later on, he told me I could keep it.

"Afterwards he told me his wife was dead. I was very much astonished, but I do not think I said anything to him about it. He gave me some furs of his wife's to wear, and I have been living with him ever since as his wife. My father and mother do not know what I am doing, and think I am a housekeeper at Hilldrop Crescent."[56]

A few minutes after Miss Le Neve had signed her name to this statement she, with Crippen, Sergeant Mitchell and myself were seated in a "growler"[57] on the way to Hilldrop Crescent,[58] Crippen was seated by Miss Le Neve's side,[59] and neither made any attempt to disguise the affectionate relationship which existed between them.

My own mind was pretty fully occupied. I was trying to get the hang of a case which was becoming more difficult at every turn.

I certainly had no suspicion of murder. You don't jump to the conclusion that murder has been committed merely because a wife has disappeared and a husband has told lies about it.

But he had lied. I couldn't get this fact out of my mind, and I was determined, if humanly possible, to find out why he had gone to such lengths to throw dust into the eyes o Belle Elmore's friends.[60]

At 39 Hilldrop Crescent I found nothing. The house was one of eight rooms.[61] Mitchell and I entered each room in turn,[62] searching the wardrobes, dressing-tables, cupboards, and every other likely place,[63] Crippen and Miss Le Neve escorted us, and the doctor seemed quite eager to help.

56   "Dr Crippen readily gave permission to search the house." appeared here in *STWN*, 15
      September 1934. This sentence was out of place.
57   A four-wheeled hansom cab.
58   Full stop here in *TWN*.
59   "by the girl's side" in *STWN*, 15 September 1934.
60   "of Belle Elmore's friends." in *TWN*, 15 September 1934. A typographical error in the book.
61   The 1911 census return recorded nine rooms. Sandy McNab, who moved into number 39
      after Crippen, said that the house had twelve rooms. (*ETWN*, 19 November 1910).
62   "One by one Mitchell and I entered each room" in *TWN*, 15 September 1934.
63   Full stop here in *TWN*, 15 September 1934.

There was plenty of evidence that Belle Elmore had a passion for clothes. In the bedrooms I found the most extraordinary assortment of women's clothing, and enough ostrich feathers to stock a millener's shop. The whole would have filled a large van.

There were two rooms in the basement, the breakfast room and the kitchen. There, also, was the coal cellar, situated immediately under the steps leading to the front door.

This was one of the last places I visited, I had no special motive in looking there on this occasion. It was just that I wanted to make certain that I had covered the whole of the house.

There was no access to the cellar from the outside, except through the coal-hole. Inside it was reached by a short passage which led from the kitchen to the back door. The cellar door was right at the end of the passage.

The place was completely dark,[64] I remember that I had to strike matches to see what it contained and what sort of a place it was. I discovered nothing unusual. There was a small quantity of coal and some wood which looked as though it had been cut from the garden trees.

Neither Crippen nor Miss Le Neve came into the cellar. Both had followed Mitchell and me down the passage, and as I struck matches, poked around and sounded the flooring with my feet, they stood side by side in the doorway.

What were Crippen's thoughts at that moment?[65] Only he among us knew that Mitchell and I were actually standing on what remained of Mrs. Crippen.

I am not at all sure that I should now be alive to tell the tale had I at that moment discovered the cellar's grim secret.

I believe that as Crippen watched us with such apparent unconcern he had a loaded revolver in his pocket, and that revolver would have been used upon Mitchell and myself had we made the find which Crippen feared.[66]

---

64   Full stop here in *TWN*, 15 September 1934.

65   Ethel Le Neve later suggested: "I think that Walter Dew gave Dr Crippen the idea that he was not worth a very great deal of powder and shot. It was true his visit had sent us flying from London to Holland [sic-Belgium], but Dr Crippen probably believed that Walter Dew would blunder along, and finding nothing would drop the case." (*ETWN*, 30 October 1920).

66   Le Neve denied this. She had heard the story that Dew had seen "the gleam of something bright in the doctor's hand, which afterwards disappeared as if he had thought better of his

After the doctor had disappeared I made a more thorough search of the house, and in a drawer in one of the bedrooms I found a fully loaded six-chamber revolver,[67] while in another drawer Mitchell found forty-five ball cartridges.

That same drawer was searched by me on the first occasion. The revolver was not there then. Where was it? My theory is, as I have said, that it was in Crippen's pocket ready to be used as a last resort by a man who was ruthless in the extreme when his own safety demanded it.

He certainly had both of us at his mercy. Impossible to miss us at that range with the flickering candle-light making us into perfect targets.

Happily we left the cellar with our suspicions unaroused as to the close proximity of those fearful remains under our feet.[68]

Before leaving Crippen that night, I said to him: "Of course I shall have to find Mrs. Crippen to clear this matter up."

He replied: "Yes, I will do everything I can. Can you suggest anything? Would an advertisement be any good?"

I told him I thought that was an excellent idea, and together we composed the following advertisement with the idea of its being inserted in various American newspapers:

"Mackamotzki. Will Belle Elmore communicate with H. H. C.–or authorities at once. Serious trouble through your absence. Twenty-five dollars reward to anyone communicating her whereabouts to ——"

I left that draft advertisement with Crippen. It was never published.

Next day Crippen and Miss Le Neve disappeared, and the real hunt began.

II

IT was quite late in the evening when Sergeant Mitchell and I,

plan. There is no truth in the story that he intended to shoot them." (*ETWN*, 16 October 1920).

67   "six-chambered revolver" in *TWN*, 15 September 1934. All of Dew's contemporary reports described it as a five-chambered revolver.

68   "as to the close proximity of those fearful remains under our feet" was not in *TWN*.

after examining 39 Hilldrop Crescent, said good night to Crippen and Miss Le Neve.

It had been a gruelling day for us both.[69] We had been on the go since early that morning.

I was dog tired, yet sleep I could not. My mind refused to rest. The events of the day kept cropping up.

What was behind it all? There was something, I now felt sure. Crippen had a secret which he was cunningly trying to hide. There would be no rest for me until I had found out.

Yet it has been stated in print that following the happenings of that day my inclination was to drop the inquiry on the ground that I was satisfied with the doctor's explanation.

What actually happened completely disproves any such suggestion.[70]

Next day–Saturday–one of the first things I did was to circulate a description of Mrs. Crippen as a missing person to every police station in London. I spent the remainder of the day on further inquiries, and on the Sunday occupied myself by analysing in detail the statement Dr. Crippen had made.

As a final proof that I was far from satisfied, I went early on the Monday morning to Albion House with the object of seeing Crippen again.

Then came the bombshell. Crippen had flown. Miss Le Neve was also missing. Pretty obvious the couple had gone away together.

I got the big news from Dr. ——, Crippen's partner in the dentistry business.[71]

Dr. —— was probably more surprised than I was. Only that morning he had received the following letter which told its own story:

"Dear Dr. —— , I now find that in order to escape trouble I shall be obliged to absent myself for a time. I believe that with the business as it is now going you will run on all right so far as money matters go. . . . I shall write you later on more fully. With kind wishes

---

69   "The day had been a gruelling one for us both." in *STWN*, 22 September 1934.

70   Ethel Le Neve agreed. Years later she wrote: "Walter Dew, however, never loosened his grip on the case from the moment he left the house at Hilldrop Crescent." (*ETWN*, 30 October 1920).

71   Dr. Gilbert Rylance.

for your success,–Yours sincerely, H. H. Crippen."

I got some valuable information bearing on the flight from a dental mechanic employed by the firm.[72] He told me that when he arrived at the office just before nine on the Saturday morning Dr. Crippen, to his surprise, was already there.

He asked Crippen if there was any trouble. He replied, "Only a little scandal."

Crippen then did a strange thing. He sent the mechanic out to buy clothing for a "boy". The order was for a brown tweed suit, a brown felt hat, two shirts, two collars, a tie and a pair of boots.

"I took the parcel to the back room on the third floor," the man told me. "There was nobody there at the time. The room is shut up on Saturdays."

The purpose of the purchase[73] is now well known. Sometime during the Saturday morning Miss Ethel Le Neve, at the suggestion of Crippen repaired to the back room and transformed herself into a "boy". Then when all was quiet, she joined Crippen and the pair of them slipped unobserved through one of the rear exits. That same day they travelled together to the Continent.

My quarry had gone, but the manner of his going pointed to guilt.

My view was that a completely innocent man with nothing to fear would have seen the thing through. A man of Crippen's calibre would certainly have done so. I had already seen enough of him to know that he was not the type to do anything foolishly rash.

Here was the real clue.[74]

His decision was a sudden one. Of that I felt convinced. A fair deduction seemed to be that he had been scared by the events of Friday.[75]

The flight of Crippen and Miss Le Neve created a big sensation. The newspapers featured it. It was the talk of the country.

I came in for criticism.[76] Certain people with no knowledge

72   William Long.
73   "those purchases" in *TWN*, 22 September 1934.
74   "the first real clue." in *TWN*, 22 September 1934.
75   Additional sentence here in *STWN*, 22 September 1934: "He had summed me up, decided I was a persistent sort of chap, and had got cold feet."
76   "I came in for more criticism." in *STWN*, 22 September 1934. In the House of Commons William Thorne M.P. accused Dew of "grave neglect of duty" for allowing Crippen to

of police procedure and less of the law blamed me for allowing Crippen to go. I ought to have arrested him, they said. Ridiculous!

There was up to this time no shred of evidence against Crippen upon which he could have been arrested or even detained. Futile to talk of arresting a man until you know there has been a crime.

No person can be charged with murder unless the body, or some portion of the body, or some very strong evidence that murder has been committed, is available.

The first thing I did was to cause a full description of Belle Elmore to be circulated right throughout the country.

Why not of Crippen and Miss Le Neve?

That was still impossible. Although their running away pointed strongly to guilt in some form or another, we still lacked evidence to bring any charge against them.

After talking over the new development with Superintendent Frank Froest, I took Mitchell with me and set out once more for Hilldrop Crescent.[77] The house was now empty. The French maid had gone. I had to get the key from the landlord.[78]

I was eager to lose no time. Crippen's absence was in one way a great advantage. It gave me great scope.[79] I now had the free run of the house. No Crippen at my elbow to hamper me and perhaps throw me off the scent.

If Crippen had stood his ground and continued to live quietly at Hilldrop Crescent my difficulties would have been infinitely greater. Maybe the mystery would never have been solved, for with nothing more definite than suspicion to go upon it would have been exceedingly difficult to get the necessary sanction to make a thorough search.

The proof of the value to me of Crippen's blunder lies in the result. Within forty-eight hours of my receiving the news that he had gone I had found the remains of Belle Elmore in the coal cellar.

During this time Mitchell and I returned to the house again and

---

escape. Home Secretary Winston Churchill responded by saying it was an inappropriate matter to discuss as Dew was not available to defend himself at that time. (PRO, HO 144/1718).

77   "for 39 Hilldrop Crescent." in *STWN*, 22 September 1934.

78   Frederick Lown.

79   "Look at the scope it gave me." in *STWN*, 22 September 1934.

again. We searched the building from top to bottom, combing every room[80] and examining every nook and cranny of the garden.

At first our quest seemed hopeless. The only evidence found bearing at all on Mrs. Crippen's disappearance was the advertisement which Crippen had written out in my presence offering a reward of twenty-five dollars for information leading to the discovery of his wife.

There was one place in the house which had a peculiar fascination for me. This was the coal cellar. I have already described its location. It was at the bottom of a short dark passage[81] leading from the kitchen to the back door.

It might well be asked why I concentrated so persistently on the coal cellar. I have asked myself the same question hundreds of times. Maybe it was my sixth sense.[82]

If, as I must confess, I was now beginning to suspect Belle Elmore had been murdered, there was nothing at all to suggest that the crime had been committed at the house. Indeed, as from the facts as then known, and following the thorough searches I had made, it seemed more than probable that Crippen must have chosen some other place.

Perhaps it was instinct. Anyway, that cellar stuck in my mind.[83] Even in bed, what little I got of it during those hectic days, I couldn't keep my mind from wandering back to the cellar.

And I suppose it was this same instinct which sent me back to the house on the Wednesday following Crippen's disappearance.

Mitchell and I had been making inquiries in the neighbourhood of Camden Town. We were both completely fagged out. Both of us had been on the go for two whole days and the greater part of two nights.

My personal inclination was to go home and sleep for twenty-four hours. But that was impossible. It would remain impossible so long as the mystery of Mrs. Crippen remained unsolved.

"Let us go along to the house and have another go at the cellar,"

---

80   "tooth-combing every room" in *STWN*, 22 September 1934.

81   "the end of a short dark passage" in *TWN*, 22 September 1934.

82   This last sentence was not in *TWN*. Coincidentally Ethel Le Neve said Dew was a "detective with a sixth sense." (*ETWN*, 30 October 1920).

83   "stuck well in my mind." in *STWN*, 22 September 1934.

I said to my companion, and a short time later we were on our hands and knees probing once more at the bricks which formed the cellar floor. I was armed with a poker, and with this worked away too tired to say a word.

Presently a little thrill of excitement went through me. The sharp point of the poker had found its way between two of the bricks, and one of them showed signs of lifting.

I toiled away more hopefully now, all sense of fatigue vanishing in the excitement of hope. The brick came out. Then another and another. After this my work became easy.

Mitchell ran to get a spade from the garden. With this I worked steadily for a few minutes. Then came evidence nauseatingly unmistakable. The stench was unbearable, driving us both into the garden for fresh air.

I was now as excited as I ever allowed myself to be. I knew that I was on the eve of a great discovery. What we had found already could mean only one thing, and that was more than enough to account for the sudden flight of Dr. Crippen.

When we had sufficiently recovered we resumed our task,[84] and this time we stuck the putrified atmosphere long enough to unearth a large piece of what I easily recognized to be human remains.

Again we had to fly, and before re-entering the cellar a third time both Mitchell and I were fortified with a long drink of brandy which I sent for.

I knew that I had solved the mystery. What other explanation could there be of the presence in Dr. Crippen's coal cellar of the parts of a human body?[85]

I sent for the Assistant Commissioner, Sir Melville Macnaughton,[86] and for Dr. Thomas Marshall, divisional police

---

84   "our gruesome task" in *STWN*, 22 September 1934.

85   Dew later admitted to barrister Cecil Mercer: "If Crippen had taken the trouble to order a ton of coal, he'd be a free man to-day. The police aren't coal-heavers, and to empty that cellar, when full, would have been a fearful job." (Yates, *As Berry and I Were Saying*, p. 250).

86   Sir Melville Leslie Macnaghten (1853-1921), assistant commissioner of the C.I.D. from 1902-1913 and a former Metropolitan Police chief constable. The correct spelling of his surname is Macnaghten and that is how it appeared throughout the newspaper serialisation. In his book *Supper With the Crippens*, (p. 128), David James Smith stated that in his memoirs Macnaghten: "forgets to mention Walter Dew, whose name is oddly absent from MacNaghten's story. MacNaghten may, of course, have been jealous of the attention his Chief Inspector enjoyed afterwards. Or he may have felt that Dew's conduct had brought

surgeon for the Kentish Town district. I also sent for assistance in the further excavation of the cellar.

When the Assistant Commissioner and the doctor had arrived the work was resumed.[87] The whole floor of the cellar was dug up.

We found only masses of human flesh. The head was missing. No bones were ever discovered.[88] Identification seemed impossible.

Yet who could doubt that the cellar, about which I had had that strange hunch, had yielded Crippen's secret, and that what we had found represented all that remained of the once charming and vivacious Belle Elmore?

To prove this, however, was quite another thing.

We were helped in this, as I shall show later, by other finds under the cellar floor. These included a pyjama jacket, part of a woman's undergarment and some hair curlers.

Soon the news leaked out that something big was happening at 39 Hilldrop Crescent. A huge crowd gathered in the street outside speculating as to what all the police activity was about.

Police officers were left in charge of the house, and the next day the remains were removed to the mortuary, where they were examined by Dr. Marshall and Dr. Pepper,[89] who were able to go so far as to say that the murdered person–there could now be little doubt that it was murder–was a female.

Again the whole complexion of the case had changed. The finding of the remains of a woman in the coal cellar at 39 Hilldrop Crescent, linked with the fact that Belle Elmore had mysteriously disappeared, automatically made Crippen a "wanted" man. Miss Ethel Le Neve, because she had run away with him,[90] was in the same category.

Scotland Yard into disrepute." However, Macnaghten did mention Dew by name on the first page of his chapter on the Crippen case, writing: "no meeting has ever been equal to that of Chief Inspector Walter Dew with the murderous doctor on the deck of s.s. *Montrose*." (Macnaghten, *Days of My Years*, p. 189). Macnaghten did refer to Dew as "the Chief Inspector" for the rest of the chapter, but he didn't use most officers' names throughout his book, referring to them instead by their ranks.

87   "the grim work was resumed." in *STWN*, 22 September 1934.

88   "No bones were discovered." in *TWN*, 22 September 1934.

89   Dr. Augustus Pepper (1849-1935), a surgeon at St. Mary's Hospital and Home Office pathologist.

90   "Ethel Le Neve, because it appeared she had run away with him" in *STWN*, 22 September 1934.

I began at once the stupendous task of preparing and sending to all parts of the world a composite circular on which were given photographs, full descriptions and specimens of the handwriting of Crippen and Miss Le Neve. The circular asked that, if seen, both should be detained for murder.

The document was headed in big type "MURDER AND MUTILATION", and gave the fullest possible aids to identification.

Crippen, for instance, was described as "Somewhat slovenly in appearance. Wears his hat on the back of his head. Very plausible and quiet spoken. Remarkably cool and collected demeanour, Carried firearms, &c."[91]

Of Miss Le Neve the circular said she "Dresses well, but quietly, and may wear a blue serge costume. May have in her possession and endeavour to dispose of same: a round gold brooch with points radiating zig-zag from centre; and two single stone diamond rings, and a diamond and sapphire (or ruby) ring, stones rather large."

And having done everything possible to set the police forces of the whole world on the hunt for the missing couple, I took on the almost equally big task of searching for evidence that would satisfy a jury that the woman who had met her fate in that gloomy looking house[92] in Hilldrop Crescent was indeed Crippen's wife.[93]

I never doubted that what we had found explained the disappearance of Belle Elmore. The woman was missing. Her husband had told untruths about her disappearance, retracting, in the statements he made to me, the story that she had gone to America and died there. His explanation had been entirely unsatisfactory.

Add to that the fact that, following the interest I had shown in the case, he himself had run away and you will see how difficult it was to arrive at any other conclusion than that we had stumbled upon the little doctor's guilty secret.

---

91 "Carries firearms &c." in *TWN*, 22 September 1934. Presumably a typographical error in the book.

92 Just "that house" in *STWN*, 22 September 1934.

93 Additional sentences here in *STWN*, 22 September 1934:

"I never despaired of accomplishing this task, though I am not at all certain that I should have succeeded but for a stroke of luck which the hunting detective sometimes enjoys.

It was the chance remark of a woman overheard by me which provided the strongest link in the chain of identification."

The inference that the woman had been murdered was strong. Bodies were rarely buried in such a way[94] unless there is something criminal to conceal. And from that it was only a step to the deduction that the runaway husband had been guilty of the crime.

But suspicion and surmise were not enough. It was my job to get the proofs.

First we had to establish that the remains were those of a woman. Next that the woman was Belle Elmore. Thirdly that it was a case of murder, and finally, if murder had been done, that Crippen had committed the deed.

The first problem was settled by the doctors. They were able to say that the victim was a woman. The second took much longer to solve. Crippen had seen to that. He had set out deliberately to destroy all the evidence of identity. The remains were headless, limbless, and boneless. Even to this day we do not know how or where other parts of the body were disposed of.

There are two theories. One is that he burned them in the kitchen grate at 39 Hilldrop Crescent, though none of the neighbours to whom I spoke ever noticed the offensive smell one would have expected if such were the case.

The other theory is that Crippen threw the missing remains overboard from a cross-Channel steamer. On 23rd March he took Miss Le Neve over to Dieppe for Easter.

It took days of hard work to accumulate the circumstantial evidence which eventually satisfied the jury that the dead woman could be none other than Crippen's missing wife.

The hair curlers we found in the cellar had long human hair in them. The hair was naturally a dark brown,[95] but it had been bleached to a lighter colour. Belle Elmore's hair was a dark brown and had been similarly treated.

The undergarments we discovered[96] were shown to friends of Belle, and they were able to say that they were such as she was in the habit of wearing.

---

94 "Bodies are rarely buried in such a way" in *STWN*, 22 September 1934.

95 *STWN*, 22 September 1934, had: "In the coal cellar grave we found some curlers with a long human hair in them; some feminine under-garments and parts of a man's pyjama suit. The human hair in the curlers was naturally a dark brown"

96 "we discovered" was not in *STWN*.

In a box in Crippen's bedroom I found an old pair of pyjama trousers with broad blue stripes. The jacket was missing. The pyjama jacket found with the remains was, on examination, discovered to be of the same material and colour as the trousers found in Crippen's bedroom.

All this was valuable evidence, but it was far from being conclusive.[97]

Then I had a rare piece of luck. I had attended the formal inquest, and after the proceedings[98] were over I was standing idly outside the court close to a group of women who were discussing the case.[99]

One of the women was Mrs. Paul Martinetti, who had been a close friend of Belle Elmore, and I pricked up my ears when I overheard her say something about Belle[100] having undergone a serious operation.

I called Mrs. Martinetti to one side and asked her if I had heard aright.

"Oh, yes," she replied. "Belle had an operation years ago in America. She had quite a big scar on the lower part of her body. I have seen it."

Here was something really vital. If that scar could be found on those gruesome remnants of human flesh lying in the Islington Mortuary it might provide the missing link in the chain of evidence of identification.

I told one of the medical men in the case of the conversation about the scar and sometime later a microscopical examination was made of a portion of the flesh by Dr. or Professor Pepper and others, when it was discovered that a scar existed, showing that whatever body it belonged to that person had undergone a severe abdominal operation. This assisted enormously to prove that the remains found in the cellar were those of Mrs. Crippen, and was one of the most important pieces of evidence as to identification.[101]

97   This sentence was not in *STWN*.

98   "the brief proceedings" in *STWN*, 22 September 1934. A reporter at the inquest wrote that Dew "wears a heavy moustache, speaks rapidly, and carries the stamp of his calling in voice and gesture." (*The Umpire*, 24 July 1910).

99   "eagerly discussing the tion. [sic]" in *STWN*, 22 September 1934.

100   "Belle Elmore" in *STWN*, 22 September 1934.

101   *TWN*, 22 September 1934 had: "I lost no time in passing the information on to the medical men engaged in the case. They had already observed something which resembled an

This was a big step forward. But it was progress only in one direction.

The big question remained unanswered. There was no clue at all as to the whereabouts of Crippen and Miss Le Neve.

Perhaps I ought to make it clear that four years before the Great War, when these events took place, life was very different in many ways from what it is to-day.

The present generation, for instance, can scarcely appreciate how easy it was then for anyone to travel unhindered to any part of the world. Passports were not necessary[102] except when entering Russia.

So that Crippen and Miss Le Neve had the world before them. They might have gone almost anywhere, provided they had sufficient money to pay their passages.

I had discovered that Crippen had some money. On the day he went away he cashed a cheque for £37 with the manageress of Munyon's Remedies,[103] the concern for which Crippen worked on commission. The cheque was signed both by him and Belle Elmore. It was a joint account.

Whether the signing of his wife's name on this cheque was a forgery or not was never discovered. Crippen was not the sort of man to let a little thing like that stand in his way. A man who had been guilty of murder would not stop at forgery. But it is just as likely he had looked far enough ahead to induce his wife to sign a sequence of cheques before the crime.[104]

We made other discoveries all pointing to the elaborate preparations Crippen had made. As long previously as 2nd February–two days after the crime–he had pawned a ring and earrings for £80,

operation scar and now, after further microscopic examination, were able to say that the murdered woman, like Belle Elmore, had at some time undergone a severe abdominal operation."

102   "not actually necessary" in *STWN*, 22 September 1934.

103   "Miss Marion Curnow, the manageress of Munyon's remedies" in *STWN*, 22 September 1934.

104   In 1911 the Post Office discovered that eight withdrawals of money had been made from Cora Crippen's account from 5 April–17 June 1910. They concluded that Ethel Le Neve had forged Cora's signature but she was not prosecuted as it was believed she had been acting under Dr. Crippen's influence at the time. (PRO, T 1/11335). At Hilldrop Crescent on 11 July Sergeant Mitchell found a sheet of paper with Belle Elmore's name written on it several times, as if somebody had been practising writing it. (PRO, DPP 1/13).

and a week later he had pledged a brooch and rings for £115. It seemed that Crippen even then was making ready for just such an emergency as eventually arose.

My theory from the first was that Crippen would make for a foreign port. He was a foreigner, and as such far more likely than an Englishman to seek refuge abroad.

A careful watch was kept on all the ports. But this step was taken too late. The birds had already flown. The fugitives were actually out of the country before I received the information that they were missing.[105]

There has never been a hue and cry like that which went up throughout the country for Crippen and Miss Le Neve. The newspapers were full of the case. It was the one big topic of conversation.[106] On the trains and buses one heard members of the public speculating and theorizing as to where they were likely to be.

All the elements to fire the public imagination were present. They were intrigued by the relationship between the doctor and his former secretary; repelled by the gruesome find in the coal cellar, and mystified as to how the victim had met her death. Every day that passed increased the fevered interest in the hunt.

We were doing everything humanly possible. The whole world was flooded with circulars asking for the detention of the runaways on a charge of murder. These bills were copied and published in many languages. The hunt had become world-wide.

I was working harder than at any time since the day when Mr. and Mrs. Nash came with their seemingly trivial complaint to Scotland Yard.[107]

As the man in sole charge of the biggest murder mystery of the century, I felt that Dr. Crippen had thrown out a challenge. I was ready to accept it.

I gave every ounce of effort.[108] For sixteen—sometimes more—

---

105 Additional sentence here in *STWN*, 22 September 1934: "Even so, at that time there was nothing on which to base an arrest."

106 "the one big topic of conversation on all lips." in *STWN*, 22 September 1934.

107 This sentence was not in *STWN*.

108 "I was ready to accept it, though it demanded every ounce of my personal effort." in *STWN*, 29 September 1934.

hours out of every twenty-four, I was directing the police campaign to track Crippen down.

I shall never forget the hours I spent with Dr. Augustus Pepper, who had now been called in to assist Dr. Marshall with the medical side of the case, at the Islington Mortuary, examining again and again every portion of those terrible remains.

The doctors played a big part in sealing Crippen's doom. It was the analysis made by Dr. William (now Sir William) Willcox[109] which established the cause of death. This revealed traces in the remains of hyoscin, a then little-known narcotic poison, of which one quarter to one half a grain is a fatal dose.

Death, Dr. Willcox was able to say, was undoubtedly due to poisoning by hyoscin.

This discovery meant more work. We had now to try and trace the purchase of hyoscin by Crippen. We were successful. It was found that on 17th or 18th January of the same year Dr. Crippen had called at a chemist in New Oxford Street, and ordered hyoscin.[110]

He called again on the 19th and collected the drug. The quantity was five grains, served in the form of crystals either in a tube or a box.

He signed the sale of poisons register as follows: "Name of purchaser, Munyons, per H. H. Crippen. Address of purchaser, 57-61 Albion House. Purpose for which it is required, homœopathic preparations."

This was the only purchase of hyoscin Crippen was ever known to have made.

The net was closing. The evidence was being slowly accumulated. But still Crippen was at large.

We were now satisfied that the remains were those of Belle Elmore.

We knew that she had been murdered, and the method employed by her slayer.

We also had evidence to show that Dr. Crippen, the man whose actions had made him a suspect, had at the material time actually

---

109   William "Wilks" Willcox (1870-1941), senior Home Office scientific analyst. Incorrectly spelled "Wilcox" in *TWN*.

110   The chemist was Lewis & Burrows, 108 New Oxford Street.

been in possession of the rare drug by which death had been caused.

It would have been quite impossible for Sergeant Mitchell and myself to make unaided the scores of inquiries and investigations the case demanded. Long before this I had called in as permanent assistants, Sergeants Crutchett and Hayman, while many other officers were engaged under my direction temporarily. We were all working with a common purpose – the catching and conviction of Crippen.

I have stressed the hard work we all put in in order to correct an erroneous impression which may have been caused by anyone reading the official record of the trial. During my examination in chief at the Old Bailey I am reported to have said in reply to a question by Mr. R. D. Muir, counsel for the prosecution, that I did not take "any further specific steps after 14th July." This, of course, is quite wrong. We were inundated with work the whole of the time Crippen was at large. Maybe I misunderstood the question on this point.[111]

Why, it was two days later, on 16th July, that I personally applied to the Bow Street Magistrate for warrants for the arrest of Crippen and Miss Le Neve on charges of murder and mutilation.[112]

I am afraid that if no further steps had been taken after the date mentioned the fugitives would never have been caught.

I was so hard pressed personally that I am sure that I would never have been able to carry on in such a hopeful spirit without the unstinting encouragement given to me by my chiefs, the late Sir Melville Macnaughton, the Assistant Commissioner, and Mr. (now) Sir Trevor Bigham, the Chief Constable of the Criminal Investigation Department.[113]

Not once did they interfere or question any step I decided to take. In the circumstances I am more than happy that I did not let them down.

Murder cases are not without their humorous incidents. There was one even in this grim case.

111   This last sentence was not in *TWN*. The quote Dew referred to appeared in the *NBT*, p. 42.

112   But, as Cecil Mercer pointed out, "the crime of mutilation is quite unknown to the law." (Yates, *As Berry and I Were Saying*, p. 239).

113   Sir Frank Trevor Bigham (1876-1954), served as chief constable from 1909-1914. He was knighted in 1928.

On two occasions a gentleman who was unfortunate enough to resemble Crippen facially, was brought to Scotland Yard on suspicion of being the wanted man. On the first occasion he took the experience in good part, but when the same thing happened a second time he was highly indignant,[114] and said it was getting a habit.[115]

I did what I could to pour oil on troubled waters by offering the man my profound apologies, and after a while I was able to make him see that the police officer who had made the mistake was really only doing his duty.

This was not the only man mistaken for Crippen. I dare not think of the scores of false alarms. Not a day passed without Crippen and Miss Le Neve being reported to have been seen in some part of the country. Sometimes they were alleged to have been in a dozen places at the same time.

All this meant extra work. One couldn't afford to ignore even the slenderest chance, and all such reports were carefully inquired into.[116]

The first week was completely without result[117] so far as the missing man and woman were concerned. More days went by. Still no clue.

I began to get a little anxious. Every day that passed increased the chances of the runaways.

The second week had almost gone. We had reached the Friday when there came the electrifying news for which I had been hoping.

It was eight o'clock in the evening. Almost completely worn out with the strain of work,[118] I was chatting with a confrere in my office at the Yard when a telegram was handed to me.

As I read its contents a wave of optimism swept over me. My fatigue instantly vanished.

The telegram was from the Liverpool police and repeated to me a wireless message[119] they had received from Captain Kendall, of the

114 "naturally, highly indignant" in *STWN*, 29 September 1934.
115 "and said it was getting a habit." was not in *TWN*.
116 "So the days passed." appeared here in *STWN*, 29 September 1934.
117 "completely negative" in *TWN*, 29 September 1934.
118 "strain of sleepless work" in *TWN*, 29 September 1934.
119 "a message" in *TWN*, 29 September 1934.

Montrose,[120] bound from Antwerp to Quebec and then somewhere in the Atlantic.

The gist of the message was that Captain Kendall had good grounds for believing that Dr. Crippen and Miss Le Neve were passengers on his ship.

Later Captain Kendall sent further messages, not to the police, describing how his suspicions were aroused.[121] Here is a summary of his interesting story.

"The man on the *Montrose*, supposed to be Crippen, answers all the descriptions given in the police report, as does also his companion, Miss Le Neve.

"I discovered them two hours after leaving Antwerp, but did not telegraph to my owners until I had found out good clues.

"They booked their passage in Brussels as Mr. John Robinson and Master John Robinson,[122] and came aboard at Antwerp in brown suits, soft grey hats and white canvas shoes.

"They had no baggage except a small handbag bought on the Continent. My suspicion was aroused by seeing them on deck beside a boat.

"Miss Le Neve squeezed Crippen's hand. It seemed to me very unnatural for two males, so I suspected them at once. . . .

"During lunch I examined both their hats. Crippen's was stamped 'Jackson, Boulevard le Nord', Miss Le Neve's hat bore no name but it was packed round the rim with paper to make it fit. Miss Le Neve has the manner and appearance of a very refined, modest girl. She does not speak much, but always wears a pleasant smile. Her suit is anything but a good fit. Her trousers are very tight about the hips and are split a bit down the back and secured with a large safety pin. . . .

"They have been under strict observation all the voyage,[123] I have not noticed a revolver in the man's hip-pocket. He continually

120 Henry George Kendall (1874-1965). In 1914 Kendall was the captain of the *Empress of Ireland* when it collided with another vessel in the St. Lawrence River with the loss of 1,012 lives.

121 These were sent to the *Daily Mail* who published them on 1 August. The *Mail* had contacted Kendall by wireless to ask him for his story. (McKenzie, *The Mystery of The Daily Mail*, p. 36).

122 Just "Master Robinson" in *TWN*, 29 September 1934.

123 Full stop here in *TWN*, 29 September 1934.

shaves his upper lip, and his beard is growing nicely. I often see him stroking it, seemingly pleased. The mark on his nose through wearing spectacles has not worn off since coming on board. . . .

"All the 'boy's' manners at table were most ladylike. Crippen kept cracking nuts for her and giving her half his salad, and was always paying her the most marked attention.

"On two or three occasions when walking on deck I called after him by his assumed name, Mr. Robinson, and he took no notice. I repeated it and it was only owing to the presence of mind of Miss Le Neve that he turned round. He apologized for not hearing me, saying the cold weather made him deaf.

"At times both would sit and appear in deep thought. If Crippen looks at Miss Le Neve she gives him an endearing smile, as though she were under his hypnotic influence."

The telegram I received was briefer and more to the point,[124] but it told me what I had been moving Heaven and earth to discover. I jumped at once into a cab and drove to the residence of Sir Melville Macnaughton. I handed the Assistant Commissioner the telegram. He read it with raised eyebrows and then, turning to me, asked: "What do you think?"

"I feel confident it's them," I replied.

"So do I," agreed Sir Melville, and then.[125] "What do you suggest?"

"I want to go after them in a fast steamer," I said eagerly. "The White Star liner *Laurentic* sails from Liverpool to-morrow. I believe it is possible for her to overtake the *Montrose* and reach Canada first."

Sir Melville Macnaughton smiled, probably at my keenness. Then he moved to his desk, sat down and started to write. A few minutes later he handed me a document which authorized me to pursue just the course I had suggested.

The Assistant Commissioner held out his hand. I seized it gratefully, "Here's your authority, Dew," he then said, "and I wish

---

124   Kendall had sent a wireless message to the managing director of his shipping company who forwarded it to the Liverpool police. It read: "Montrose. 130 miles West of Lizard. Have strong suspicion that Crippen London Cellar Murderer and accomplice are amongst saloon passengers. Moustache shaved off, growing beard. Accomplice dressed as boy, voice, manner and build undoubtedly a girl." (PRO, MEPO 3/198).

125   Comma here in *TWN*, 29 September 1934.

you all the luck in the world."[126]

Thrilled with the prospect of the chase ahead, I hurried back to the Yard, and a few minutes later a telegram had been sent to the Liverpool police asking them to book me a passage in the *Laurentic* under a *nom de plume*, and enjoining them to keep my departure a strict secret.

After handing over at the Yard and impressing everyone there with the importance of secrecy in case Crippen, if he were on board, should be acquainted with my intentions, I went home to snatch a few hours sleep. Early next morning I left for Liverpool, and so intent was I on keeping my mission dark, that all I told my wife was that I had to go abroad on a matter of great urgency.[127]

But despite all my precautions the news did leak out, and next morning the newspapers broadcast my mission to the world.

At Liverpool I was met by Chief-Inspector Duckworth, of the Liverpool City Police, who smuggled me on board, where I found that a passage had been booked for me in the name of Mr. Dewhurst.[128]

So began the chase for the elusive doctor, the first time in history that wireless had been used to set the police on the track of a murderer.

On the whole I had a most pleasant voyage, thanks largely to the kindness and consideration shown me throughout by the *Laurentic*'s captain and purser. These officers and the chief officer and wireless operator were the only folk on board who knew my identity and shared my secret, with perhaps one other exception.[129]

126 Macnaghten used to say that "the two best detectives were Inspector Luck and Detective Chance." (Berrett, *When I Was at Scotland Yard*, p. 261).

127 Kate Dew would have soon realised what he was working on from newspaper reports. On 2 August Dew telegraphed Scotland Yard and asked them to inform her where he could be contacted in Quebec. (PRO, MEPO 3/198).

128 "Not quite the best nom-de-plume that could have been chosen!" in *STWN*, 29 September 1934.

129 "with perhaps one other exception" was not in *TWN*. It was widely reported in the newspapers that Dew was on board the *Laurentic*. A journalist later claimed that he was an old friend of Duckworth who told him: "If I go aboard and signal to you before the ship casts off you'll know that the Scotland Yard man is aboard." Duckworth waved to the journalist from the ship's rail. (*Worthing and District Review*, January 1948). There were press reports about Dew's identity being known to the passengers, to which he responded: "Whatever may have appeared in the press to the contrary, I may say that my identity was not known until about a day before my landing at Father Point." (PRO, MEPO 3/198).

Wireless in those days was in its infancy. I was terribly anxious to get into touch with Captain Kendall of the *Montrose* and to advise him of the plans I had made. The captain of the *Laurentic* gave me every facility, and I spent hour after hour in the wireless room while attempts were being made to "get through" to the ship on which the suspects were travelling.

It was hopeless. The answering signals simply would not come.[130]

As the liner neared the pilot station known as Father Point, on the St. Lawrence River, on Friday afternoon,[131] where I had decided to disembark in the hope of intercepting the *Montrose*, I was again assailed by doubts. Had we beaten the *Montrose*? I was assured by the captain that there was little doubt on the point.

I knew before we landed that we had won the race. The pilot cutter which met the *Laurentic* at Father Point was filled with reporters and camera men, who obviously would never have been there had the *Montrose* already arrived.

One thing they[132] could not understand. They were thirsting for information. I refused to say a word. They demanded to know why, and I had the greatest difficulty in the world in convincing them that the granting of an interview at that stage would have got me into hot water at home.

They do things very differently in America. I prefer the British way.

At Father Point I was met by Inspector McCarthy and Inspector Dennis,[133] of the Quebec City Police.

Father Point I found to be a desolate spot on the St. Lawrence. All it boasted was a few wooden shacks, a wireless station and a lighthouse.

I was accommodated in one of the shacks. The reporters crowded into the others. The place was lonely, but it was far from peaceful. The lighthouse foghorn combined with the vocal and musical efforts of my friends the reporters made sleep impossible.

---

130   Although wireless technology played such an important part in Dew's greatest case, his wife said that he "did not seem to care for the wireless... he never had one of his own." (*Worthing and District Review*, January 1948).

131   "on Friday afternoon" was not in *TWN*.

132   "One thing these reporters" in *STWN*, 29 September 1934.

133   Spelled "Denis" in the case files.

The wireless operator at Father Point became very enthusiastic. He quickly got into touch with Captain Kendall of the *Montrose*, and it was very reassuring to receive a message from him to the effect that he was more convinced than ever that he had the fugitives on board.

The *Montrose*, I learned, was due to reach Father Point on the Sunday morning, and Captain Kendall readily agreed to see that in the meantime no wireless message was communicated to the suspects.

While waiting, there was one disconcerting development.

On the Saturday evening the representative of an English newspaper, whose name I regret I have forgotten, gave me some very unsettling information. He said that some of the lads of the American Press were concocting a scheme to get on board the *Montrose* before she arrived at Father Point.

These reporters[134] meant by hook or by crook to be the first to tell the world whether it really was Crippen and Miss Le Neve on board, and to get a big scoop for their papers by interviewing the couple.

Their plan, I was told, was to rig up a kind of raft, float it down the St. Lawrence and get picked up by the *Montrose* as shipwrecked mariners.

Now I don't pretend to know whether there ever was any serious intention to carry out this ambitious scheme, but from what I had seen of the American newspaper men I did not put it beyond them. In any case it was up to me to do my best to prevent it.[135]

After giving the matter a lot of thought I decided that the best thing to do was have a personal talk with the pressmen and try to dissuade them.

They were surprised that I had discovered their secret, but listened understandingly as I pointed out the danger to my mission of such an enterprise.

"If you gentlemen[136] abandon this mad idea of yours," I said, "I

---

134   "These fellows" in *TWN*, 29 September 1934.
135   Additional sentence here in *STWN*, 29 September 1934: "The last thing I wanted was for Crippen to be forewarned of my coming, or, indeed, to know that his real identity had been discovered. Faced by the certainty of arrest on a charge of murder, it was quite probable that he would commit suicide."
136   "If you fellows" in *TWN*, 29 September 1934.

will see that you get the news you want at the first possible moment. I'll give you a signal from the *Montrose* to tell you whether the people are Crippen and Miss Le Neve or not. We can easily arrange the details."[137]

To my great relief the wild scheme was abandoned on the conditions I had suggested. I am pleased to say they kept their word.

As Crippen knew me, I had to devise some means of getting on board without his recognizing me.

I got over the difficulty by borrowing the uniform of a genial old pilot. This made a capital disguise.

All the details for my boarding the *Montrose* were arranged with Captain Kendall by wireless. The plan was for me to be rowed down the St. Lawrence in a large boat with the real pilot and Canadian officers[138] and board the liner in mid-stream.

The *Montrose* was sighted shortly after nine o'clock on the Sunday morning. A thrill of excitement ran through me as the big ship hove into view.

My boat swung into mid-stream. The *Montrose* seemed to grow rapidly in bulk as we approached her. Presently we could distinguish forms moving about on her decks.

The liner was visibly slowing down. That meant my boat had been spotted. A ladder was thrown over the side. We drew alongside. The pilot went up the ladder; I followed.[139]

I went straight to the bridge, where Captain Kendall was awaiting me.

We shook hands. Our words of greeting had barely been exchanged when my attention was caught and riveted by a little man who had emerged unconcernedly from behind a funnel on the deck below.

There was something about the little man which seemed familiar.

Captain Kendall was watching me closely, but he said no word.

---

137   Additional sentence here in *STWN*, 29 September 1934: "I knew that each man had booked a passage on the Montrose from Father Point to Quebec, and that there was no power on earth to prevent them boarding her there."

138   "with the real pilot and Canadian officers" was not in *TWN*.

139   Additional sentence here in *STWN*, 29 September 1934: "It seemed like going up the side of St. Paul's." Dew used the same analogy in Chapter 4 of *From Pitch and Toss to Murder* when describing boarding a boat, (*ICC*, p. 204), and when writing an article about the Crippen case in 1926. (*Daily Express*, 23 November 1926).

Together we moved in the direction of the man now walking slowly up and down. He looked like Crippen. Yet he was different. This man had no heavy sandy moustache, and he was wearing no glasses.

Presently only a few feet separated us. A pair of bulgy eyes were raised to mine. I would have recognized them anywhere.

The little man was Crippen. I thrilled with the realization that this was no wild goose chase after all. My search was ended. Miss Le Neve, I felt certain, would not be far away.

During my long career as a detective, I have experienced many big moments, but at no other time have I felt such a sense of triumph and achievement.[140]

Poor Crippen was still in ignorance of the fate so close at hand. My pilot's uniform was proving an effective disguise. He had not yet recognized me.

"Good morning, Dr. Crippen," I said. The little man gave a start of surprise, and a puzzled look came into his eyes as they scanned me. For a second longer doubt and uncertainty were registered on his face. Then a sudden twitching of his Adam's apple told me that recognition had come to him.

Even though I believed him to be a murderer, and a brutal murderer at that, it was impossible at that moment not to feel for him a pang of pity. He had been caught on the threshold of freedom. Only twelve hours more and he would have been safely at Quebec.[141]

"Good morning, Mr. Dew," Crippen replied, and his voice was as calm and quiet as it had been on the occasion of our first meeting at Albion House.

"You will be arrested for the murder and mutilation of your wife, Cora Crippen, in London, on or about February 1st last,"[142] I told him.

To this he made no reply, and offered no resistance as he was handcuffed and taken as unobtrusively as possible to a vacant

---

140 Additional sentence here in *STWN*, 29 September 1934: "My emotions then more than repaid me for all the anxieties and all the efforts of the previous weeks."

141 Additional sentence here in *STWN*, 29 September 1934: "My coming had blighted all his hopes. He must have suffered mental torture. Yet he remained unmoved. He made no scene. The man's iron control never for a moment deserted him."

142 "February 2" in *TWN*, 29 September 1934.

cabin.[143] An officer from Quebec (Inspector Dennis)[144] was placed in charge and the door was locked.

Now for Miss Le Neve. Inspector McCarthy and I proceeded at once to the cabin she and Crippen had occupied. I knocked at the door and then walked in. Miss Le Neve was standing just inside, probably awaiting Crippen's return from his morning walk.

As I entered she looked up.

"I am Chief-Inspector Dew," I said formally.

There was no need for the introduction. It was clear from the frightened look in her eyes that she had already recognized me.

With a shriek she collapsed and would have fallen to the floor had I not caught and supported her.

I sent at once for the stewardess, a big pleasant woman,[145] and with her assistance the unhappy girl was soon restored to consciousness.

Miss Le Neve as I had expected, was dressed as a boy in a neat dark-brown suit, and she looked the part reasonably well.[146]

This was soon changed. I got the stewardess to lend her some female clothing, and stood outside the door while she changed into a woman again.

The clothes were not a good fit, but Miss Le Neve was very grateful. She had become tired of masquerading as a boy.

I told Miss Le Neve she would be arrested on a charge of murder, and cautioned her:[147] "You are not obliged to say anything, but what you do say will be taken down in writing and used either for or against you."

To this she made no reply.

I then went back to Crippen, and read to him the warrant, and cautioned him in the same way. He also made no reply.

Next Inspector McCarthy and I carefully searched Crippen.

---

143 After Dew's death in December 1947 a reporter visited his widow and was shown "the very handcuffs, now rusty with age, with which he secured Crippen after boarding the Montrose." (*Worthing and District Review*, January 1948).

144 "An officer from Quebec was placed in charge." in *ETWN*, 29 September 1934. *STWN* had: "The second officer from Quebec was placed in charge."

145 "a big, pleasant woman" was not in *STWN*.

146 He hadn't always thought that. In a report written at the time of the arrest Dew said that he "found it difficult to believe that any person with an average amount of intelligence could ever have believed her to be a boy." (PRO, MEPO 3/198).

147 "warned her" in *TWN*, 29 September 1934.

Pinned on his under-vest we found several articles of jewellery. These included a rising sun brooch, four rings, and a paste butterfly brooch.

In one of his pockets we found two cards on which significant words had been written.

On one side of the cards was printed, "E. Robinson & Co., Detroit, Mich., presented by Mr. John Robinson", and on the back, in Crippen's own pencilled handwriting this appeared:

"I cannot stand the horror I go through every night any longer, and as I see nothing to-night ahead and money has come to an end, I have made up my mind to jump overboard to-night. I know I have spoiled your life but II (there were two I's) but hope some day you can learn to forgive me. Last words of love.

Yours, H."

On the other card, or rather piece of card, had been written:

"Shall we wait till to-night about 10 or 11? If not, what time?"

He was then taken to another cabin, and on the way said: "I am not sorry; the anxiety has been too much." I then read the warrant in detail to him, but he made no reply. Inspector McCarthy then put the handcuffs on him, and I said, "We must put these on, because on a card found on you, you have written that you intend jumping overboard." He replied, "I won't. I am more than satisfied, because the anxiety has been too awful."[148]

Shortly afterwards Crippen said, "How is Miss Le Neve?" I said, "Agitated, but I am doing all I can for her." He said, "It is only fair to say that she knows nothing about it; I never told her anything."[149]

---

148 *TWN*, 29 September 1934, had: "At the time these messages seemed to have only one possible construction. They surely meant that Crippen had contemplated, and made plans for committing suicide. I took possession of the cards, and warned him that, as he appeared to be thinking of jumping overboard, it was my duty to keep him handcuffed.

To this Crippen replied: "I would not. I am more than satisfied, because all the anxiety has been too awful.""

149 This paragraph did not appear in *ETWN*, but appeared slightly later in *STWN*, 29 September 1934: "One of the first things he asked me after I returned to his cabin was how Miss Le Neve was. I told her she was very agitated, but I was doing all I could for her.

His next remark was designed to shield her from all possible consequences. "It is only fair to say," he said, "that she knows nothing about it. I never told her anything.""

When he was in the witness-box giving evidence on his own behalf at the Old Bailey, Crippen gave an ingenious, if unconvincing explanation of the message relating to suicide. He said both messages were written at the suggestion of one of the quartermasters of the *Montrose*, with the object of hoodwinking the police into thinking he had committed suicide.

His story was that this friendly quartermaster had told him that his secret had been discovered, and that the police would be awaiting him at Quebec.

They had then formulated a scheme for staging a bogus suicide and evading capture. The quartermaster, Crippen declared, had promised to stow him away and smuggle him ashore at Montreal. Then when the police came on board Miss Le Neve would hand them the cards with the suicide messages, and they would have no option but to think their quarry was dead.

But Crippen could not give the quartermaster's name, and the story he told was so vague that no doubt is left in my mind that the quartermaster episode was a pure invention designed to explain away a damning piece of evidence.[150]

My belief is that Crippen really did intend to take his life and would have done so before the *Montrose* reached Quebec.[151]

Whatever may be said and thought about Crippen, one can only admire his attitude towards the girl who had shared his great adventure.

III

FROM then until the end Miss Le Neve[152] was his greatest, indeed it seemed to me, his only concern. He was continually inquiring after her, and embarrassingly grateful for any little thing I was able to do for her while at Quebec and during the journey home.

Dr. Crippen's love for the girl, for whom he had risked so much,

---

150   Additional sentence here in *STWN*, 29 September 1934: "It is certainly significant that no attempt was made by the defence to get the mysterious quartermaster to the Old Bailey to give evidence on the prisoner's behalf."

151   Additional sentence here in *STWN*, 29 September 1934: "In the circumstances it was indeed fortunate for me that I had made plans to intercept the vessel at Father Point."

152   "Ethel Le Neve" in *STWN*, 29 September 1934.

was the biggest thing in his whole life.

With my capture of Dr. Crippen and Miss Le Neve my troubles were by no means over.

My first and most pressing bother was the newspaper men, to whom I had given the promised three blasts on the ship's siren.[153] When they came on board the *Montrose* they began to badger me to be allowed to interview and photograph the prisoners.

I flatly refused and, because of my attitude, I am afraid I became somewhat unpopular.[154] They seemed to think they should be allowed to carry on just as they would have done in the United States.[155] I had very different views and expressed them pretty strongly.

All they got from me was that the suspected passengers had been identified[156] as Crippen and Miss Le Neve and had been placed under arrest.

By this time each prisoner was safely locked from sight in a separate cabin under the charge of police officers.

Later on, when Miss Le Neve was in her cabin with the stewardess, Captain Kendall came along to ask if he could do anything for her.[157] He then said to her, "Have you seen the letter from your father in the newspapers?" She replied: "No, I have not seen any papers whatever since I left London. I know nothing about it. If I had seen anything in the papers I should have communicated at once."

Then she turned to me and amplified this by saying: "I assure you, Mr. Dew, that I know nothing about it. I intended to write to my sister when I arrived in Quebec."

The letter to which Captain Kendall had referred was in the

---

153 This second part of the sentence was not in *TWN*.

154 Bernard Grant of the *Daily Mirror* had followed Dew to Canada and confirmed this in his autobiography: "Not one word would he say on the subject of his prisoners, and he left no doubt in my mind as to his feelings towards all pressmen. War had been declared between himself and the American and Canadian newsmen, and that war was both bitter and personal." (Grant, *To the Four Corners*, p. 37). Dew told Chief Constable Bigham at Scotland Yard that his refusal to speak to the journalists resulted in abuse being "showered upon me by these gentry, and the most outrageous lies have been printed." (PRO, MEPO 3/198).

155 "badger me to be allowed to carry on just as they would have done in the United States." in *STWN*, 6 October 1934.

156 "definitely identified" in *STWN*, 6 October 1934.

157 "do anything for the female prisoner." in *STWN*, 6 October 1934.

nature of an appeal, pleading with her to come home, and promising that everything would be forgiven.[158]

By this time, another wireless message[159] was on its way to England reporting the success of my mission.

I learned on my return that the news caused great excitement, even in such an unemotional place as Scotland Yard.[160]

The *Montrose* arrived at Quebec at ten o'clock on the Sunday night. The news had preceded us and great excitement prevailed. Through the crowds which thronged the quay my two prisoners were conveyed to police headquarters, where they were detained for the night.

Next morning they were brought before the magistrates and remanded, both agreeing to waive extradition proceedings and return to England as soon as possible.

Crippen was then taken to the prison on the Plains of Abraham.

In ordinary circumstances[161] Miss Le Neve would have been taken to the same prison. But she was ill. Inspector McCarthy, of the Quebec City Police, offered to look after the girl, with his wife,[162] in their own home until such time as she had recovered sufficiently to stand the rigours of gaol. I was very pleased with this arrangement, for it was far from my wish to subject her[163] to any unnecessary suffering.

Quebec during the days that followed became almost impossible for me. The excitement and interest of the public was such that I experienced great difficulty in getting any privacy.

There were many things to be done. Certain formalities had to

---

158   The letter was written on 17 July and read: "Dear Ethel.–Should this letter by any chance come before your notice, I fervently appeal to you with all a father and mother's love to return to London or give yourself up to the police authorities in whatever country you may be.

Every hour that you stay away you are making the situation terribly worse for yourself. Do wire me instanter.

Assured to you my devotion and protection through this your trouble. Your affectionate Dad." (*Daily Mail*, 18 July 1910).

159   "a wireless cable" in *STWN*, 6 October 1934.

160   "a normally phlegmatic place as Scotland Yard." in *ETWN*, 6 October 1934.

161   "In normal circumstances" in *TWN*, 6 October 1934.

162   "with his wife" was not in *ETWN*. *STWN*, 6 October 1934, had "and Inspector McCarthy and his wife offered to look after the girl in their own home."

163   "subject Crippen's companion" in *STWN*, 6 October 1934.

be gone through with the authorities at Quebec and Ottawa, while I had to make arrangements for conveying the prisoners[164] back to England. In the latter connexion I was constantly in touch with Scotland Yard by cable.

It was arranged that Sergeant Mitchell, who had worked with me in the early inquiries, and two women warders[165] from Holloway Prison should be sent to Canada to assist me on the voyage home.

When in Quebec I visited Crippen and Miss Le Neve almost daily,[166] getting for both of them articles they needed. Crippen's chief demand was for books. He was a gluttonous reader.

It was a very harassing time. In upholding the prestige of British justice and British police methods, and steadfastly refusing to discuss Crippen and Miss Le Neve or to give any information whatever concerning the case, I got into the bad books of some of the newspapers.

What everyone in Quebec wanted to know and especially the newspapers, was how Crippen and Miss Le Neve were to be conveyed to England.

I was determined that this secret should be kept.

In the absence of genuine information, all kinds of stories were invented. One ridiculous rumour which gained currency, and was believed by a lot of people, was to the effect that the prisoners would be taken to St. John's, Halifax, and thence to England on a cattle boat.

In the meantime, in spite of being shadowed everywhere I went,[167] I was proceeding quietly with my own secret plans.

I got quietly into touch with the White Star agent at Quebec, and was pleased to find that he was a man in whom I could place implicit reliance.

Then, having ascertained from the Canadian authorities when my warrants and documents from Governor-General[168] would be ready and the prisoners handed over to me, I got my White Star

---

164 "my prisoners" in *TWN*, 6 October 1934.

165 "women officers" in *ETWN*, 6 October 1934, "female officers" in *STWN*, 6 October 1934.

166 Just "daily" in *TWN*, 6 October 1934.

167 Dew complained that journalists "intrude into my hotel and force their questions upon me at meals." (PRO, MEPO 3/198). No detail was too trivial for the Press. They even reported that Dew had "fresh Canadian eggs and salt pork" for breakfast. (*Daily Mail*, 1 August 1910).

168 "from the Governor-General" in *TWN*, 6 October 1934.

Line "confederate" to book passages for the whole party in the liner *Megantic*, a sister ship of the *Laurentic*, which was sailing from Montreal for Quebec and England on Saturday, 20th August.

No one studying the liner's passenger list would have been any wiser. Miss Le Neve was to travel as Miss Byrne; Crippen's passage was booked in the name of Nield,[169] while I had become temporarily a Mr. Doyle.[170]

The next problem was where and how to board the liner. I was particularly anxious that this should not be done either at Montreal or Quebec.

In consultation with my White Star Line friend, I worked out a neat little scheme which, I hoped, would secure for us the secrecy I wanted.

The plan was to hire a small tug, or river boat, which the whole party would join at a wharf some miles up the St. Lawrence from Quebec. We were then to steam towards Montreal and board the *Megantic* on her way down the St. Lawrence to Quebec.

You may take it from me that I had very good reasons for the action I took.

I had had plenty of opportunities for sensing public opinion in Quebec. The people there were incensed against Crippen. They looked upon him as a monster in human form. By some[171] he had already been judged and found guilty. The ghastly murder and mutilation of Belle Elmore, followed by his flight from justice with Miss Ethel Le Neve as his companion, had roused public feeling against him to fever point.

It was the same the world over. I have never known anything like it. Only those who can remember the case and the intense excitement and bitterness it engendered, can have any conception of the widespread antipathy towards the little man who was now in my charge.

It was my job to get Crippen safely to England. To be certain of

---

169 "Field" in *TWN*, 6 October 1934 and *The Times*, 29 August 1910. Dew had used the name Silas P. Doyle, leading a disgruntled American journalist to call him "Sillyass P. Doyle." (Grant, *To the Four Corners*, p. 45).

170 The passenger list held at the National Archives gives their correct names, although Mitchell's first name was incorrectly recorded as "Charles". (PRO, BT 26/422).

171 "By them" in *TWN*, 6 October 1934.

doing this it was necessary to avoid any sort of public demonstration in Quebec at this time, and I knew well enough that there would have been a demonstration, possibly developing into an ugly situation, if the time of Crippen's departure had become known.

This was a risk I dared not take.

Late on the Friday night I made arrangements for two closed carriages to be at a certain rendezvous in Quebec the following morning at six o'clock. Inspectors McCarthy and Dennis,[172] Sergeant Mitchell, and the two women officers and myself met at the appointed time and drove to the prison, where by previous arrangement with the Governor, Crippen and Miss Le Neve were all in readiness to leave.

I was relieved to see the vicinity of the prison completely deserted. This told me that my secret, which of necessity had had to be shared with several others, had been kept. To the loyalty of those who stood by me in this matter I wish to pay a belated tribute.

The prisoners were hurried to the waiting carriages unseen by a single curious eye,[173] and soon we had left Quebec well behind us. We drove for several miles through quiet country roads until we reached the wharf where our small steamer was waiting. There was not a soul in sight as our party made its way quickly on board.[174]

The little vessel was headed upstream and, after traveling for several miles, the big liner came into view. The pre-arranged signal was given and the *Megantic* slowed down.

At that moment, I looked downstream and saw a small steamer rapidly approaching us. I was suspicious of that steamer, and not without reason.[175]

By the time the *Megantic* had been brought to a standstill and a gangway lowered to our small craft so that we might board her, the strange steamer had drawn quite close. On board I saw a young man with a camera, and recognized him as the representative of a British newspaper.

---

172 Dennis was not mentioned in *TWN*.
173 "unseen by a single curious eye" was not in *STWN*. According to Le Neve, Dew "was smiling all over his face, and seemed very pleased to think that he had beaten the newspaper men on the very last lap." (*ETWN*, 27 November 1920).
174 "as our party went on board." in *STWN*, 6 October 1934.
175 "and not without reason." was not in *STWN*.

I discovered later that this enterprising young photographer had succeeded in getting a snap of Crippen as he was climbing the gangway to the *Megantic*.[176] He deserved it, though how he got the information which resulted in his being on the spot at the critical moment I have never discovered.

This photograph was the only one taken of Crippen or Miss Le Neve from the moment of their arrest until later they landed at Liverpool.

On board the *Megantic* I was warmly greeted by the genial captain, under whose direction my charges were taken to the staterooms reserved for them. Miss Le Neve was in the custody of the two women warders, while Mitchell and I had charge of Crippen.[177]

There was great excitement at Quebec when we arrived. The docks were thronged with people eager to get a glimpse of the prisoners. They did not succeed. At four o'clock we were off again, after I had rushed to my hotel, paid my bill, and collected my belongings.[178]

From the time we boarded the *Megantic* Crippen was never out of sight of Mitchell or myself, and Miss Le Neve always had one or other of the women officers with her.

I had plenty of opportunity now to study both my prisoners, though naturally I saw more of Crippen.

But I made a point of going into the girl's cabin frequently during the day and asking if there was anything she wanted.[179]

By this time Miss Le Neve had recovered from the shock of her arrest, and her health had considerably improved. She was now almost as calm and collected as Crippen himself There was

---

176 This was Bernard Grant, a *Daily Mirror* photographer, who wrote about the incident in his autobiography. (Grant, *To the Four Corners*, pp. 39-44). Dew told Grant he was glad it hadn't been an American or Canadian photographer who had got the photograph. (*Ibid.*, p. 42). Grant said of Dew: "I hold him in the very highest respect as an officer who would allow nothing to interfere with what he considered to be his duty." (*Ibid.*, p. 45).

177 "while Mitchell had control of Crippen." in *TWN*, 6 October 1934.

178 "At four o'clock we were off again." In *TWN*, 6 October 1934.

179 Le Neve said of Dew: "I saw a great deal of him. In course of time I grew to like him." (*ETWN*, 30 October 1920). Dew "was very nice and fatherly, and we talked about anything but the Hilldrop Crescent affair." (*ETWN*, 27 November 1920). She went so far as to address Dew as "father." (*Lloyd's Weekly News*, 13 November 1910).

no weeping, no hysterics, such as might have been excused in a woman undergoing such an ordeal.

Meals were brought to both in their cabins. Crippen ate well and apparently slept well. I found him a good conversationalist, able to talk on almost any subject. For the most part we confined ourselves to general topics–books, the weather, the liner, the progress we were making, and so on–but several times every day he asked about Miss Le Neve.

Never a word was spoken about his wife. This was a subject, of course, which was completely taboo so far as I was concerned, and Crippen himself showed no inclination to discuss the woman for whose death he was going home to stand his trial.

One would never have guessed from Crippen's demeanour and manner, on that homeward voyage, that he was under arrest for murder, and[180] that he had on his conscience a burden which few men could have borne without wilting.

The more I saw of this remarkable man the more he amazed me.

During the whole journey back across the Atlantic in the *Megantic*, Crippen and Miss Le Neve never spoke to one another. They only saw each other once. This was at Crippen's request.

One evening between eight and nine–I think it was the Wednesday–I was taking him for exercise on the boat-deck. One of his hands, as was the invariable custom, was handcuffed to mine or Mitchell's.[181]

We had been discussing general subjects when suddenly the little doctor's manner changed. A curious note[182] crept into his voice as he turned to me and said: "I hope you won't mind, Mr. Dew, but I want to ask you a favour."

"Not at all," I replied. "You know I will do anything I possibly can."

I waited for the question, but it did not come. My companion continued to walk by my side in silence, his eyes staring dreamily at the foam-flecked waves. Presently he spoke again.

"No," he said, "I think on second thoughts I'll wait till Friday."

---

180   "that he was under arrest for murder, and" was not in *STWN*.

181   "or Mitchell's" was not in *TWN*.

182   "A serious note" in *TWN*, 6 October 1934.

"Just as you wish," I replied. "But I can answer now just as well as Friday. Why not get it off your chest?"

There was another pause. It was unusual for Crippen to be like this. I began to wonder what it was he had on his mind.

Then a little haltingly, he unburdened himself.

"When you took me off the ship (the *Montrose*)," he said, "I did not see Miss Le Neve. I don't know how things may go. They may go all right or they may go all wrong with me.[183] I may never see her again, and I want to ask you if you will let me see her. I won't speak to her.[184] She has been my only comfort for the last three years."[185]

I admit I was touched. Where is the man who could have listened unmoved to such a request in such circumstances? It confirmed what I had already guessed—that in the heart of the little man I was holding for murder there was a very deep and real affection for the girl who had supplanted the wife he was alleged to have killed.

There was nothing to hinder my granting Crippen's request, and I agreed at once, providing Miss Le Neve herself raised no objection.

The doctor was embarrassingly grateful.

The next day I went to see Miss Le Neve and told her of the request her fellow prisoner had made. Her eyes lit up as she eagerly replied: "Oh, yes, please arrange it, Mr. Dew. I should like it very much."[186]

And so it came about that there was staged somewhere in mid-Atlantic one of real life's strangest little dramas.

Crippen was brought to the doorway of his cabin, Miss Le Neve stood in hers. The distance between them was probably thirty feet. There for a minute or so this tragic pair remained with eyes only for one another.

I had to be present. But somehow as I looked on I felt an interloper.

---

183   "with me" was not in *ETWN*.

184   Additional sentence here in *TWN*, 6 October 1934: "And he added with more feeling than I have ever previously heard in his voice". *STWN*, 6 October 1934 had "more feeling than I had ever previously heard".

185   "during the past three years." in *TWN*, 6 October 1934.

186   *STWN*, 6 October 1934, had a more muted response from Le Neve: "'Yes, please arrange it, Mr Dew,' she said."

Not a word was spoken. There were no hysterics on either side. Just a slight motion of the hand from one to the other. That was all.[187]

Then back to their improvised cells to await what fate had in store for them both.

I have often wondered what passed through Crippen's mind during those tense moments when his little dream was realized, and he was able to gaze again on the face of the woman he loved so devotedly. Perhaps he guessed even then that the association for which he had risked so much would never be resumed.

IV

I WAS greatly impressed on the voyage home by the unswerving loyalty of Crippen to Miss Le Neve.

Every morning he asked first thing how Miss Le Neve was. He never seemed to care much what happened to himself, so long as her innocence was established.

One incident sticks out in my memory. When off the coast of Ireland we ran into a heavy storm. Most of the passengers became ill, including my girl prisoner.[188]

Crippen was a good sailor. He remained unperturbed through it all, or would have remained unperturbed had he not learned of Miss Le Neve's condition. The news that she was seasick caused him great concern. He told me the best remedy was champagne, and that the patient should lie flat.[189]

For a moment it didn't strike me that he had it in his mind that champagne should be given to Miss Le Neve.

He saw this, and looked pleadingly at me as he said: "Oh, Mr. Dew, please give her a little champagne and I will be eternally grateful to you."

Once again my little prisoner had succeeded in touching me.

---

187   There was only Dew's word that this encounter took place. At the time Dew ambiguously wrote: "I have kept them – as far as I was concerned – apart from one another ever since." (PRO, CRIM 1/117). The story did not appear in any contemporary official account. It was repeated in Bloom, *The Girl Who Loved Crippen*, pp. 161-162.

188   Le Neve said that Dew was also sea-sick. (*ETWN*, 27 November 1920).

189   "should lie in a prone position." in *TWN*, 13 October 1934.

He had worries enough of his own. A terrible charge was hanging over his head. Yet he was able to forget all that in his anxiety for the comfort of the woman he loved.

I told him that if the storm did not abate and Miss Le Neve got no better, I would do as he suggested.

I then went along to Miss Le Neve's cabin to see how she was. She seemed worse. So I kept my promise and ordered a small bottle of champagne. The wine had a marvellous effect. The first glass seemed to relieve her suffering, and soon she was quite herself.[190]

Crippen was like a dog in his gratitude. He could scarcely have expressed greater pleasure had I told him that he could go free.

Most men, in the course of such a journey with such a prospect at the end of it, would have shown signs of breaking down. There would have been moments when, however cheerful generally, they would have been compelled to give way to fits of depression.

Dr. Crippen never did. His nerves must have been made of iron. Except that he was under constant supervision and was handcuffed when he was taken out for exercise, he lived the life of a normal passenger.

He mystified me. He seemed quite happy. He gave no trouble, and never once tried the patience of Sergeant Mitchell or myself.[191]

The impression he gave was that of a man with a mind completely at rest. Most of his time he spent reading. I used to fetch his books myself from the ship's library, being careful, of course, never to get him one with a crime or murder plot. He loved novels, especially those with a strong love interest.

By arrangement with the captain the boat-deck was placed at our disposal every evening between eight and nine. It was then the prisoners took their exercise. We gained access to the deck by some private steps, and were never under the gaze of prying eyes.

This was appreciated by both. Neither was the type which revels in publicity. Crippen was a man of retiring disposition. There was

---

190   In later years Dew gave his wife champagne when she was ill, possibly because of what Crippen had taught him. (email from Kathleen Arthur to author, 6 September 2005).

191   This came as a relief to Dew who had seen Crippen stripped and was surprised at his powerful physique. He told barrister Cecil Mercer: "Well, I'm a much heavier man, but I should have been very sorry to have had to take Crippen on." (Yates, *As Berry and I Were Saying*, p. 243).

nothing he detested more than being subjected to the public gaze.[192]

Crippen always took his exercise first. Miss Le Neve would follow, and the only difference was that she was accompanied by the female officers, though I myself was always close at hand.

I had many talks with my female prisoner. Miss Le Neve, too, bore herself bravely, but her case was not quite the same. Her conscience was clear. Her fortitude was born of the knowledge of her own innocence and her faith in the integrity of the British Justice to which she was being surrendered.

So the days passed. Liverpool was rapidly approaching.

I expected exciting scenes when we landed. My experience in Canada had warned me of what was likely to happen when we got home.

But I was quite unprepared for the amazing reception we received. The quayside was one vast concourse of people. Crippen and Miss Le Neve seemed to have acted like a magnet to the whole of the city.

When he saw the crowds Crippen showed his first signs of nervousness.

"This is terrible, Mr. Dew," he said, "I can't face it. Is it not possible to give me something with which to cover my face?"

Thereupon I handed him my heavy ulster. This came down to his ankles, and the upturned collar so covered his face that little could be seen of his features, now pale and harassed looking.

Officers from Scotland Yard and others from the Liverpool City Police came on board to congratulate me and give me a hand.

When all was ready we made a dash for the waiting train, facing a battery of cameras as we made our way down the gangway.

Crippen must have realized from the booing and jeering that accompanied our brief passage that the populace was incensed against him.

He made no comment, but he seemed relieved when we reached the shelter of the compartment of the train that was to take us to London.

192　However, an American journalist attending Crippen's trial at the Old Bailey noted that he "gazed about the crowded court with evident satisfaction. He appreciated that he was the center of attention, and returned the curious stares of the brilliant assemblage with a faint smile." (*The American Law School Review*, 1920, p. 557).

London's welcome was even more antagonistic. The boos of the terrific crowd at Euston Station could be heard before the train had drawn to a standstill. Then, met by officers from Scotland Yard, we were driven rapidly[193] to Bow Street Police Station.

Here was another tremendous crowd. More boos and more jeers. The police had taken every precaution. This was just as well, for an ugly rush was made towards the cab in which Crippen and I were travelling. Fortunately, the double gates leading to the rear of the station had been opened and we dashed through. The gates were then slammed in the faces of the angry mob.

Crippen and Miss Le Neve were immediately charged. Neither made any reply.

So ended what was probably history's most thrilling chase of a murderer.

I have already paid tribute to Crippen's demeanour from the moment of his arrest until I handed him over at Bow Street Police Station. I feel I should also add that he never once showed any animosity towards me. There was nothing in the nature of resentment, because it was chiefly as a result of my efforts that he was tracked down and caught. He was intelligent enough to realize that I had only done my duty.

Nor did he utter one word about the hostility of the public. He accepted it all as part of the price he had to pay.

It was with a big sigh of relief that I passed Crippen and Miss Le Neve to the care of others. My personal responsibility was ended.

But I was not foolish enough to think that all my worries in connexion with the case were over. Far from it.

My first experiences were pleasant. Soon after my return I received a letter from Mr. Bigham, now knighted,[194] the Chief Constable, warmly welcoming me back and congratulating me on the success of my mission.

A little later I received an enthusiastic welcome from my old chief, and I might with truth say, friend, the late Sir Melville Macnaughton.[195] He was very pleased with the way things had gone.

---

193 "driven in cabs" in *STWN*, 13 October 1934.
194 "now knighted" was not in *TWN*.
195 Macnaghten was known as "Good old Mac" at Scotland Yard and was held in great affection among his men. One of them, James Berrett, wrote: "Nothing mattered to him but ability and

Then I hurried home, where I received the best welcome of all from my delighted family. Alas, some of them are no more. One of my sons, a lad of twenty, was killed in the Great War, and my wife died a few years ago.[196]

My family little realized the worries and anxieties the Crippen case had caused me. It was a practice of mine never to discuss my cases in the family circle.[197]

So far as I know my wife never entered a police station in her life, and I am sure that with one exception my children have not. The exception was my eldest son, who recently retired on pension from the Special Branch of the Yard with the rank of inspector.[198]

There was far more in the Crippen case than my spectacular dash across the Atlantic.

On the Sunday morning I was in conference with my chief and subordinates at the Yard, discussing various aspects of the case in preparation for the trial.

Early on the Monday morning I was at the Yard again, and afterwards went on to Bow Street Police Court to give evidence of arrest at the first magisterial hearing.

There was no lessening in public interest and excitement. The street was thick with people. The court could have been filled a hundred times. I have seen nothing like it. No other murderer's personality has been quite so magnetic as that of Dr. Crippen.

The Bow Street magistrate of those days was the late Mr.

---

the will to use it. School education was almost a negligible factor. "You can't make a detective," he would say, "unless he has the ability in him. He must be born with the detective instinct if he is to be successful."" (Berrett, *When I Was at Scotland Yard*, p. 261). Dew, who was a failure at school, held a similar view. (*ICC*, p. 213).

196   Stanley Dew was killed on 26 May 1915 at which time he was twenty-one. Kate Dew died from cancer on 12 July 1927 at 3 Vincent Road, Croydon. She was sixty-one years old.

197   "never to introduce matters or to discuss my cases in the family circle." in *TWN*, 13 Oct 1934. Dew's daughter Kate confirmed that her father "was usually very reluctant to give any information or express any opinion on the work on which he was engaged." (*Daily News* (Durban), 12 November 1938).

198   Dew's eldest son, also named Walter, was born in Bethnal Green on 7 October, 1887 and joined the Metropolitan Police on 29 June 1908. He retired on 19 November 1933 (PRO, MEPO 21/69) and died at Farnborough Hospital in Kent on 31 August, 1954. On his retirement a newspaper said he: "Looks scarcely older than the twenty-five years service he has put in. Tall, lithe, and very quick in action. Knows lots of secrets of Whitehall and thereabouts. Has guarded crowned heads and statesmen. Holds a decoration from King of Denmark." (*Daily Express*, 15 November 1933).

Marsham, a giant of a man with a ruddy face and an old-fashioned style of dress which gave him the appearance of a prosperous farmer. I say he was big–he was in every sense of the term. One of the finest gentlemen I have ever met. Later the Chief Magistrate, Sir Albert de Rutzen was the magistrate who presided.[199]

Mr. Travers Humphreys (now Sir Travers Humphreys and a High Court Judge) appeared to prosecute,[200] and among the legal luminaries present was the late Sir Charles Mathews, the Director of Public Prosecutions, and a man from whom at all times I received the greatest kindness and consideration.[201]

The court was packed with a widely varied, cosmopolitan crowd. All conditions of people had fought and jostled to catch a glimpse of the ordinary little man who was holding the stage, and the demure young woman who stood by his side in the dock.

Extra police were required to keep the crowds in order.

Soon after 10.30 the prisoners were ushered into the dock. Crippen came first. He had donned a grey frock-coat and looked smarter than I had previously seen him looking.[202]

Then came Miss Le Neve. She was wearing a navy blue costume and a big hat, with a large motor veil which almost completely concealed her features.

Here again was the Crippen I had learned to know so well–self-possessed and alert. Occasionally he leaned forward to talk in whispers to his solicitor, but most of the time he had eyes only for the little woman who stood by his side.[203]

---

199   This last sentence was not in *TWN*.

200   Richard Somers Travers Christmas Humphreys (1867-1956). A supremely able prosecuting barrister, Humphreys was the junior counsel in the Crippen case. He later worked on the high-profile cases of Frederick Seddon, George Joseph Smith and Roger Casement. Humphreys was knighted in 1925 and became a judge in 1928.

201   Sir Charles Willie Mathews (1850-1920), a barrister who held the position of director of public prosecutions from 1908-1920.

202   The word "looking" was not in *ETWN*. *STWN*, 13 Oct 1934, had: "He looked smarter than I had previously seen him."

203   According to one reporter, when Crippen entered the court Dew "leaned over, nodded, and smiled. He appeared to be anxious to catch the eye of the man round whose ankles he was trying to place the shackles. He seemed to respect him.

The nod was quickly returned by the man in the dock, and he met the look in Dew's eyes with face broadened and with a pleasant smile over it." (*TWN*, 10 September 1910). *The Saturday Post*, 29 January 1916, said that it was Crippen who was eager to catch Dew's eye every day. (See Appendix 2).

My knowledge of the man had taught me that the only thing likely to break his iron nerve was signs of distress shown by the woman who had shared his life so disastrously for herself.[204]

The proceedings were brief.

Mr. Travers Humphreys, in opening the case, said the facts pointed to the female prisoner having been an accessory after the fact of murder, and intimated that this was the probable line on which the prosecution against her would proceed.

This course was followed at the next hearing. The charge of murder against Miss Le Neve was then dropped.

At the first hearing I gave evidence of arrest and on that both prisoners were remanded in custody.[205]

Crippen and his companion were then taken to the cells and with their disappearance the crowd dispersed. This was all they got in return for hours of waiting. Perhaps they were satisfied. But I have never been able to understand the mentality of such people.

I have particularly in mind a charming, cultured, and highly-connected woman who could always be found in any court when a really important case was on. She was at all the Bow Street hearings of the Crippen case, and was present at the trial at the Old Bailey, and even listened to the last fight made for Crippen's life in the Appeal Court.

What, I wonder, was the allure in her particular case?

Personally, I detested the atmosphere and surroundings of criminal courts, and always made a point of getting away at the first possible moment.

This same lady once paid me one of the nicest compliments I have ever received. During one of the many chats I had with her, she said: "I like to talk to you, Mr. Dew, because you are one of the few men I know who has had to handle pitch who has not become besmirched."

I hope sincerely that she was right.[206]

---

204 "the woman at his side." in *STWN*, 13 October 1934.

205 A reporter observed Dew enter the witness-box "clutching his brown handbag, which he opened in a business-like way, and proceeded to tell of the arrest. A homely-looking man, with a manner of putting his head on one side when he speaks, as if he were calculating every word. He told his story in a slow matter of fact tone." (*TWN*, 3 September 1910).

206 This sentence and previous paragraph were not in *STWN*.

Before passing to the famous Crippen trial at the Old Bailey, I feel I ought to say that during my absence in Canada my colleagues had done invaluable work in strengthening the chain of circumstantial evidence already in existence against Crippen.

It was during that time that the doctor's purchase of hyoscin came to light, and it was then also that some exceedingly useful evidence was obtained relating to the part of a pyjama jacket found with the remains.

The pyjama suit was definitely identified as having been sold to the Crippens by Messrs. Jones Bros., of Holloway,[207] and their representative was not only able to give the date of the transaction, but to say that the trousers I had found in a box in Crippen's bedroom, and the jacket discovered with the remains were parts of the same suit.[208]

Another important step taken during this period was the bringing to this country from America of Belle Elmore's sister.[209] She was able to give strong evidence relating to the scar upon which we were relying so much for the murdered woman's identification.

After the evidence had been completed before the Bow Street magistrate, both prisoners were committed for trial.

V

THE scenes at the Crippen trial at the Old Bailey were indescribable. Great masses of people had gathered outside the

207 "by a Holloway firm" in *STWN*, 13 October 1934.

208 Travers Humphreys said that prosecutor Richard Muir was not satisfied with the initial statements supplied by Jones Bros. staff about the pyjamas and "made more than one attempt through Dew to obtain further information, but without success... we decided as a last effort to write out a series of questions to be put to a responsible representative of the company." (Humphreys, *A Book of Trials*, p. 59). After Crippen's trial the Director of Public Prosecutions' office telephoned Scotland Yard and requested a report on the investigations into the sale of the pyjamas. Sergeant Mitchell wrote the report which said that he had taken the initial statement from the company secretary on 12 September and it had been Mitchell who returned to Jones Bros. on 17 October (the day Muir and Humphreys wrote their list of questions) "By request" to speak to the buyer who confirmed the date of the sale. (PRO, MEPO 3/198). Humphreys held Dew responsible for the delay, suggesting there was an "apparent lack of interest in the case shown by Dew after his return from Canada." Dew had allegedly informed Humphreys that Jones Bros. were unable to provide a sale date or confirm that they were definitely the ones bought by Crippen. (Humphreys, *Criminal Days*, pp. 108-109).

209 Theresa Hunn, Cora Crippen's younger sister.

building, with not the slightest hope of being admitted.

No. 1 Court was crowded. The public gallery was crammed, and every available space in the well of the court occupied. Even the seats allotted to counsel were packed with K.C.s and other leading legal men who were content to be spectators.

In the front row sat Mr. R. D. Muir (later Sir Richard Muir, and now, alas, no more),[210] and behind him was his junior, Mr. Travers Humphreys (now Sir Travers and a judge),[211] who had cleverly piloted the prosecution's case through the police court and inquest stages.

On the other side were Mr. A. A. Tobin (now Sir A. A. Tobin, the County Court Judge at Westminster),[212] Mr. Huntley Jenkins, and Mr. Roome.

The judge was Lord Alverstone, the Lord Chief Justice,[213] one of the kindliest of men.[214]

Crippen had been brought from the cells below, and stood in the dock facing the judge with a prison officer[215] on each side of him. It had been decided to try Crippen and Miss Le Neve separately.

Crippen was told by the Clerk of Arraigns that he was indicted with the wilful murder of Cora Crippen on 1st February.

"How say you? Are you guilty, or not guilty?" asked the clerk.

Crippen's voice was firm and clear as he replied: "Not guilty, my Lord."

The trial had begun.

The little man was facing his ordeal just as I had expected him to face it. His face was a mask. Outwardly he was the most calm and self-possessed person in the court.

---

210   Richard David Muir (1857-1924), a formidable and relentlessly hard-working prosecutor. When Crippen found out he was going to be facing Muir he said: "I wish it had been anyone else but him. I fear the worst." (Browne & Tullett, *Bernard Spilsbury*, p. 48). Muir was knighted in 1918.

211   Dew gave virtually the same description of Humphreys twice in *ICC*, pp. 60 & 63.

212   Alfred Aspinall Tobin (1855-1939). It is believed that Tobin was appointed because the celebrated Edward Marshall Hall was unavailable. Tobin became the Member of Parliament for Preston in 1910. He was knighted and became a judge in 1919.

213   "the Lord Chief Justice of England" in *STWN*, 20 October 1934.

214   Richard Everard Webster (1842-1915). Known as "Dicky" and a singer in his church choir, Alverstone possessed a prodigious memory and sharp mind. A former attorney general, he retired in 1913 because of ill health.

215   "a sturdy prison officer" in *STWN*, 20 October 1934.

The preliminaries over, Mr. Richard Muir rose to open the case for the Crown. In a quiet, but masterly way, he laid the facts before the judge and jury.

Crippen listened with a tense expression on his face. And well he might. For although Mr. Muir's manner was matter of fact, the points he stressed were deadly.

In conclusion he asked three vital questions:

"What had become of Belle Elmore?"

"Whose remains were those in the cellar?"

"If they were Belle Elmore's what explanation of their being found in that place was there, mutilated as they were?"

Keeping these questions before their mind he thought the jury would be able to apply the evidence to their verdict when the time came.

Then, link by link, came the chain of evidence. One of the early witnesses was a doctor friend of Crippen's.[216]

I saw him personally and got from him a statement which he now bore out in evidence. Its importance lay in its reflection of Crippen's attitude following his wife's disappearance and reported death.

The doctor, having heard that Mrs. Crippen had died in March, wrote her husband the following letter, a copy of which was now produced as an exhibit:

"Dear Peter,—[217] Both Maud and myself were inexpressibly shocked to learn of poor Belle's death. We hasten to send our heartfelt condolences on your great loss. As two of her oldest friends, why ever did you not send us a line?

"Do please give us some details of how and where she died. Maud is very much upset and very anxious to hear. Only quite casually we heard she had suddenly left for America, and were daily expecting a letter or a card from her.

"Maud could not understand it as Belle always wrote her on such important occasions, so could only think Belle wanted to cut all her old friends.

---

216 "of Mrs. Crippen's." in *STWN*, 20 October 1934. This was Dr. John Burroughs, honorary physician to the Music Hall Ladies' Guild.

217 Crippen was known to his friends as Peter.

"And now to learn she is no more. It is all so sudden that one hardly realizes the fact. We should so like to send a letter of condolence to her sister, of whom she was so fond, if you would kindly supply her address. Yours sincerely."

To this letter Crippen replied as follows:

"My Dear Doctor,–I feel sure you will forgive me for my apparent neglect, but really I have been nearly out of my mind with poor Belle's death so far away. She was not with her sister, but out in California on business for me, and quite like her disposition, would keep on[218] when she should have been in bed, with the consequence that pleuro-pneumonia terminated fatally.

"Almost to the last she refused to let me know there was any danger, so that the cable that she had gone came as a most awful shock to me.

"I fear I have sadly neglected my friends, but pray forgive, and believe me most truly appreciative of your sympathy. Even now I am not fit to talk to my friends, but as soon as I feel I can control myself I will run in on you and Maud one evening.

"I am, of course, giving up the house, and every night packing things away. With love to both, and again thanking you for your kindness, I am, as ever, yours, Peter."

Has there ever been anything more hypocritical than this letter, written by Crippen at a time when what remained of his wife's body was lying under the floor of the coal cellar but a few feet away from the room in which he lived?

The medical evidence occupied a long time. It was highly important, for it was left chiefly to the doctors to prove that the remains found in the cellar were not only those of a female, but of Mrs. Crippen.

In addition to Dr. Pepper, Dr. Willcox, and Dr. Marshall, evidence was given on these points by another medical man who was then comparatively unknown. He was Dr. Bernard Henry Spilsbury, pathologist of St. Mary's Hospital. Since then Dr. Bernard Spilsbury has become Sir Bernard Spilsbury, and has probably given more vital evidence in big criminal cases than any other living doctor.[219]

---

218 "keep up" in *STWN*, 20 October 1934 and in the *NBT*.

219 Bernard Henry Spilsbury (1877-1947). Spilsbury carried out over 25,000 post-mortems over the course of his career. He gave evidence in the cases of Frederick Seddon (1911), George

But even in those early days Sir Bernard impressed me. He gave his evidence in the same confident, self-assured manner[220] which has characterized so many of his later court appearances. The impression he gave was that he was a man who knew what he was talking about.

Every effort was made by the defence to shake Dr. Spilsbury and his colleagues on this occasion, but in spite of the fact that several eminent medical men were on the side of the prisoner, the testimony of the prosecution medical experts withstood every assault in cross-examination.

Indeed, the case against Crippen as a whole remained unbroken at any vital point, and I felt even at this stage that the chances of the little man in the dock were slender in the extreme.

The witness-box is something of an ordeal at any time. It is doubly so when a man's life is at stake. It was with a feeling of intense relief that I was allowed to stand down after occupying the box for considerably more than two hours.[221]

When the last prosecution witness had been called.[222] Mr. Tobin rose in a tense silence to make his opening address for the defence. It was both powerful and clever.

He gave Crippen's explanation for fleeing the country. This, briefly, was that he had become alarmed by my visit. He realized he was in a bad position because of the lies he had told to his wife's friends, and saw that I was determined to find Mrs. Crippen. I had said to him: "Crippen, I must find your wife," and it was these words ringing in his ears that had driven him to the decision to flee.

"Feeling that there was that high mountain of prejudice which he had erected by his lies against himself, he did what innocent

Joseph Smith (1915) and Major Herbert Armstrong (1922) among many others. Spilsbury was knighted in 1923. He committed suicide on 17 December 1947, the day after Walter Dew died.

220   "same confident manner" in *STWN*, 20 October 1934.

221   One reporter noted that Dew was always the first person to arrive at court and that when he gave his evidence he was "very suave, perfectly cool, and self-possessed... Mr. Dew is scrupulously fair to the prisoner." (*The Pall Mall Gazette*, 19 October 1910). Another described Dew as "an amiable, kindly-faced man, who gave his evidence in a rather low tone. He is not a romantic or highly-coloured personality." (*The Daily Graphic*, 20 October 1910). This view was supported by a reporter at the magistrates' court hearing who somewhat harshly described Dew as "the bland detective." (*The Bystander*, 14 September 1910).

222   Full stop here in *ICC*. *TWN* had a comma.

men, threatened with a charge, have done before. He resolved in his folly to flee.[223] What more natural than he should take with him his mistress?

"The rest followed as a matter of course–the disguise, the shaving of his moustache, the dressing of Miss Le Neve in boy's clothes."

Mr. Tobin also made a powerful point of Crippen's demeanour during my first search of 39 Hilldrop Crescent, when in his presence I actually visited the coal cellar.

"Here," said counsel, "was a supposed murderer, readily and willingly going with the chief-inspector to the house where, if he were the murderer, he knew that part of his wife's remains were buried. He went into all the rooms with Dew, and they went into the cellar together.

"If he were a murderer, if he had buried those remains in the cellar, he knew the spot in the middle of the cellar there under his very eye as he stood there!

"Yet he never turned a hair, never showed the slightest sign of agitation, or fear, or terror. Was not that beyond all powers of belief?"

Next Mr. Tobin tried to explain away the two cards I found on Crippen at the time of his arrest, on one of which he had written: "I have made up my mind to jump overboard to-night."

The prosecution contention was that these messages could mean only one thing–that Crippen, filled with remorse or possibly fearing arrest at Quebec, had decided to take his own life.

But Mr. Tobin maintained this was not the explanation at all.

"They were not written for the eyes of Miss Le Neve," he declared. "They were not written to convey to Miss Le Neve his intention to commit suicide. There would be no necessity to write those cards to Miss Le Neve, because they were together.[224]

"They were both written in pursuance of a plot to enable Crippen to get hidden and smuggled ashore to escape up country, and there be afterwards joined by Miss Le Neve when everything had blown over.

---

223 "to fly." in *STWN*, 20 October 1934 and in the *NBT*.
224 This paragraph was not in *STWN*.

"Two days before the arrest Crippen had learned from the quartermaster the he (Dr. Crippen) was to be arrested on landing at Quebec. There was then no question of Miss Le Neve's arrest at all. He expected that he (Crippen) was alone to be arrested, and the quartermaster was persuaded, or pretended to be persuaded, to believe that Crippen was entirely innocent.

"And it was arranged that just before the vessel reached Quebec, Crippen was to be concealed amongst the cargo in the ship, and that the longer card was to be found in his cabin indicating to those who found it that Crippen had jumped overboard.

"Whether the quartermaster was a guilty participator, or only pretended to be, did not matter."[225]

On completing his speech Mr. Tobin at once called Dr. Crippen. The prisoner left the dock, and proceeded unhurriedly to the witness-box. He was perfectly cool and collected, and gave his evidence in a low and distinct voice.[226]

After tracing his early life in much the same way as he had done in the statement he made to me, he was brought up to the vital points of his story and asked if the statement he had made to me was a true or a false statement.

Crippen replied: "It was quite true. Inspector Dew was very imperative in pressing upon me that I must produce my wife, or otherwise I would be in serious trouble. He also said that if I did not produce her quickly the statements I made would be in the newspapers the first thing I knew."

As a matter of fact I never, during the whole course of that first interview with Crippen, made any reference to publishing anything in the newspapers. Obviously, this was a thing I should never have dreamed of doing.

"Was Inspector Dew's coming on board at Father Point a surprise to you?" was another question Crippen was asked during his examination-in-chief.

To this he replied: "It was at Father Point—well, I did not expect him at all. I thought there had been a cable to the Quebec police. I

---

225   Additional sentence here in *STWN*, 20 October 1934: "The story of Crippen's, as I have previously said, I regarded as a pure invention, as Crippen could not give the name of the quartermaster and his story was altogether too vague."
226   "low but distinct voice." in *TWN*, 20 October 1934.

did not expect Inspector Dew. That was a surprise to me."

Asked what he meant by saying to me at the time of his arrest, "I am sorry; the anxiety has been too much?" the prisoner said, "I expected to be arrested for all the lies I told. I thought probably it would cast such a suspicion on me and perhaps they would keep me in prison–I do not know how long, perhaps a year–until they found the missing woman."[227]

Crippen's long examination concluded with two pointed questions.

"Did you ever at any time administer hyoscin to your wife?" he was asked. The reply was, "Never."

"Those remains that were found at your house in Hilldrop Crescent–have you any idea whose they were?"

"I had no idea. I knew nothing about them until I came back to England," was the emphatic reply.

Then followed one of the most searching cross-examinations ever heard in a murder trial.[228]

I shall never forget the duel[229] between Crippen and Mr. Richard Muir. Counsel for the prosecution was relentless. Crippen was clever, but not clever enough. There were gaps in his armour which Mr. Muir's skill was able to pierce.

This was Mr. Muir's first question:[230] "On the early morning of the 1st of February you were left alone in your house with your wife?"

Crippen agreed.

She was alive?–She was.

And well?–She was.

Do you know of any person in the world who has seen her alive since?–I do not.

Do you know of any person in the world who has a letter from her since?–I do not.

Do you know of any person in the world who can prove any fact showing that she ever left the house alive?–Absolutely not. I have

---

227   These three paragraphs were not in *STWN*.
228   This sentence was not in *STWN*.
229   "the Old Bailey duel" in *STWN*, 20 October 1934.
230   "The opening was dramatic enough." appeared here in *STWN*, 20 October 1934 instead of "This was Mr. Muir's first question."

told Mr. Dew all the facts.

A little later Crippen made his first blunder. He was asked at what time he came home on the evening of the first of February. He first said the time would be about seven-thirty. Pressed on the point he then said it might have been 7.25 or 7.35, but it was close on 7.30.

Mr. Muir immediately confronted the prisoner with the statement he had made to me. In this he stated: "I came to business the next morning, and when I went home between 5 and 6 p.m. I found she had gone."

"Is that right?" demanded counsel.

Crippen could only reply that if he had said that to me it was probably right.

The lapse on Crippen's part was by no means vital, but it showed thus early in his long ordeal of cross-examination that he was not quite sure of himself and his facts.

When later, Crippen was being questioned about the remains found in the coal cellar of his house the Lord Chief Justice interposed with this pointed question: "Do you really ask the jury to understand that your answer is that without your knowledge or your wife's, at some time during the five years, those remains could have been put there?"

Crippen hesitated before replying. Then speaking slowly, he said: "I say it does not seem possible–I mean it does not seem probable, but there is a possibility."

Two pairs of pyjamas were handed to Crippen. He said they were his and had been bought by himself the previous September.

Then he was shown the pair of pyjama trousers which matched the jacket found with the remains. These the witness said, had been bought long previously, he believed in 1905, soon after they went to Hilldrop Crescent.

Crippen little realized the significance of that reply. Mr. Muir warned him that his answer was highly important, and gave him every opportunity to retract. But Crippen insisted that the two suits were part of a lot of three bought the previous September and that the trousers had been bought much earlier.

A few seconds later the witness must have realized what a pit he had dug for himself, for Mr. Muir then dropped this bombshell:

"Now I am going to put this to you, so that you will have the opportunity of altering your answers if you desire to alter them, that those three sets which are now before you, one of them incomplete, were manufactured in November, 1908, and the cloth of which they were made never came into existence before 1908."

Poor Crippen was obviously staggered, and he replied weakly: "I can only say that I do not think it possible that this is so, of this set, for the reason that this is so much worn and these are not."

Again Mr. Muir gave Crippen an opportunity to alter his answers, intimating that if necessary it was possible to call evidence on the point, but Crippen stuck to his original statement.[231]

The effect of this episode on the court and upon Crippen was obvious. To the man in the witness-box, fighting desperately for his life, it must have come as a tremendous shock to realize that such a piece of damning evidence could have been obtained from a commonplace pair of pyjama trousers.

Mr. Muir next turned his attention to Crippen's flight, and some of the questions and answers were so striking that I propose to give them verbatim.

"When did you make up your mind to go away from London?" Crippen was asked.

"The morning after Inspector Dew was there–the 8th or 9th of July."

Are you sure about that?–Yes.

Had you the day before been contemplating the possibility of going away?–I would not like to say that I had made up my mind. When Inspector Dew came to me and laid out all the facts that he told me, I might have thought, "Well, if there is all this suspicion and I am likely to have to stay in gaol for months and months and months, perhaps until this woman is found, I had better be out of it!"

The Lord Chief Justice: "You must answer this question, Mr. Crippen. Do you really say that you thought you would have to stay in gaol for months and months? Do you say that?"

"Quite so, yes," said Crippen.

"Upon what charge?" challenged Mr. Muir.

231   This sentence was not in *STWN*.

"Suspicion," was the reply.

"Suspicion of what?" asked counsel.[232]

"Suspicion of being concerned in her disappearance," said Crippen.[233]

"What crime did you understand you might be kept in gaol upon suspicion of?–I do not understand the law enough to say. From what I have read it seems to me I have heard of people being arrested on suspicion of being concerned in the disappearance of other people."

"The disappearance of other people?–Well, I am doing the best I can to explain it to you. I cannot put it in a legal phrase."

The Lord Chief Justice here intervened.

"Nobody," he said, "wants you to put it in a legal phrase. The simple question is: What was the charge you thought might have been brought against you after you had seen Inspector Dew?"

"I could not define the charge, except that if I could not find the woman I was very likely to be held until she was found. That was my idea."

"Because of what?" Mr. Muir still persisted.

But Crippen was unable to amplify his previous replies. He merely repeated that Mr. Dew had told him he would be in serious trouble, and said that no other idea than that entered his head.

Later, however, Crippen added that his flight was prompted also by the fact that he had said (presumably in his statement to me) that Miss Le Neve was living with him. She had told her people she was married to him, and it would put her in a terrible position. "The only thing I could think of was to take her away out of the country where she would not have this scandal thrown upon her."

Mr. Muir: You thought you were in danger of arrest?–Yes.

And so you fled the country?–Yes.

Under a false name?–Yes.

Shaved off your moustache?–Yes.

Left off wearing your glasses in public?–Yes.

Took Miss Le Neve with you?–Yes.

Under a false name posing as your son?–Yes.

---

232 "asked counsel." was not in *STWN*.

233 *STWN*, 20 October 1934 had "Suspicion of what Inspector Dew said. "This woman has disappeared. She must be found." "Suspicion of what?" persisted counsel. "Suspicion of being concerned in her disappearance," said Crippen."

Went to Antwerp?–Yes.[234]

And so, hour after hour, the cross-examination went on. On the whole, Crippen came out of the ordeal well, but there were times when the penetrative questioning of Mr. Muir laid bare the weaknesses of his case.

No person, with experience of criminal court procedure, could have escaped the impression that the little doctor was seeking cleverly, if unconvincingly, to give innocent interpretations to facts all pointing strongly to his guilt.

A lesser man–that is lesser in education and self-control–would have collapsed completely under the searching cross-examination for the Crown.[235]

VI

AFTER the searching cross-examination by prosecuting counsel, Crippen's ordeal was not over.

He was re-examined by Mr. Tobin for the defence, and then the Lord Chief Justice took up the rôle of questioner.

Crippen agreed that Belle Elmore, to her friends and the outside world, was amiable and pleasant. He said he found her gone when he came home on the evening of 1st February. Except for a watch and a few rings, he said, he noticed nothing missing from the house.

At long last it was over, and Crippen left the witness-box and crossed to the dock as impassive as ever.

In his heart, Crippen must have known that many of his answers had been unsatisfactory but he did not show it.

To me he was still a puzzle. In my whole dealings with him I saw nothing which by the wildest stretch of the imagination could be said to suggest that he had in his make-up the capacity for so terrible a crime.

I noticed one curious thing about Crippen when he was giving evidence. He never once referred to the dead woman as "my wife",

---

234 *STWN*, 20 October 1934, had: "And so you fled from the country under a false name, shaved off your moustache, left off wearing your glasses in public, took Miss Le Neve with you under a false name posing as your son?" "Yes."

235 "the searching cross-examination of the Counsel for the Crown. But Crippen had still to face the questioning of the Lord Chief Justice." in *STWN*, 20 October 1934.

or "Mrs. Crippen". Throughout, he spoke of her as "this woman", or "that woman".[236]

There have been many conjectures as to Crippen's motive for murdering his wife. I do not propose to discuss these.

There never has been an adequate motive for murder. There certainly was no reason for Crippen to kill his wife. He had no strong ties to keep him in England, so he could have taken all he wanted in the way of jewellery and left for any part of the world, taking Miss Le Neve with him. If he had done this, I doubt if anyone would have tried to stop him or to bring him back.

All it is necessary for me to say is that I have never wavered from the opinion that Crippen was guilty.

I believe[237] he harboured an intense hatred for his wife. The cause does not matter. It was, however, sufficient to cause him to take her life, and to do so in a way which he hoped would escape discovery.

Dr. Crippen was in many ways a modest man. In others he was egotistical. I shall always believe that he was vain enough to think he had the cleverness to commit the perfect crime. But murderers, however clever, invariably make fatal blunders. Crippen made many. One of the worst, perhaps, was in trying to destroy the ghastly remains of his wife by placing a quantity of lime with them in the cellar. He also did something else in connexion with the lime, but I don't think it is in the public interest to say more on this subject; but it formed a strong link in the chain of evidence that led to his condemnation.[238]

The question has been asked, and it might be asked again: "Why, holding such an opinion about Crippen, did you go out of your way to show him acts of kindness after he was in your custody?"

The truth is that I showed no more courtesy or kindness to Crippen than I have done to any of the hundreds of other prisoners who have passed through my hands.

I have always maintained that it is the duty of a police officer to treat a prisoner with consideration and fairness and consider him

236   "It was always "this woman" or "that woman."" in *STWN*, 27 October 1934.
237   "Deep down I believe" in *STWN*, 27 October 1934.
238   These last four sentences were not in *TWN*. The "something else" was that Crippen had added water to the lime which made it a preservative instead of a destroyer of flesh.

innocent until he has been found guilty.

It is the police officer's job to catch the suspect and to see that he or she appears before the proper tribunal.[239] Hence the enormous amount of trouble I went to in order to ensure that Dr. Crippen was brought safely back to England.

Four days of the Crippen trial, each of them packed with drama, had passed. The case was now drawing to its close.

Perhaps he knew what it would be before Saturday, 22nd October, 1910, the day on which the verdict was given and sentence was passed. My own impression is that from the very first he had little hope for himself. That remark of his on the ship which brought him back[240] to England stuck in my mind.

"When you took me off the ship I did not see Miss Le Neve, and I don't know how things may go. They may go all right and they may go all wrong with me, and I may never see her again."

When Crippen said that, he had no conception of the strength of the case against him.

Now, on the final day of the trial, having listened to witness after witness for the prosecution, and having heard the powerful arguments of Mr. Muir, his last hope of renewing his association with the woman he loved must have vanished.

Nor was there anything in the scrupulously fair summing-up of the Lord Chief Justice to revive his waning hopes of eventual freedom. The Lord Chief Justice made it quite clear to the jury how important was the question of identity.

"If the body in the cellar," he said, "was not the body of Cora Crippen, but of some other person, Dr. Crippen is entitled to go out of this court." Again: "You are to draw no conclusion whatever against Dr. Crippen unless you are satisfied that the remains in the cellar are the remains of his wife, and that he, in fact, murdered his wife in the way suggested. He is not here on any other charge than that of murdering his wife."

His Lordship then proceeded to deal exhaustively with the evidence on the vital question. He emphasized that the pyjama jacket found with the remains was identical, even to the pattern and

---

239 This was echoed in a comment Dew made about Crippen to his second wife: "It is not for me to judge the man. I knew nothing about him." (*Worthing and District Review*, January 1948).
240 "brought us back" in *TWN*, 27 October 1934.

number of threads, with the trousers found in Crippen's bedroom and admitted to be his.

The operation scar was described by the Lord Chief Justice as "the battle-ground in this case".

He was right.

Upon that scar hinged the identity of the dead woman. At this stage one might have gone further and said that upon it depended the issue of the whole case. Once satisfied on this point, the jury seemed to have little alternative but to bring in a "guilty" verdict.

When he came to deal with the statement Crippen had made to me, the Lord Chief Justice had this to say:

"Now, it has been for years a test applied in these courts, and it ought to be applied. How did the man behave when the charge was brought against him? You have heard his answers to Mr. Muir and to his own counsel and to me. 'I have read romances, and I thought I might be arrested and kept in gaol for months on suspicion because of my wife's disappearance,' his story being that she had left him.

"Gentlemen, we are not children, and he is not a child. Is that argument satisfactory to you? You have it that, living there in the same name, carrying on his business, consorting with Miss Le Neve for practically six months, the day after the inspector goes to his house he alters his name and flees, goes to Antwerp, appears under the name of Robinson, induces Ethel Le Neve to disguise herself as a boy, passes her off as his son, and endeavours to escape to Canada, and he would no doubt have got there but for Inspector Dew being able to catch him . . ."

One could go on indefinitely reviewing and giving extracts from the trial, but I think I have quoted sufficient to show its inevitable trend.

There is, however, one point I would like to make. Neither the Lord Chief Justice nor Mr. Muir nor anyone else,[241] made the slightest suggestion that Crippen should have been detained before he ran away. Indeed the Lord Chief Justice ridiculed the idea of any charge being brought at that time.

Yet, mark you, a very few stupid people still tried to blame me for not arresting Crippen on or about 8th July.

---

241   "nor Mr Muir, nor, for the matter of that, anyone else" in *STWN*, 27 October 1934.

Sir Melville Macnaughton, my chief, apparently under the impression that I was upset by these foolish innuendoes, said to me one day: "Never mind, Mr. Dew, you will always find a lot of yapping curs at the heels of a better dog."

The matter was left at that.

But I suppose the best answer to my irresponsible critics is that it was through my efforts that the body was found and the complete chain of evidence against Crippen forged.

The Lord Chief Justice wound up his summing-up[242] by warning the jury that the benefit of any doubt must be given to Crippen.[243]

The jury took just twenty-seven minutes to decide that Crippen must die. I was surprised by the swiftness–unusual in a murder case–of their return.[244]

All eyes were now turned on Crippen. How the majority of those present reacted to that moment of drama I cannot say, but I know my own heart beat a little faster as I looked again at the man whose fate was now sealed.

He took his "medicine" in the manner I expected. There was nothing in his outward appearance to show that it was of him those fateful words of the foreman of the jury had been spoken. His bulgy eyes never flickered. The muscles of his face did not twitch. And when he spoke in answer to the clerk's question: "Have you anything to say why the Court should not give you judgement of death, according to law?" his words came clearly.

"I am innocent," he said.

And when he was asked if he wished to say anything, the same calm clear voice replied: "I still protest my innocence."

Then the judge, under his black cap, passed sentence of death, and Crippen turned and walked from the dock with a face as expressionless as it was on that day in July when I first met him at

---

242 "his calm and dignified summing-up" in *STWN*, 27 October 1934.

243 Additional sentence here in *STWN*, 27 October 1934: "and in an atmosphere made tense by the knowledge that the fate of the little man in the dock was in their hands the jury filed slowly out of the Court."

244 Lord Alverstone was pleased with the quick verdict. After his summing-up he had retired to his rooms for a cup of tea with his friend Henry Leveson Gower, the Surrey and England cricketer. Alverstone said to Gower: "Shrimp, I hope the Jury will not be much longer as I have promised to give away some billiard prizes at 4.30." Alverstone got to the billiard hall in time. (Gower, *Off and On the Field*, p. 154).

Albion House.

So passed from sight Dr. Hawley Harvey Crippen, the murderer with the strangest complex I have ever known. And so ended the drama of my most thrilling adventure as an officer of the law.

Crippen appealed, but without success. He was hanged at Pentonville Prison on 23rd November, 1910. How he met his death I do not know. Happily, it was not part of my duties to be present at that grim scene.

But knowing the man as I had learned to know him, I have no doubt that he bore himself bravely, and that his self-control never deserted him on that cold November morning when he breathed his last.[245]

Why was this strange little man known as "Doctor" Crippen? This is easily answered. When I searched 39 Hilldrop Crescent, I found a diploma of the Hospital College of Cleveland (Ohio) which had been presented and registered in July, 1900, in the office of the Clerk of Kings, by Hawley Harvey Crippen, as his authority to practice physic and surgery, &c. Other documents found showed that Crippen had been instructed in a course of medicine and kindred sciences. From this it will be gathered that he was not drawing on his imagination in describing himself as a doctor, at any rate, so far as the U.S.A. was concerned.[246]

Crippen died with the consolation of knowing that Miss Ethel Le Neve was free. Exactly a month before he was executed, she stood her trial before the Lord Chief Justice at the Old Bailey. She was charged with being an accessory, or, as Mr. Muir, who again prosecuted, put it, "with assisting Hawley Harvey Crippen to escape from justice at a time when she knew that he had been guilty of the murder of his wife".

She was defended by that brilliant lawyer and orator, Mr. F. E. Smith, later Lord Birkenhead, and now, like so many others who

---

245   Executioner John Ellis recorded that: "If he had ever shown cowardice or collapse he displayed none now.

I could see him smiling as he approached, and the smile never left his face up to the moment when I threw the white cap over it and blotted out God's light from his eyes for ever." (*TWN*, 19 July 1924). However, Crippen had been prevented from committing suicide the night before by his warders. (PRO HO 144/1718/195492).

246   This paragraph was not in *TWN*.

were prominently associated with the Crippen case, no more.[247]

Miss Le Neve must have suffered great agony of mind as she stood demurely in the dock on such a charge.

But after listening to the brilliant speech of "F. E." I do not think she could have had many anxieties as to the result. And when the judge had summed up there could not have been a person in court who was not prepared for the verdict of "Not Guilty" returned by the jury after a brief absence from the court.

I am quite certain that most people, including myself, felt satisfied that justice had been done. Poor Miss Le Neve had suffered enough. Her association with Crippen had cost her many weeks of mental torture and doubt.

Shortly after the trial, Miss Le Neve called to see me at Scotland Yard. She thanked me for what she described as "My kindness and consideration to her through her ordeal".[248] And she added that Dr. Crippen, whom she had seen at Pentonville, begged to add his thanks.

Though, as I have already said, I do not think I did anything for either of them deserving of special thanks, I did appreciate Miss Le Neve's call. It was nice to know that in spite of the trouble I had been instrumental in bringing on them both by capturing them,[249] neither she nor Crippen bore me any animosity.

I wonder if Crippen died with Miss Le Neve's name on his lips? His last published letter certainly showed that his thoughts of her transcended all anxiety for himself.

"In this farewell letter to the world, written as I face eternity (he wrote) I say that Ethel Le Neve has loved me as few women love men, and that her innocence of any crime, save that of yielding to the dictates of the heart, is absolute. To her I pay this last tribute. It

---

247   Frederick Edwin Smith (1872-1930). A Member of Parliament and barrister, Smith cut a glamorous figure when appearing in court. Smith was Winston Churchill's closest friend and rose to high office, serving as solicitor general and attorney general. He was knighted in 1914 and created Baron Birkenhead in 1918.

248   Le Neve always spoke highly of Dew, saying: "Walter Dew turned out to be a very nice man and a real friend to a poor girl in distress." (*ETWN*, 16 October 1920). He was "one of the straightest, kindliest men I ever met." (*TWN*, 30 October 1920). She described Dew as "one of the smartest men that ever passed along the corridors of Scotland Yard." (*ETWN*, 13 November 1920).

249   "by capturing them" was not in *TWN*.

is of her that my last thoughts have been. My last prayer will be that God will protect her and keep her safe from harm and allow her to join me in eternity."

And his last letter to Miss Le Neve herself was one of the most remarkable documents ever written in a condemned cell:

"Time is short now,[250] and there is so much that I would say.

"There are less than two days left to us. Only one more letter after this can I write you, and only two more visits, one to-night before you read this letter, and one to-morrow.

"When I wrote to you on Saturday I had not heard any news of the petition, and though I never at any time had hope, yet deep down in my heart was just a glimmer of trust that God might give us yet a chance to put me right before the world and let me have the passionate longing of my soul.

"Your letter, written early Saturday, came to me last Saturday evening and soon after the Governor brought me the dreadful news about ten o'clock.

"When he had gone I kissed your face in the photo, my faithful and devoted companion in all this sorrow.

"Oh, how glad I am I had the photo. It was some consolation, although in spite of all my greatest efforts it was impossible to keep down a great sob and my heart's agonized cry.

"How am I to endure my last look at your dear face? What agony must I go through at the last when you disappear for ever from my eyes! God help us to be brave then. That is my constant prayer."[251]

---

250   "so short now" in *STWN*, 27 October 1934 and in the *NBT*.

251   Additional text here in *TWN*, 27 October 1934, under the sub-heading (in *ETWN*) "What Crippen Cost the Nation": "Before drawing my narrative to a close there is one other point I would like to touch upon. Wild statements have been made from time to time as to the cost of the Crippen case to the nation. Only the other day I read that something like £10,000 was spent in the search for Crippen up to the time the wireless message was received from Captain Kendall, and that "the trial that led to his conviction and execution added thousands to the bill of costs to the public."

I cannot allow this to go unchallenged. It was a gross over-estimate. I doubt very much if my own cab fares before the famous wireless message was received amounted to more than £2, and I am certain that the whole expense entailed in the inquiries up to the time of the wireless did not amount to more than £300, if that."

This had been provoked by an article in the *Daily Mail* on 10 July 1934, and it was possibly a last-minute addition to the *TWN* text. Dew wrote an angry letter to the *Mail* which they did not publish. (See Appendix 1). It seems unlikely that this was what inspired him to

There is little more to add. The Crippen case placed the coping-stone on my thirty years' service in the police force. It seemed a fitting moment to retire.

My decision caused surprise. My chiefs, Sir Edward Henry,[252] Sir Melville Macnaughton and Mr. Trevor Bigham, all wished me to remain, while the late Sir Charles Mathews, the Director of Public Prosecutions, sent for me and asked me to reconsider my decision.

But there were special private reasons which compelled me to stick to my resolution, and so later in the same year I retired on full pension. I was given an exemplary certificate of character. This meant that I had gone through my whole career without a single complaint being made against me.[253] I was proud of this, and proud, too, of the fact that I had at one time and another, received considerably more than a hundred commendations from judges, magistrates, the commissioner, war lords, the Admiralty, and the Directors of Public Prosecutions in whose periods I served.

My career provides a strange and gruesome coincidence. As a young officer, just appointed to the Criminal Investigation Department, I was stationed in the Whitechapel Division. This was at the height of the "Jack the Ripper" terror. My inquiries in connexion with that unsolved mystery brought me to the notice of the higher authorities at Scotland Yard, and helped my advancement.

My last job as a chief inspector at the "Yard" was the capture of Crippen.

Mutilation of the bodies was a feature of both crimes.

write his memoirs and set the record straight, as they were published so soon after. Perhaps he had already written the articles and added his comments about the *Mail*'s claims because he had the opportunity to do so.

252 Sir Edward Richard Henry (1850-1931), Metropolitan Police commissioner from 1903-1918. Henry was a pioneer in establishing fingerprinting as a means of identification.

253 This is confirmed in the Metropolitan Police Removal Register. (PRO, MEPO 4/343).

THE CRIME OF
DR CRIPPEN

39 Hilldrop Crescent, Camden Town.
(I Caught Crippen)

Top: *Lil Hawthorne who told Walter Dew*
about Cora Crippen's disappearance.
(Author's collection)

Middle: *Superintendent Frank Froest.*
(The Police Encyclopaedia)

Bottom: *A fanciful depiction of Dew's first meeting*
with Ethel Le Neve, from a 1930s magazine.
(Family Star)

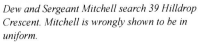

Dew and Sergeant Mitchell search 39 Hilldrop Crescent. Mitchell is wrongly shown to be in uniform.
(The Illustrated Police News)

The discovery of Cora Crippen's remains in the cellar. Only Dew and Mitchell were present.
(The Illustrated Police News)

SCENE AT THE INQUEST.
INSPECTOR DEW.-"EACH PIECE OF FLESH
WAS NO BIGGER THAN THAT BAG"

A plan of the trans-Atlantic chase.
(Thomson's Weekly News)

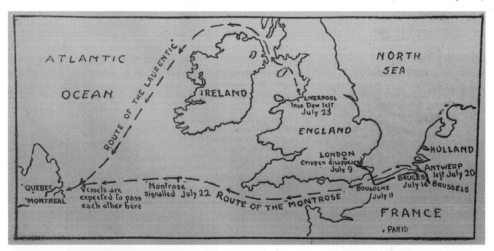

Top: "Mr. Dewhurst"
boards the Laurentic.
(The Illustrated Police News)

Bottom: A disguised Dew
approaches the Montrose.
(The Daily Graphic)

An imaginative depiction of Dew confronting
Crippen on board the Montrose.
(Le Petit Journal)

*Right: Mitchell, Crippen and Dew board the Megantic
for the return voyage.*
(To the Four Corners)

Below: Dew's appearance causes Ethel Le Neve to faint.
(The Illustrated Police News)

MISS LE NEVE FAINTS IN HER CABIN.

Dew escorts Crippen off the Megantic at Liverpool.
(I Caught Crippen)

PHOTOGRAPHS OF CRIPPEN'S RETURN.

DAILY GRAPHIC

ONE PENNY

LONDON: MONDAY, AUGUST 29, 1910.

REGISTERED AS A NEWSPAPER.

No. 6464.—Vol. LXXXIII.

CRIPPEN LANDS AT LAST.

A STRIKING PHOTOGRAPH OF "DR." CRIPPEN AS HE WAS CONDUCTED ON TO THE LANDING STAGE BY INSPECTOR DEW AT LIVERPOOL ON SATURDAY; OWING TO HIS HIGH COLLAR AND HAT IT WAS AT FIRST THOUGHT THAT CRIPPEN WAS MASKED   ("Daily Graphic" photograph.)

613

Walter Dew giving evidence at Bow Street.
(The Bystander)

Bow Street Magistrates' Court and Police Station.
(The Queen's London)

Crippen and Le Neve
in the dock at Bow Street.
(I Caught Crippen)

Right: Walter Dew outside the Old Bailey during Crippen's trial.
(Stewart P. Evans)

Below: Magistrate Sir Albert de Rutzen, playwright Sir William Gilbert and Sir Melville Macnaghten watching the proceedings.
(The Bystander)

The Old Bailey, scene of Dr. Crippen's and Ethel Le Neve's trials.
(Author's collection)

THE HUNT
FOR JACK THE RIPPER

THE HUNT
FOR JACK THE RIPPER[254]

In writing of the "Jack the Ripper crimes", it must be remembered that they took place fifty years ago, and it may be that small errors as to dates and days may have crept in.[255]

I

IN the early part of 1887 I was transferred to the "H", or Whitechapel Division of the Metropolitan Police, and attached to Commercial Street Police Station.[256]

From Paddington and Bayswater I was sent to a district which, even before the advent of Jack the Ripper, a year later, had a reputation for vice and villainy unequalled anywhere in the British Isles.

I had attained my first ambition as a police officer, being now a member of the famous Criminal Investigation Department–a detective officer.[257]

But the natural elation with which I viewed my promotion was

---

254 Called "My Hunt For Jack the Ripper" in *TWN* and on the contents page of *I Caught Crippen*.

255 This short preamble did not appear in *TWN*, 19 January 1935, which had instead: "THE most terrifying killer of all time–That was Jack the Ripper, the phantom-like fiend who stalked the streets of Whitechapel, London.

Again and again he came in the silence of the night on his mission of murder and mutilation. His victims were all women.

For years the Ripper kept the whole country in a state of terror, and even to-day there are women in the East End who remember and tremble at the very mention of the name.

Ex Chief Inspector Dew, who was stationed in Whitechapel during the whole of the Ripper atrocities, was the first policeman on the scene at one of the murders. "It was the most terrible sight I have ever seen," says Mr Dew, who gives a vivid account of the actual crimes and the awful state of the district at the time they were committed."

256 Dew's transfer to H Division was noted in Metropolitan Police Orders for 2 June 1887 and confirmed in the orders of 7 September 1887. (PRO, MEPO 7/49, pp. 132 & 212).

257 "a plain clothes detective officer." in *TWN*, 19 January 1935.

tempered by my knowledge of the neighbourhood to which I had been sent to win my detective's "spurs".

I knew that I might have to spend many years there.[258] For myself I did not care so much. My chief concern arose from the fact that I had just married, and the thought of taking my wife to live in that hot-bed of crime[259] filled me with foreboding.[260]

Whitechapel, Spitalfields and Shoreditch were now my hunting-ground, with hundreds of criminals of the worst type as my quarry.

I knew Whitechapel[261] pretty well by the time the first of the atrocious murders, afterwards attributed to Jack the Ripper, took place. And I remained there until his orgy of motiveless killing came to an end.

All his victims were women of the unfortunate class. Some of them had known better days.

There were no lower depths to which these hapless women could sink.

Why did the Ripper choose them as his victims? I do not know. This is one of the questions which will never now be answered.

Few of them were pretty or young.[262] Indeed, with one exception, all the women lured by the killer to their deaths were approaching or past middle age.

The exception was Marie Kelly, aged between 20 and 25[263] and quite attractive. I knew Marie quite well by sight. Often I had seen her parading along Commercial Street, between Flower-and-Dean Street and Aldgate, or along Whitechapel Road. She was usually in the company of two or three of her kind, fairly neatly dressed and invariably wearing a clean white apron, but no hat.

Marie Kelly was the most horribly mutilated of all Jack the

---

258   "I knew from the experience of others that I might have to spend many years of my life there." in *STWN*, 19 January 1935.

259   "in the heart of that hotbed of crime" in *STWN*, 19 January 1935.

260   Dew had married coachman's daughter Kate Morris at Christ Church, Notting Hill, on 15 December 1886. They subsequently moved to 166 Finnis Street, Bethnal Green and later to 38 Leopold Buildings, Bethnal Green.

261   "I had got to know Whitechapel" in *STWN*, 19 January 1935.

262   "Few of them were pretty. Few of them were young." in *STWN*, 19 January 1935.

263   "Marie Kelly, a girl aged anything between 20 and 25" in *STWN*, 19 January 1935. Kelly used the name Marie Jeanette Kelly and was also known as Mary Jane Kelly. She claimed to have visited France which may account for the affectation.

Ripper's victims. I know because I was the first police officer on the scene of that ghastly crime in Miller's Court, a cul-de-sac[264] off Dorset Street.[265]

What I saw when I pushed back an old coat and peeped through a broken pane of glass into the sordid little room which Kelly called her home, was too harrowing to be described. It remains with me–and always will remain–as the most gruesome memory of the whole of my police career.

After the lapse of so many years I find it difficult to say just when the name of Jack the Ripper became associated with the Whitechapel murders, but it was certainly in the early days of the mystery.

The name originated from the messages chalked on the walls, and the many letters received by the police and others bearing this terrifying signature. It fitted, and because it fitted, it stuck. Even to this day it lives in the minds of many as a symbol of fear and horror.[266]

I feel I must say a few words in defence of the police–of whom I was one–who were severely criticized for their failure to hunt down the wholesale murderer. There are still those who look upon[267] the Whitechapel murders as one of the most ignominious police failures of all time.

Failure it certainly was, but I have never regarded it other than an honourable failure.

Let us take a quick look at the men upon whom the responsibilities of the great man-hunt chiefly fell.

The officers sent from Scotland Yard were Chief-Inspector Moore, Inspector Abberline and Inspector Andrews, assisted, of course, by a large number of officers of subordinate rank.

In addition to them was Detective-Inspector Reid,[268] the local

---

264 "a mean cul-de-sac" in *STWN*, 19 January 1935.

265 There is only Dew's word for his being the first on the scene as there is no mention of him in surviving files on the Mary Kelly murder. He attended the scene with Inspector Walter Beck who said at Kelly's inquest: "I was the first police officer called to 13 Millers Court."

266 "And even to this day it lives in the minds of many–mainly those women who remained in Whitechapel throughout the long ordeal–as a symbol of horror and fear." in *STWN*, 19 January 1935.

267 "Even today there are those who look upon" in *STWN*, 19 January 1935.

268 Edmund John James Reid (1846-1917). He joined the Metropolitan Police in 1872 and

chief, who worked under the direction of his colleagues from the Yard.

Looking back to that period, and assisted in my judgement by the wideness of my own experience since, I am satisfied that no better or more efficient men could have been chosen.

Chief-Inspector Moore[269] was a huge figure of a man, as strong minded as he was powerful physically. He had much experience behind him, and was in every way a thoroughly reliable and painstaking officer.

Inspector Abberline[270] was portly and gentle speaking. The type of police officer–and there have been many–who might easily have been mistaken for the manager of a bank or a solicitor.[271] He also was a man who had proved himself in many previous big cases.

His strong suit was his knowledge of crime and criminals in the East End, for he had been for many years the detective-inspector of the Whitechapel Division, or as it was called then the "Local Inspector".[272] Inspector Abberline was my chief when I first went to Whitechapel. He left only on promotion to the Yard, to the great regret of myself and others who had served under him. No question at all of Inspector Abberline's abilities as a criminal hunter.[273]

Inspector Andrews[274] was a jovial, gentlemanly man, with a fine

retired in 1896. Reid was the head of the Whitechapel C.I.D. from 1887-1895. He had previously held that position in the neighbouring Bethnal Green Division. (PRO, MEPO 21/25).

269 Henry Moore (1848-1918). He joined the Metropolitan Police in 1869 and retired in 1899. Moore was an inspector at the time of the Whitechapel murders. He was not promoted to chief inspector until 1895. (PRO, MEPO 21/28).

270 Frederick George Abberline (1843-1929). He joined the Metropolitan Police in 1863 and retired in 1892. Abberline had previously been stationed at Whitechapel from 1873-1887. (PRO, MEPO 21/21).

271 Dew himself was once similarly described: "He is a slight man with a quiet voice, and might be taken for a keen solicitor rapidly making his way." (*Daily Mail*, 31 October 1907). Dr. Crippen's mistress Ethel Le Neve said of Dew's appearance: "if you saw him you would never dream for a moment that he was a detective. Tall and quiet looking, there is nothing out of the common about his appearance, and, looking into the kindly brown eyes, you would never dream that behind them the brain of the man pulsates with human voltage." (*ETWN*, 30 October 1920).

272 "had been for many years the divisional detective-inspector of the Whitechapel Division." in *TWN*, 19 January 1935.

273 This last sentence was not in *STWN*.

274 Walter Simon Andrews (1847-1899). He joined the Metropolitan Police in 1869 and retired in 1889. (PRO, MEPO 21/19).

personality and a sound knowledge of his job.

These three men did everything humanly possible to free Whitechapel of its Terror. They failed because they were up against a problem the like of which the world had never known, and I fervently hope, will never know again.

There was criticism, too, of the Chief of the Criminal Investigation Department, Sir Robert Anderson,[275] and the Chief Commissioner, Sir Charles Warren,[276] later of Spion Kop fame. This was equally undeserved.

It would be futile to attempt to tell the full story of the Ripper crimes without first giving a picture of the neighbourhood in which they were committed. Whitechapel in those days was full of slums in which vice of all kinds was rampant. Sordid narrow streets, still narrower courts, filthy and practically unlighted.

Woe betide any innocent wayfarer venturing alone down any of those dark and sinister passages.

So bad was the reputation of Flower-and-Dean Street that it was always "double-patrolled" by the police. A single constable would have been lucky to reach the other end unscathed.

Happily, Whitechapel is a different place to-day.[277]

You would look in vain now for Dorset Street. It is still there, but under another name. The street came into such ill-repute after the Miller's Court murder that the authorities decided, apparently, that it no longer deserved to be called after such a delightful county.[278]

One of the greatest problems of the police in the bad old days were organized gangs. Lawless characters banded together,[279] and under some fancy name went about robbing[280] and blackmailing honest tradesmen, assaulting innocent pedestrians, garrotting and fleecing drunken sailors, and preying upon the defenceless foreign

---

275 Dr. Robert Anderson (1841-1918). Appointed as assistant commissioner of the C.I.D. in September 1888, having previously held positions at the Home Office, the anti-Fenian intelligence department and the Prison Commissioners. He was knighted in 1901 when he retired.

276 General Sir Charles Warren (1840-1927). A distinguished archaeologist and soldier who was appointed Metropolitan Police commissioner in 1886 and resigned in November 1888.

277 How would Dew know this? Later in the book he wrote, "since I left Whitechapel I have avoided the scenes of the Ripper murders as I would a plague." (*ICC*, p. 135).

278 It was renamed Duval Street in 1904.

279 "banded themselves together" in *TWN*, 19 January 1935.

280 "went about in groups robbing" in *STWN*, 19 January 1935.

element, chiefly poor Polish Jews.

In most cases the attacks would be so sudden that the victim never saw the faces of his assailants, and even if he did he was more often than not too scared to give any assistance to the police.

There were other gangs who made their homes in Whitechapel and operated elsewhere. One such was the "Blind Beggar Mob", a title derived from a public-house in the Mile End Road at which they used to meet.[281]

The "Blind Beggars" were not quite the mean thieves I have described. There is snobbery even among thieves, and these swell mobsmen, who carried on their criminal operations in the West End and the provinces, would have resented being classed with the crooks who confined themselves to the East End.

Crime was rampant, but it did not go unchecked. A study of the Old Bailey calendar of the time would confirm this. I had the pleasure of seeing scores of them sentenced to long terms of imprisonment and lashes with the cat.

I say I saw this with pleasure, for had I not seen the suffering of many of their victims?

If the criminals were known to the detectives, the detectives were also known to the criminals. We were all given nicknames, some of them very apt.

A sergeant named Thick, who was a holy terror to the local law-breakers, was known as "Johnny Upright", because he was very upright both in his walk and in his methods.[282]

A detective named Caunter was nicknamed "Tommy Roundhead", and he certainly had an unusually round head.[283]

Another was always spoken of as "The Russian".[284] He had a

---

281   The pub is actually on the Whitechapel Road and is still open. It is best remembered as the location of the murder of George Cornell by Ronnie Kray in 1966.

282   This was William Thick (1845-1930). He joined the Metropolitan Police in 1868 and retired in 1893. (PRO, MEPO 21/22). Coincidentally Dew was described in a similar way by his second wife as being "straight as a gun barrel in physique, he was as straight as a die in his character." (*Worthing and District Review*, January 1948).

283   This was Eli Caunter (1852-1908). His name was misspelled as "Counter" in *TWN*, 19 January 1935. He joined the Metropolitan Police in 1872 and was a sergeant at the time of the Whitechapel murders. Caunter retired in 1898. (PRO, MEPO 21/27).

284   "Another, named Leach, was always spoken of as "The Russian."" in *STWN*, 19 January 1935. Presumably Detective Sergeant Stephen Leach (1851-1910). He joined the Metropolitan Police in 1872 and retired in 1897. (PRO, MEPO 21/26). An 1889 photograph

very thick, long auburn beard which I am afraid must have been a severe handicap when he was struggling with a prisoner.

My own nickname was "Blue Serge", simply because when I arrived in the division I invariably wore a suit of that material.

Then there was "The Shah", one of the most picturesque personalities ever to patrol the criminal haunts of Whitechapel.

I have seen it stated that there were some parts of the East End the police themselves were afraid to penetrate.

Rubbish!

I could recount story after story of single police officers walking calmly into the very dens of the gangs and claiming their men.[285]

In every district[286] you will find at least one police officer who can and does do this with impunity. The Shah did it repeatedly. He was a finely built man with jet black hair and moustache, one of the best-looking police officers I have ever seen. It was his appearance which had earned him his nickname.

He knew everyone. Everyone knew him. If you said to him, "Ginger Jim is wanted for 'snatchin' '.[287] Bring him in if you see him," the odds were that when you returned to the police station Ginger Jim would be there.

The Shah seemed to bear a charmed life. He went alone into places of the utmost danger. Yet I never once heard that he was molested or assaulted. Other police officers attempting to do the same would have needed a dozen policemen to get them and their prisoners away–and then only after a fight.[288]

Of course it must not be thought there were no decent honest folk in Whitechapel and Spitalfields. There were–plenty of them. Foreign Jews never giving any trouble,[289] prosperous furriers, Spitalfields silk weavers–all these were law-abiding citizens.

Such then, in the days of which I write, was Whitechapel.

Bucks Row, George Yard, Hanbury Street, Berners Street,[290]

---

of Leach shows that he later abandoned his beard and settled for a more manageable moustache.

285   "claiming their man." in *TWN*, 19 January 1935.

286   "In every one district" in *STWN*, 19 January 1935.

287   "snatching." in *TWN*, 19 January 1935.

288   "and then only after a fight" was not in *STWN*.

289   "never giving any trouble" was not in *STWN*.

290   Berner Street, spelled as "Berners" in *ICC* and *TWN*.

Mitre Square and Miller's Court became the scenes of definite Ripper crimes, and in every case he left behind the mutilated form of what had once been a woman.

It is not easy to say which was the fiend's first murder.

The difficulty is that it was not until some time had elapsed that the country awoke to the terrible realization that a wholesale murderer was abroad.

A single killing in the streets of Whitechapel of that time was not unknown,[291] and had the Ripper been content with one or even two such crimes his name would never have been whispered in terror.

On Easter Monday, 1888, a woman was found lying unconscious outside a big cocoa warehouse in Osborne Street,[292] a turning leading out of the Whitechapel High Street, and merging after a short distance into Brick Lane.[293]

The man who made the discovery called the police and a doctor, and it was realized at once that the poor victim was bleeding to death. She was conveyed to the London Hospital where she lingered for two days in great agony.

The injuries were unusual. Examination showed that the woman was suffering from terrible wounds in the lower part of her body. It was impossible to say with what they had been caused, but the theory of the medical men was that some sort of blunt instrument[294] had been used.

Detectives waited by the bedside in the hope that the woman[295] would rally sufficiently to give them some clue as to her assailants. She died, however, without regaining consciousness.

Emma Smith was the murdered woman's name. At least that is the name by which she was known to associates and to the proprietor of the lodging-house in Church Street,[296] Spitalfields, in which she made her home.

---

291   "was no uncommon thing" in *TWN*, 19 January 1935.
292   Usually spelled Osborn, as it is throughout *TWN*.
293   She was not found in the street, but had managed to get back to her lodgings at 18 George Street before being taken to the London Hospital.
294   "blunt knife" in *TWN*, 19 January 1935.
295   "the poor woman" in *STWN*, 19 January 1935.
296   "the low lodging-house" in *STWN*, 19 January 1935. It was in George Street, not Church Street.

Emma, a woman of more than forty,[297] was something of a mystery. Her past was a closed book even to her most intimate friends. All she had ever told anyone about herself was that she was a widow who more than ten years before had left her husband and broken away from all her early associations.

There was something about Emma Smith which suggested that there had been a time when the comforts of life had not been denied her. There was a touch of culture in her speech unusual in her class.

Once when Emma was asked why she had broken away so completely from her old life she replied, a little wistfully: "They would not understand now any more than they understood then. I must live somehow."

So, more lonely even than most of her fellows, she walked the streets of Whitechapel.

On that Easter Monday, Emma Smith entered into none of the holiday festivities. She remained at the lodging-house waiting until the evening, when necessity would drive her once more into the streets.

Evening came. Emma, arrayed in her poor finery, sallied forth to her death.

It was a rule of such lodging-houses as that in which Emma Smith lived that the women must return not later than 1 a.m. if they wished to retain their beds. One o'clock came. There was no sign of the widow. No one worried. Women of that kind often found excuses for remaining out all night and saving the fourpence which they paid for their beds.

And it was not until the next day that her fellow-lodgers learned the real reason of Emma's failure to return. But they never guessed[298] that what had happened the previous night was the beginning for them of years of unmitigated terror. They never suspected that the hand which had struck Emma Smith down was to strike again and again.

The public did not suspect it. Nor did the police. How could they do so? The crime itself, save for the unusual nature of the injuries, was no novelty in Whitechapel.

---

297 "more than forty years of age" in *STWN*, 19 January 1935.
298 "Even then they never guessed" in *STWN*, 19 January 1935.

Some even now doubt that the murder of Mrs. Smith was the handiwork of the Ripper. In some respects the crime differed from those which followed.

This woman, although mutilated, had not suffered the horrifying maltreatment meted out to the later victims. And none of the other bodies were found in such an open and frequented thoroughfare as Osborne Street.

Dark alleys and sinister courts were the places the monster selected to bring swift death to the other hapless women who fell into his clutches. The scenes of the crimes seemed to have been deliberately chosen.

But it must be remembered that if this was a Ripper murder it was the first. The need for caution was not so great. Afterwards, when the great hunt was on, hundreds of police[299] were nightly patrolling the streets confident that sooner or later the fiend would fall into their power.

In its brutality and its lack of motive the murder in Osborne Street had the stamp of the Ripper upon it.

It is true that the first assumption of the police was that the woman had been attacked by one of the Whitechapel blackmailing gangs, and there was some support for this theory in the fact that no money was found in the victim's purse. But it is more than likely that Emma Smith was as penniless when she left her lodgings that night as when her body was found. An empty purse was far from being a novel experience to women of her type.

It has always been inconceivable to me that such a person could have been killed for gain. With robbery as the motive, a very different type of victim would have been chosen.

As in every case of murder in this country, however poor and friendless the victim might be, the police made every effort to track down Emma Smith's assailant. Unlikely as well as likely places were searched for clues. Hundreds of people were interrogated, many of them by me personally. Scores of statements were taken. Soldiers from the Tower of London were questioned as to their movements. Ships in the docks were searched and sailors questioned.

All this led nowhere. Not a single clue was discovered.

---

299   "thousands of police" in *TWN*, 19 January 1935.

No one appeared to have seen the fatal blow struck, and no one seemed able to give a description of any man with whom the victim[300] might have been seen.[301]

The silence, the suddenness, the complete elimination of clues, the baffling disappearance all go to support the view which I have always held that Emma Smith was the first to meet her death at the hands of Jack the Ripper.

I have another theory. It is that the Ripper having, like a tiger, tasted blood, remained unsatisfied until his dread knife had cut short the lives of one after another of his victims.

At the inquest proceedings the Coroner made a statement which was strangely prophetic. After commenting on the violence and mystery of the crime he went on to express his uneasiness at the possibility of some particularly brutal murderer being at large in the district.

The verdict, as in all such cases, was "wilful murder against some person or persons unknown," and the case of Emma Smith, friendless and unclaimed by relatives even in death, would never have found a place in the chronicle of big crimes had it not been for the events which followed of which I am to write.

II

EXCEPT by the police who were still working secretly in their efforts to track the murderer down, the tragedy of Emma Smith, the victim of the Osborne Street crime,[302] was forgotten almost as soon as her mutilated body had been lowered into a pauper's grave.

By most people the crime was merely regarded as a more than usually unpleasant incident in a district in which acts of violence were of daily occurrence.

One might have expected some concern among the women of Emma Smith's class, any one of whom it seemed, might have been the victim. There was none. They gossiped about it at street corners, but they showed no sign of fear.

---

300   "the street walker" in *STWN*, 19 January 1935.
301   Except for Smith herself who, before dying, described being attacked by two or three men, one of them aged about nineteen. This scuppers Dew's belief in her being a Ripper victim.
302   "the victim of the Osborne Street crime" was not in *STWN*.

Indeed the conduct of these women throughout the period of the crimes was to me one of the most remarkable features of the whole drama.

It is true they became panic-stricken following each of the later murders. Sheer terror was reflected in their faces as they walked about, no longer singly, but in groups.

But soon their courage returned. The groups gave place to couples, and then, as time passed with no further evidence of the Ripper, they were to be seen venturing once more alone.

Some of them tried to make a joke of the business. They would call across the street to me, "I'm the next for Jack."

Though much of this was bravado cloaking a secret fear, I had to admire their attitude.

Then, just as we were all fervently hoping–these poor women more than anyone–that we had heard the last of Jack the Ripper, there would be another murder. The panic was renewed, only to be followed once more by a recovery of confidence.

Other East End women whose lives were never in danger from the Ripper's knife showed far more fear than the unfortunates who never knew when they went out at night whether it would be their turn to encounter the dread phantom.

I know from my own personal experience what took place in the East End, or that part of it bounded on the one side by Commercial Road, Whitechapel Road, Leman Street, &c., and on the other side by Shoreditch High Street, Bethnal Green Road, Club Row (a place notorious for the number of stolen dogs marketed there), and Brick Lane,[303] to the proximity of Hoxton, Old Street and Hackney Road.

It was within these boundaries that all the murders took place

---

303   On 31 January 1888 Dew had been called to the Two Brewers pub in Brick Lane to investigate a shooting. The pub's manager, Robert Matthews, had twice shot a former potman named Henry Blaming with a revolver. Earlier that day Blaming had been acquitted at the Old Bailey of raping Matthews' young daughter Eliza. Blaming deliberately chose to go to the Two Brewers where he laughed at Robert Matthews which provoked the shooting. He received bullet wounds in the abdomen and left buttock and spent ten weeks in the London Hospital. Matthews told Detective Constable Dew "I wish I had killed him." He was tried at the Old Bailey for felonious wounding and intent to murder and eventually found guilty of unlawful wounding. Matthews was sentenced to six weeks in prison with hard labour after the jury strongly recommended mercy due to the provocation he had received. (*The Times*, 2 February, 12 & 26 April 1888).

with the exception of the one in Mitre Square, which came under the jurisdiction of the City of London police.

It was only to be expected that the knowledge that in their midst stalked a human devil who could pass noiselessly among them and murder at will, was too much for the overwrought nerves of many women and children.

A large number flew from the district as from a plague, and thousands of those whom circumstances compelled to remain, made it a habit for a time[304] never to venture out alone after dark.

Mothers were fearful for their daughters whose work compelled them to travel home in darkness; husbands were anxious about their wives; young men for their sweethearts. The terror was contagious. It communicated itself to the children who ran home with fear in their eyes at the slightest scare, and were awakened by fearful nightmares after they had been put to bed.

All this I admit, and yet I say that, bearing in mind the unprecedented circumstances, the people as a whole behaved in a manner which was highly praiseworthy.

The vast majority, although frightened, showed outwardly the same stoic calm that was in evidence during the war.

The worst panic was among the foreign element, and this, after all, is only what one could expect.

Of excitement, of course, there was plenty especially immediately following a crime. Thousands of people from all parts of London rushed to the spot where the latest victim had been discovered.

This happened after the tremendous publicity given in the newspapers, and when the name of Jack the Ripper was on the tongues of people everywhere.

For some months after the Osborne Street murder Whitechapel lived its normal life. Even the police had abandoned hope of solving that mystery.

Then came the first real evidence that Whitechapel was harbouring a devil in human form.

Emma Smith had been murdered on Easter Monday. The Ripper came again on August Bank Holiday of the same year.

A curious coincidence this. Does it mean that these two nights

---

304   "for years" in *TWN*, 26 January 1935.

were deliberately chosen? Did the fact that the people of the East End were on holiday in some way facilitate the crimes?

Whatever may be said about the death of Emma Smith there can be no doubt that the August Bank Holiday murder, which took place in George Yard Buildings, less than a hundred yards from the spot where the first victim died, was the handiwork of the dread Ripper.

Again a woman of the streets was the victim. Her name–or at least the name by which she was known locally–was Martha Turner.[305] Her body was found early in the morning on the first landing of a squalid block of buildings in George Yard.

These buildings were just off High Street, Whitechapel, and thus quite close to the police station to which I was attached. Originally the buildings had been a weaving factory. This had been converted into mean flats housing innumerable poor class families.

George Yard had a caretaker, and every night at eleven o'clock it was his duty to turn out the few gas jets with which the landings were lighted.

On this holiday[306] most of the families were still out celebrating when the lights were extinguished, and when they did return they had to climb the stairs to their apartments in unaccustomed darkness.

One couple, a Mr. and Mrs. Mahoney returned at two o'clock in the morning. They saw nothing unusual. Silence then settled upon the drab building until, an hour or so later, Albert Crow,[307] whose duties as a cabman had kept him out late, came home and climbed wearily up the stairs.

Dawn was now breaking. And by the faint light which filtered through the landing window, Mr. Crow saw something lying against the wall. He went closer and saw that it was a woman. She was lying outstretched on her back.

Had this not been the morning following a public holiday Mr. Crow might have made a more thorough examination. But, jumping to the conclusion that the woman had celebrated too freely and was in a drunken sleep, he passed on to his flat without giving the matter

---

305 She had separated from her husband Henry Tabram and taken the name Turner from a man she had lived with on and off for some years.

306 "On this holiday night" in *TWN*, 26 January 1935.

307 This was Alfred George Crow.

another thought.

That the woman was dead, and that she had met a ghastly fate was discovered in a strange way.

Also living in the buildings was a woman named Reeves. She had gone to bed early, but she could not sleep. She was filled with a strange foreboding. Two or three times she awakened her husband and communicated her fears to him. He merely laughed, turned over, and went to sleep again.

But the premonition of tragedy was so strong in Mrs. Reeves' mind that shortly before five o'clock she awakened her husband once more. Her distress was now such that her husband, solely with the idea of pacifying her, decided to investigate.

He was still sceptical as he went down the stairs, but when he reached the first-floor landing he saw something, now fully revealed by the bright morning light,[308] which drove the smile of incredulity from his face and sent him hurrying for a policeman. P.C. Barrett was the officer he found. Together they returned to the buildings. Hardened though he had been by his police experiences in Whitechapel the sight by which the constable was confronted completely unnerved him, just as later I was unnerved by the terrible thing I saw in that little room in Miller's Court.

The dead woman was lying in a pool of blood. Her clothing had been disarranged, and even without close examination the signs of horrible mutilation were obvious.

A doctor and detectives were sent for, and the usual hue and cry which follows a murder was raised.

The poor creature, the doctor was able to say, had been dead many hours. Fiendish violence had been used by her murderer, whose task had been made easy by the woman's own caution. It required small deduction to assume that the woman and the man had met in Whitechapel Road or Commercial Street, and that she had taken him to this backwater known as George Yard to escape the watchful eyes of passing policemen and others.

Many of the Ripper's victims simplified his task in this way. An unlighted alley; the back of premises which could be reached by a passage from the street; an unfrequented court; a dark archway. It

---

308   John Reeves found the body at around 4.50 a.m. so it is unlikely that the morning light was that bright. However, the body would have been visible as Crow had seen it at around 3.30.

was in such spots that all the murders took place.

Nothing could have better suited the fiend's purpose. Immune from observation and immediate discovery, he was able to kill his victims and still have sufficient time to escape.[309]

Martha Turner's injuries had been caused by a knife. There were many wounds, most of which had been caused after death.[310] The poor woman had died without a struggle and without a cry.

Any call for help must have been heard by people sleeping on the other side of the wall against which she was found lying. Her end had been instantaneous. The first wound had been fatal. The others had been inflicted merely to satisfy the blood lust of her assailant.

Dr. ———,[311] who practiced among the poor of Brick Lane, and was the first medical man on the scene, realized at once that this was the work of no ordinary murderer.

Murder and mutilation had probably taken less than a minute. Then, his foul deed accomplished, the Ripper must have stolen swiftly and silently down the stairs and made his way to the home which was never discovered. By the time the body was found he was probably safe in his own bed gloating over the thing he had done.

The police, made eager by the horrible nature of the crime, began their inquiries at once. I played my own small part. At first we seemed to make a little progress. Then we came up against a blank wall.

It was known that Martha Turner had been in the habit of frequenting low public-houses in the company of soldiers and sailors. The preliminary investigations were therefore made among the sailors at the various docks and the soldiers stationed at the Tower of London.

Then came what seemed to be a confirmation of this theory. One of the murdered woman's companions stated that on the night of the crime she had left Martha with a soldier quite close to George Yard.

---

309   "sufficient time to make his escape." in *TWN*, 26 January 1935.
310   "Altogether there were thirty-nine wounds, most of which had been caused after death." in *TWN*, 26 January 1935.
311   This was Dr. Timothy Killeen. Named as "Dr Keleene" in *TWN*, 26 January 1935.

Lest such a statement should malign soldiers as a class, I hasten to add that it was not a practice of the Tower soldiers to frequent the East End and associate with women of Martha Turner's type. The majority of them had too much decency and too much common sense to penetrate at night into the haunts of Whitechapel. But there were always a few, generally among the younger ones, who were not so mindful as they should have been of their own reputations or of the dignity of their uniform.

The woman who gave us this clue, which turned out to be useless, was known as Pearly Poll. Her story was that she had spent the evening with Martha Turner, and that at eleven o'clock they had met two soldiers. The four remained together until nearly midnight, when Pearly and her companion went off, leaving Martha and her soldier friend outside the buildings in which the murder took place.

Such evidence could not be ignored, and in the hope that she would be able to identify the two soldiers, Pearly Poll was taken to the Tower of London, where all the soldiers stationed there were then paraded before her. Pearly failed to identify the two men, but knowing the difficulties of identification at any time, and especially in the case of men in uniform, the police still hoped that they were on the right track. The fact that a soldier would probably have been wearing his bayonet, a weapon with which the injuries might have been inflicted, seemed to point in the same direction.

Several days passed without a clue[312] being found. Again the police were baffled. The newspapers began to criticize and talk of inefficiency. Then the public took up the cry.

This was grossly unfair. The police were doing everything humanly possible. For the sake of their own prestige, quite apart from their natural desire to avenge a heinous crime, they were determined to succeed.

There was one thing our critics overlooked. This murder, as indeed were all the Ripper murders, was an added burden thrust upon a body of men already grievously overworked. Other crimes were being committed and other criminals had to be hunted. Life for the police officer in Whitechapel in those days was one long nightmare.

---

312 "a definite clue" in *STWN*, 26 January 1935.

My only criticism of the action of the police during the hunt[313] for the Ripper was the policy of those in high places to keep the Press at arm's length. Individual officers were forbidden to give information to the newspapers. With this I have no quarrel because of the dangers of abuse, but I have always thought that the higher police authorities in ignoring the power of the Press deliberately flouted a great potential ally, and indeed might have turned that ally into an enemy.[314]

It is not usual to associate with the same person two murders taking place several months apart. And so in this case it was not for some time after Martha Turner had met her fate that the suspicion was born that Emma Smith might have been the first victim of the same murderer.

But once this suggestion was put forward it captured the public imagination in a remarkable way.

The first theory was that both women had been the victims of the same gang, and the name of the High Rip gang of blackmailers then terrorizing the district was whispered from mouth to mouth.

Soon the gang theory gave place to another, and in all probability the correct one. It was founded on the sinister suggestion that the two crimes were the work of one man, and gave rise to the fear that somewhere in their midst a bloodthirsty villain was at large.

One of the results of this was that the difficulties of the police were greatly increased. People from whom information was sought refused to talk. Their silence was imposed by terror.

They were frightened of the Ripper's vengeance.

Pearly Poll was one of those who took fright. Terrified at the thought of having to give evidence at the Coroner's inquest, she disappeared. Police hunted her[315] for days before she was eventually found hiding in Covent Garden.

Still working on the soldier theory the police took Pearly to Chelsea Barracks where, in a fit of pique, she picked out the first two soldiers she saw. They were able to prove they had been nowhere in the East End on the night of the crime.

---

313   "during the long hunt" in *STWN*, 26 January 1935.
314   "and indeed might have turned that ally into an enemy." was not in *STWN*.
315   "We hunted for her" in *TWN*, 26 January 1935.

This delay handicapped the police and helped the Ripper, who had now visited Whitechapel twice, taken his toll and vanished like a spectre.

Poor Martha Turner, like Emma Smith, remained unavenged.

Martha was a married woman living apart from her husband. How often has tragedy resulted from such separations! I have seen it again and again in the course of my career. All the victims of Jack the Ripper, with the exception of Marie Kelly, were women of this type.[316]

The husband from whom Martha had separated was a furniture packer in Greenwich named Samuel ———.[317] He was found, but could only say that he had lost all trace of his wife from the day she had left him nine years before to go and live with another man.

The inquest was held and the usual formal verdict returned.

Police efforts were not relaxed. The reverse was the case. Realizing now something of the enormity of the problem by which they were faced, the authorities drafted a large number of extra detectives from Scotland Yard and various Divisions[318] to the East End.

It would be impossible to recount here all that was done, the hundreds of inquiries made, the scores of statements taken and the long, long hours put in by us all. No clue was turned down as too trivial for investigation.

We all had heartbreaking experiences, several times I got on to something which looked like a clue, followed it up day and night, only to find in the end it led nowhere.

As always happens in such cases, so many people were eager to give information. The majority were well-meaning enough, but some notoriety seekers made statements which were patently untrue, with no other object than to get their names into the newspapers.

I have never been able to understand the mentality of such people. Our job was big enough in all conscience without having to waste time exploring false clues.

Already I had formed the view that we were up against the

---

316 Kelly was supposedly a widow.
317 Named as "Samuel Tabran" in *TWN*, 26 January 1935. His real name was Henry Samuel Tabram.
318 "and various Divisions" was not in *TWN*.

greatest police problem of the century. A third heinous crime shortly afterwards proved how right this theory was.

III

THE hope and ambition of every East-End policeman–myself included–was to catch the Ripper red-handed.

This seemed the only way. There was small chance of the killer being caught and convicted through circumstantial evidence. Of such evidence there was virtually none.

In most cases in which women are murdered, some man, by reason probably of his association with her, immediately stands suspect. But the Whitechapel victims were all strangers to their slayer, and died within a few minutes of their first meeting with him.

On 1st September, 1888, the Ripper struck a third time. His victim was found in the early hours of the morning lying in the gateway of Essex Wharf,[319] in Bucks Row, just off Brady Street, and not far from Hanbury Street, the scene later of a duplicate murder.

Bucks Row was just a few yards outside the boundary of "H" Division to which I was attached.[320] The district was squalid. The spot for such a crime was ideal. Close by were a number of slaughterhouses.

No better illustration of East-End conditions at the time could be afforded than by the behaviour of Charles ———,[321] a middle-aged carman, who was the first to see the body.

The carman was on his way through Bucks Row to his day's work when he saw a huddled mass in the gateway of Essex Wharf. He crossed from one side of the street to the other to investigate.

The light was just sufficient to show him that the form was that of a woman and that she had been mishandled. Her clothing had been disarranged and her bonnet had fallen from her head. There was something strange too about the position of the woman's head.

In any other district of London such a discovery would have sent the man dashing for a policeman. But this was Whitechapel,

319   Dew repeats this location three more times, but Nichols was found on the other side of the road to Essex Wharf.
320   That murder took place in J Division, Bethnal Green, which had been formed in 1886.
321   Named as Charles Cross throughout *TWN*, 2 February 1935.

where crimes of violence and outrage were of everyday occurrence.

The carman shook the woman. She did not stir. He decided it was a case of a woman who had fainted following assault, and, making a mental note to report the matter to the first police constable he saw, he went on his way.

A curious thing then happened. The carman had gone but a short distance when he saw another man on the opposite side of the street whose behaviour was certainly suspicious. The other man seemed to seek to avoid the carman, who went over to him, and said:

"Come and look here. Here's a woman been knocked about."

Together the two men went to the gateway where the poor woman was lying. The newcomer felt her heart. His verdict was not reassuring.

"I think she's breathing," he told his companion, "but it's very little if she is."

The couple parted, —— promising, as he walked away, to call a policeman.

All this was afterwards told in evidence by the carman. It never had the corroboration of the other man. The police made repeated appeals for him to come forward, but he never did so.[322]

Why did he remain silent? Was it guilty knowledge that caused him to ignore the appeals of the police?

In any other district and in any other circumstances this would have been a natural inference, but in the East End of London at this time the man might have had a dozen reasons for avoiding the publicity which would have followed. He might have been a criminal; or he might have been afraid, as so many were, to risk the linking of his name with a Ripper-crime.

The carman reported his early-morning discovery to a policeman, but in the meantime, P.C. Neal,[323] making his regular beat along Bucks Row, had seen the huddled form lying in the gateway.

The policeman, with the aid of his bullseye, saw what the others had overlooked. The woman's head had been almost severed from

---

322 The other man was a carman named Robert Paul and he eventually gave evidence at the resumed inquest. Is this an example of Dew's faulty memory or had he not known what had happened?

323 P.C. John Neil (1850-1903). He joined the Metropolitan Police in 1875 and retired in 1897. ((PRO, MEPO 21/26). His surname was misspelled in *ICC* and *TWN*.

the body.

Soon after P.C. Neal had given the alarm, Dr. ———,[324] whose surgery was in Whitechapel Road, was on the scene. He could only confirm the conclusion reached by the constable–that the woman was dead.

The throat injury had caused instant death, but it was the mutilation of the lower part of the body which told policemen[325] and doctor as plainly as though the woman's assailant had himself spoken, that the killer the East End feared had come again.

The remains were taken to the mortuary–what terrible places these were in those days–where further examination proved beyond all doubt that the hand which had struck down Martha Turner had also committed the crime in the gateway of the Essex Wharf.

We began our inquiries at once. Close to the scene of the tragedy several watchmen were employed. None of them had heard a sound, and some of them went so far as to declare that it was impossible for the crime to have been committed at the spot where the body was found.

But we were to learn again and again that Jack the Ripper never gave his victims a chance to advertise his dread presence.

There was later some conflict of opinion as to whether the Bucks Row victim was actually struck down there or carried to the spot after death. In my own mind I have never had any doubt that the woman died where she was found–in the gateway of Essex Wharf.

One significant discovery was made in this case. The throat had been cut from right to left, such as would have been the case had her assailant been a left-handed person. The police worked upon this clue,[326] but as in the case of all other theories and all possible clues,[327] it led nowhere.

The injuries to the throat and to the body suggested the ferocity of a madman.

What was the motive? This was the question we were always up

---

324 Named as "Dr. Llewellyn" in *TWN*, 2 February 1935. This was Dr. Rees Ralph Llewellyn (1849-1921). Why hadn't Dew named Killeen or Llewellyn in the book when he named Dr. Phillips later on and all the doctors involved in the Crippen investigation?

325 "policeman" in *TWN*, 2 February 1935.

326 "police worked upon it" in *TWN*, 2 February 1935.

327 "all other possible clues" in *TWN*, 2 February 1935.

against. There seemed to be none, unless the killer was wreaking his vengeance against a class.

The latest Ripper murder was discussed with bated breath, not only in the East End of London, but throughout the whole country.

Crowds began to gather in Bucks Row and outside the local police station, and some ignorant-minded persons tried to organize a demonstration against the police.

To some extent I can sympathize with the public. They were living in the presence of a terror which was inspiring fear among their women-folk. They could only look to the police for deliverance from the menace.

What they overlooked was that idle criticism of the police must hinder rather than help the accomplishment of the one thing police and public alike most desired.

The third Ripper victim was quickly identified as Mary Ann Nicholls,[328] a woman of thirty-eight, who shared a tiny, well-kept room in a lodging house at 18 Thrawl Street, Spitalfields. She paid fourpence a night for her bed.

Had Mary Nicholls possessed the sum of fourpence at midnight on the night of her death she might have escaped death.

At that hour she returned penniless to her lodgings, and it was force of circumstances which drove her to face the streets again.

Mary joked as she went out for the last time.

"I'll soon have my doss money," she cried. "Look what a nice new bonnet I am wearing now."

It was this same bonnet which some hours later the carman found lying beside her battered body.[329]

Only once was Mary seen after she went out at midnight. We got evidence that at 2.30[330] in the morning she was standing at a spot in Osborne Street almost identical with that at which the first Ripper victim met her death. That was some little distance from the gateway in Bucks Row,[331] where her own body was found a few hours later.

---

328 The name is usually spelled Nichols in official and contemporary sources. *TWN* and *ICC* used "Nicholls" throughout.

329 "her body." in *STWN*, 2 February 1935.

330 The time was given as 2.20 in *ETWN*, 2 February 1935; 2.30 in *STWN*.

331 "That was a mere 500 yards from the gateway in Bucks Row" in *TWN*, 2 February 1935.

Again there was the same baffling absence of clues that was a feature of all the Jack the Ripper murders. He came, no one knew whence and departed, no one knew whither.

There were definite signs now of panic among the populace. The publicity given by the newspapers and the freedom with which the cases were discussed everywhere caused the actual dangers to be magnified.

A moment's serious thought would have been sufficient to show that the only people to whom the fiend was a menace were the poor women of the streets. The three victims had all been of this class. Those that followed were the same.

But I am afraid that the respectable women of Whitechapel derived small comfort at the time from any such reflection, and everywhere extreme precautions were taken against the Ripper's coming.

As soon as darkness set in on the night following the Mary Nicholls' murder hundreds of women locked themselves in their homes. Tradesmen made a rich harvest[332] in making houses secure. Courts, which had hitherto remained in sinister darkness, were now illuminated by feeble lanterns.

The panic which seized the women of Mary Nicholls' class was understandable. They were in a sense defenceless. The very nature of their livelihood precluded them from appealing for protection to the police, though this would have been given readily enough in the case of a known danger.

Many such women fled in terror from the East End never to return. Those who remained walked about in groups, and made a picture of frightened misery.

I felt sorry for these women, exposed as they were to a danger all the more terrorizing because none knew how, where or when it came.[333]

As may be imagined, feeling against the Ripper ran high. The temper of the people was such that had the police had the good fortune to arrest him in a public place, they would have been lucky, indeed, to get him safely to a police station.

---

332 "reaped a rich harvest" in *TWN*, 2 February 1935.
333 "or when, it would come." in *TWN*, 2 February 1935.

More than one innocent man narrowly escaped lynching at the hands of an infuriated mob.

One of the suspects about this time was a man known locally as "Leather Apron".[334] He was a doubtful character known to the police.[335] Moreover, he invariably wore boots with rubber soles, this fitting in with the popular conception of the silent-working Ripper.

"Leather Apron" was a short, heavily-built man of Jewish appearance, and he had been so nicknamed locally because whenever seen he was wearing a small leather apron.

After the Martha Turner murder, "Leather Apron" disappeared from his usual haunts. His prowling the streets at night ceased.

Then came the Mary Nicholls' tragedy, and in their eagerness to find someone to fit the bill everyone in the East End seemed to jump at the same time to the conclusion that the man the police had to find was "Leather Apron".

"Get 'Leather Apron'," became the popular cry. "Lynch him!"

It became necessary for the police to find "Leather Apron" if only to protect him from the fate he was likely to suffer if he fell into the hands of the mob. His description was circulated.

This led to the man being found. He was discovered by a detective hiding in a house in Mulberry Street, and in order not to attract attention in the streets the two walked normally together to Leman Street Police Station.

"Leather Apron" appreciated the thoughtfulness of the officer who found him. He was under no delusions as to the danger which threatened him. He had been hiding, not from the police, but from the public.

It is amazing how soon news of this sort of news goes round. "Leather Apron" had not been under lock and key for more than half an hour when hundreds of people congregated outside the police station clamouring to get at him.[336]

There was widespread rejoicing. The Terror had been trapped! the menace[337] had been removed.

---

334 "Leather Apron" was a bootmaker named John Pizer (1850-1897).
335 "for his bullying and brutal methods with women." added to the end of this sentence in *TWN*, 2 February 1935.
336 "clamouring for his blood." in *TWN*, 2 February 1935.
337 "The menace" in *TWN*, 2 February 1935.

So thought the people.

They were wrong. "Leather Apron" made a statement accounting for his movements during the previous ten days, which, if true, ruled him out as a possible murderer of Mary Nicholls. Every detail in the statement was carefully checked. It was found to be correct.

In the ordinary way the man would have been released at once. The police had nothing against him then. But, with the populace in the mood it was, this would have meant the violent death of an innocent man.

So "Leather Apron" was kept in safety[338] until after the resumed inquest on Mrs. Nicholls at which his name was publicly cleared. He was then released, and so far as I know was never molested.

It was soon after this that the cry for "Leather Apron" gave place to the cry for "Jack the Ripper".

Poor Mrs. Nicholls was another married woman separated from her husband.

Her father, whose name was Smith, identified her at the inquest, though he was only able to do so by a scar on her forehead which she had received when a child.

He told the Coroner that she had been separated from her husband for seven years and had spent some time in Lambeth Workhouse. After that he had lost all trace of her, and it was not until after her death that he had learned of the sort of life she had been leading in recent years.

I am a great admirer of British juries, but occasionally one comes across a voluble juryman who barges in with silly questions of no value to the Coroner or to anyone else. I have known some adopt a very arrogant attitude, and recall an instance some years ago when I was the victim of one of these "gentlemen" who behaved as though he would like me hanged, drawn and quartered.[339]

---

338 "in custody" in *TWN*, 2 February 1935.

339 This may have referred to an incident at the resumed inquest on Cora Crippen in September 1910. A juror said: "I should like to ask Inspector Dew why it was that he allowed Dr. Crippen to go away after he called on him at Hilldrop Crescent." The coroner told him that it was not a matter for a coroner's jury to consider. However, Dew managed to reply: "I should like to answer it. I know many attacks have been made on me, and I should only be too willing to answer them... I may add that there was no actual evidence at that time of a crime having been committed. I should like to answer the question. I have a perfect explanation, if I am allowed to give it." (*The Umpire*, 25 September 1910).

The inquests on these women did not fail to produce one or two jurymen[340] who wanted to know why the police had not done this, that, or the other, though I have no recollection of any of them making a practical attempt to help.

One juryman at the inquest on Mrs. Nicholls made just such an outburst. "Why don't the police offer a reward?" he cried. "If Mrs. Nicholls had been a rich woman living in the West End of London they would have offered £1000. But she is a poor unfortunate and so they take no notice. These women have souls just like other women, and I myself will offer £25 to anyone who can tell me anything which will help."

All stuff and nonsense! The truth is that the Home Office is very chary about offering rewards, and for very good reasons, and, of course, the police cannot make such an offer without the authority of headquarters.

Let me say at once, it was not a question of money at all. Police and public–a very familiar phrase in those days–[341]were doing their best. No matter what sum of money had been offered it would have made no difference. Right-minded people don't want blood money.

There would have been money in plenty for the person responsible for bringing this monster to book. It would have rolled in from rich and poor alike, so great would have been the gratitude of the people.

Unofficially, substantial rewards were offered. Great bankers and others openly stated that they were ready to pay big money to the person giving information leading to the Ripper's arrest. Unhappily, the occasion for the redemption of these promises never arose.

Those were wretched days for me. The hunt became an obsession. I spent long, long hours on duty, only to return home worn out but sleepless.

Night after night I tossed about on my bed seeing again and again the terrible sights I had witnessed. In this I was not alone. There were dozens of other police officers whose lives Jack the

340   "one or two jurymen of this type" in *TWN*, 2 February 1935.
341   And quite familiar in *My Hunt For Jack the Ripper*. Dew used the phrase three times in that section of the book.

Ripper had made scarcely worth living.

My food sickened me. The sight of a butcher's shop nauseated me.

All this had to be hidden from the women folk. It would never have done to let them see you were worried. My aim always was to minimize the crimes. On their awfulness I kept silent.

The women were frightened enough without listening to such ghastly details as I could have given.

It was the uncanniness of the crimes that "got" the women. Their courage was undermined by the knowledge that somewhere in their midst there lurked unknown, unheard, unseen, the man who came to kill.

And it was only a few days after the Bucks Row drama that yet another victim died just as silently and mysteriously as all the others.

IV

THE scene of the Ripper's fourth coming was Hanbury Street, no more than a minute's walk from Commercial Street Police Station, and quite close to Spitalfields Church and Market.

Only the day before, the blinds of the windows in Hanbury Street had been drawn when the funeral procession of Mary Nicholls, the third victim, passed that way.[342]

If I remember rightly it was on a Saturday morning that a strongly-built woman in the early forties was found murdered and mutilated, in a fashion we had all come to dread, in the small back yard of No. 29.

The house belonged to a woman named Richardson, a respectable packing-case maker, but she and her family occupied only a small portion of the premises. Altogether seventeen persons made their homes in the building, the front door of which was kept open day and night.

---

342 "had been drawn as a silent tribute to Mary Nicholls, the third victim, whose funeral procession passed that way." in *STWN*, 9 February 1935. Dew got the date of Nichols' funeral wrong by one day. She had been buried on the afternoon of Thursday 6 September and the murder of Annie Chapman took place on the morning of Saturday 8 September. (A. Wood, "The Foulest Deed of Modern Times", *Ripperologist*, 15 (February 1998).

Through this door the murderer must have passed with his victim, thence along a dark and narrow passage to the yard at the rear which was only separated from the adjoining premises by a four-foot fence.

In some ways, this was the most daring of all the Ripper crimes. Had either he or the woman given an inkling of their presence in that small yard he could have been caught like a rat in a trap. But again he was true to the Ripper tradition. His deed was done in silence, and not a soul in the building guessed that they would awake next morning to discover the frightful evidence of his coming on their own back doorstep.

But more remarkable than his escape from the house itself is his safe passage through the streets now filled with hunters.[343]

Huge numbers of police, both from the uniformed and plain-clothes branches, were on patrol from dusk till dawn. Yet he must have passed through the ring of watchers, not once but twice. Small wonder that the superstitious-minded began to whisper that such an escape was possible only to a supernatural being.

What these people failed to see was that, however thorough a police patrol may be, it is quite impossible to keep every door in every house in every street under continual surveillance. The area of possibility was so big that there were bound to be loopholes in the precautions taken.

One may be sure that the murderer, his deed accomplished, only emerged from that dark doorway in Hanbury Street when he knew the coast was clear. If he then turned left, he was in Brick Lane in a moment or so and he could gain Commercial Street, where he had the market in front of him in the same time.

With luck—and the killer must have had the devil's own luck—a man of his undoubted cunning always had slightly more than even money chance[344] of getting away.

Mrs. Richardson's son was a porter at Spitalfields Market. His work took him abroad very early in the morning.

On this particular morning, young Richardson was about before any of the other residents of No. 29, and before leaving the premises

---

343 "then filled with hunters." in *STWN*, 9 February 1935.
344 "an even money chance" in *TWN*, 9 February 1935.

he actually went into the yard without seeing anything suspicious.

It was not until much later–the exact time was a quarter to six–that John Davis, a labourer who lived with his wife and children on the top floor, went into the yard and saw a sight which nearly turned his brain. Scarce knowing what he did, he ran into the street crying, "Murder! Murder!" at the top of his voice. Two men came in response to his cries, and as they reached him Davis collapsed in the street.

With eyes bulging almost out of his head, Davis pointed to the passage, and mumbled something about there being a dead woman in there. "I can't face it again," he gasped.

Only the work of Jack the Ripper could have inspired the fear which showed in the labourer's eyes. The two men knew instinctively what they were going to find at the other end of that dark passage.

They braced themselves and went in. And when they reached the yard they understood at once why Davis had cried, "I can't face it again."

The woman was lying to the left of the door and close to the fence. Her injuries, although these men didn't know it, were exact duplicates of those which had been suffered by Mary Nicholls.[345] The head had been almost severed from the body and, for some mysterious reason, was being kept in position by a tightly tied, coloured handkerchief.

Disarranged clothing and fearful mutilation of the body told their own story.

The cool deliberation of the killer is shown by the fact that, with every second precious to him, he had stayed to arrange to woman's personal belongings in a neat pile at her feet.

When Dr. Phillips, the divisional surgeon came, he confirmed what the police had already assumed, that there was no doubt at all that the mutilation in this case had been caused by the same hand which had maltreated the dead body of Mary Nicholls.

I knew Dr. Phillips well. He lived in Spital Square, close to

---

345   While there were similarities, the injuries of the two victims were not "exact duplicates" as Dew would have it. Chapman's intestines had been removed and placed by her body and some body parts had been removed which was not the case with Nichols.

Commercial Street Police Station, and had been the local divisional surgeon for a great many years.

He was a character. An elderly man,[346] he was ultra-old-fashioned both in his personal appearance and his dress. He used to look for all the world as though he had stepped out of a century-old painting. His manners were charming; he was immensely popular both with the police and the public, and he was highly skilled.

Doctors are supposed to be immune from the shock of gruesome sights, but I met more than one Whitechapel doctor of this period who dreaded to be called to a Ripper crime. I sympathized with them.

The fourth victim was Annie Chapman.

Until four years previously, the woman had lived a normal, reasonably happy married life. Her husband was a head coachman employed at ——— .[347]

Another man came along to win her affection and to break up her home. She left her husband for her lover, who discarded her three years later. She tried to live by needlework, but in the end she was driven to the streets. Her home was a mean lodging-house in Dorset Street.

And so another woman who had once known respectability and a happy home life met the qualifications which Jack the Ripper required in his victims, and had the bad luck to cross his path early on this September morning.

There was in the Annie Chapman case evidence that whatever her murderer's motive for killing, he might also have been ready to rob when his victim had anything worth taking.

When Mrs. Chapman left her lodging-house for the last time she was wearing two rings. They were only made of brass, but in the darkness might easily have been mistaken for gold. These rings had been torn from her fingers. But one must not lose sight of the fact that there were many other ways in which the loss of the murdered woman's rings might have been accounted for.

Indeed, all the evidence, except this, suggests that whatever he

346 Dr. George Bagster Phillips was baptised in 1835 so was in his early fifties when Dew knew him. Perhaps his old-fashioned manner and dress made him appear older to the twenty-five year old Dew. Phillips died in 1897.

347 Place given as Windsor in *ETWN*, 9 February 1935. Place not stated in *STWN*.

may have been, the Ripper was not a thief. If robbery had been any part of his motive he would have chosen victims very different from those East End women.

I was one of the large body of police officers kept busy the day after the murder interviewing all kinds of people and taking statements from them. We concentrated mostly in and around Hanbury Street.

What a task!

As often as not I required an interpreter, and you can imagine something of my difficulties in seeking anything like a coherent statement from frightened foreigners.

I was standing in Commercial Street with a fellow detective named Stacey,[348] when my attention was attracted by a young man standing close to the entrance to Dorset Street. I recognized him at once as a young scoundrel nicknamed "Squibby", who had given the police a lot of trouble at one time and another,[349] and was now "wanted" for assault on a child.

"Squibby" was an associate of notorious young thieves, and although short of stature he was stockily built, and so powerful that we used to call him the Pocket Hercules.[350]

Whenever this "charming" young fellow was arrested it took six or eight policemen to get him to the station, and by the time he was brought in he was usually devoid of every stitch of clothing, and the policemen pretty well hors de combat.

This "mighty atom" of the East End was covered from head to foot with tattoo designs.[351]

---

348 Detective Constable Thomas Stacey (b. 1858). He joined the Metropolitan Police in 1880 and retired in 1905. (PRO, MEPO 21/33). Like Dew, Stacey later worked as a private detective.

349 His nickname derived from his name George Squibb. He was also known as George Cullen and had a string of previous convictions. In July 1888 he stood trial (and was found not guilty) at the Old Bailey for breaking and entering a dwelling house from where clothes and pipes had been stolen. On the night of that crime Dew had spoken to Squibb who had "blackguarded" the plain-clothes detective. Dew threatened to arrest him if he didn't go away, to which Squibb replied, "God blind me, if you ever attempt to take me I will chevy [stab] you."

350 He was 5 ft. 4 in. tall.

351 In 1898 these were recorded as: "two Union Jacks, two guns, and wreath on chest ; head, bust of soldier, wreath, READY FOR ACTION, sailor and flag, carriages and gun on l upper

Some time previously "Squibby" had engaged in one of his periodical battles with the police. It was as a result of this that the child was injured. The assault on the girl was not deliberate. "Squibby" was amusing himself by throwing bricks at a policeman. One of the missiles was badly aimed and hit the child.[352]

Knowing he would be "wanted" for that, the miniature giant went into hiding, and the morning following the Hanbury Street murder was the first occasion following the offence that he had come under the eyes of a police officer. I have a shrewd suspicion that it was not mere curiosity that caused "Squibby" to mix among that throng of morbid sightseers. He was not the type of fellow to let an opportunity like that pass.[353]

Unfortunately for me, "Squibby's" eyes were as sharp as my own. Recognition was mutual. He knew I would be after him, and was determined to give me a hard chase. He made a sudden dash, dived between the legs of a horse, crossed the road, and ran as fast as his short legs could carry him along Commercial Street, in the direction of Aldgate.

Stacey and I gave chase, drawing our truncheons–plain-clothes men carried truncheons during the Ripper murders–as we went.

The sight of a man running away from the scene of a Ripper crime with the police officers[354] in hot pursuit sent the crowd wild with excitement. They jumped to the conclusion that the man on the run was a murder suspect.

"Jack the Ripper! Jack the Ripper! Lynch him!" The cry was started by a few and taken up by hundreds.[355]

Behind us as I ran[356] I could hear the tramp of hundreds of feet.

---

arm, ship on r upper arm ; sailor holding flag and sword on l, T. MURRAY, lion and unicorn, sailor, female and wreath on r forearm ; several other tattoo marks on each forearm ; five blue dots l calf."

352 "Squibby" had thrown a stone at P.C. Bates in Commercial Street on 1 September, but it had missed and struck a young girl named Betsy Goldstein. Dew correctly recalled that "Squibby" received a three-month prison sentence for the offence. (*Lloyd's Weekly Newspaper*, 9 September 1888).

353 These last two sentences were not in *STWN*.

354 "two police officers" in *TWN*, 9 February 1935.

355 The name Jack the Ripper is generally accepted to have come into use after it was used as a signature in a letter written on 25 September that was sent to the Central News Agency. They sent it to Scotland Yard on 29 September. The incident with "Squibby" took place on 8 September so Dew's recollection of the mob using the name is questionable.

As I was passing Fashion Street a great, burly brute did his best to trip me by thrusting his legs in front of mine. He possibly thought[357] I was the man the crowd was chasing, but more probably knew me as a police officer. I dealt him a heavy blow with my truncheon and he fell back into a baker's window.

Meantime our quarry had reached Flower-and-Dean Street, and realizing that he was bound to be caught if he continued running, he entered the front door of a house, jumped over a low wall, and entered the adjoining house.[358]

Stacey and I dashed in after him. He led us up the stairs and into a bedroom where we grabbed him just as he was making his way through a back window.

I was done in. So was Stacey. Now for a rough time, I thought. "Squibby" had never been known to be arrested without the most violent resistance.

But this was a different "Squibby". Instead of finding, as we expected, an animal of a man, foaming at the mouth and ready to fight to the last breath, his face was of a ghastly hue[359] and he trembled violently.

In a flash I saw the reason. It was not of Stacey or myself that the wanted man was afraid but of the howling mob outside.

They were crying for his blood. Their cries reached us.

"Lynch him. Fetch him out. It's Jack the Ripper," came from a thousand throats. The crowd now stretched to Commercial Street.[360]

"Squibby" saw the danger, and so now did I. His life wouldn't have been worth twopence once that mob got their hands on him.

I told him we would do what we could, but I have often wondered what would have happened had not a number of uniformed police officers followed and, as I discovered afterwards, with great difficulty held the door of the house in which we were marooned.

Precautions had also been taken against a demonstration of mob law. Urgent messages had been sent to the surrounding police stations–Leman Street and Commercial Street–and soon

---

356   "we ran" in *TWN*, 9 February 1935.
357   "probably thought" in *STWN*, 9 February 1935.
358   "he leapt over a low wall and entered the front door of a house." in *TWN*, 9 February 1935.
359   "his face was ghastly green" in *TWN*, 9 February 1935.
360   "now stretched right the way to Commercial Street." In *TWN*, 9 February 1935. *Lloyd's Weekly Newspaper*, 9 September 1888, reported that "some thousands of people gathered".

reinforcements[361] of uniformed police arrived on the scene.

The baffled crowd became more bloodthirsty than ever. The very precautions the police were taking confirmed them in their conviction that the man whose life they were demanding could be none other that the East End Terror.

The cries of "Get him! Lynch him!" "Murder him!" became more insistent than ever, and I am sure little "Squibby" was convinced that his last hour had come. No policeman who had previously had the unpleasant task of arresting him would have believed that such a change could come over a man. Abject terror showed in his eyes as again and again he appealed to me for protection.

I myself wouldn't have given much for "Squibby's" life at that moment, and I was not at all happy as to what might happen to Stacey and myself if the mob reached us.

Presently, however, the yells of the crowd became more subdued, and I ventured down to the front door of the hovel into which our prisoner had led us. The sight I saw filled me with relief. Scores of lusty policemen were clearing a space in front of the house.

Never in all my life have I more warmly welcomed the sight of the blue uniform.

Several officers came into the house, and it was only with their assistance that our scared prisoner could be induced to descend the stairs and face the street.

On emerging into Flower-and-Dean Street I realized that our dangers were far from over. At the sight of the little man being shepherded by a posse of police officers the mob seemed to go mad.

They made one mad, concerted rush which threatened for a time to break down the police barrier. Their cries became louder than ever, filthy epithets being intermixed with the demands for "Squibby's" summary execution.

We gained Commercial Street, but beyond that, despite the strong force of police, we found it impossible to go.

One thoughtful young constable solved our immediate problem by getting a four-wheeled cab from Aldgate into which we bundled our prisoner and proceeded with the police forming a "guard of honour".

361   "large reinforcements" in *TWN*, 9 February 1935.

At last it seemed that our troubles were over. But, oh dear, no! Several ugly rushes were made at the cab, and more than once it came within an ace of being over-turned.

A big, burly inspector named Babbington came to our rescue. He suggested that we should be much safer on foot than in our precarious vehicle, and with this I agreed. So out we scrambled, just along Spitalfields Market.[362]

The whole of Commercial Street was now packed by a yelling, hooting mob of frenzied people.[363] Some,[364] I have no doubt, regarded the opportunity as a heaven-sent one to have a go at the police.

A lane was formed all the way to Commercial Street police station, and after what seemed to me an interminable time, and likewise I am sure to "Squibby", we fought our way into the grimy-looking building which for once looked really beautiful to me.

The station is, or was, an island. It was immediately surrounded by the mob, now more infuriated than ever because the man they believed to be the "Ripper" had been delivered safely at the police station.

Even now they did not abandon hope of taking the law into their own hands. The police station was attacked again and again, and it was only the indomitable pluck of the men in blue which prevented an innocent man being crucified. There were many sore heads in Commercial Street that day.

I was told afterwards that from the very first police officers shouted to the crowd to say that the man who had been taken in custody had nothing whatever to do with the Ripper murders. They would have none of it. Their blood was up.

For a long time[365] the shouting crowd surrounded the police station. A few seconds after a space had been cleared it was filled again.

Inspectors went to the upper windows of the police station and tried to explain who the prisoner was, and why he had been arrested.

---

362 "just alongside Spitalfields Market." in *TWN*, 9 February 1935.
363 "most of them, without doubt, belonging to the lower order." added here in *STWN*, 9 February 1935.
364 "Some of these" in *STWN*, 9 February 1935.
365 "For hours" in *TWN*, 9 February 1935.

Several other ruses were adopted in order to induce the people to go to their homes. But nothing would convince them they had made a mistake, and it was not until many hours after "Squibby" had been placed under lock and key that the streets in the vicinity of the police station reverted to their normal peacefulness.

The moment he was put in a cell "Squibby" began to regain his composure. Much as he hated policemen he had confidence in their ability to protect him in their own police station. Eventually he was sentenced to three months' imprisonment and was quite happy about it.

"I shall be much safer in Pentonville for a bit," he said with a smile.

After this experience "Squibby" was a changed man. Whenever he met me he never failed to thank me for "saving his life", and as far as I know he never again gave trouble to police officers whose duty it was to arrest him.

I have seen many riotous crowds in my career, but none quite like the one I have described. Every man and woman in that mob was ready to tear a fellow-creature to pieces because some fool, seeing a man pursued by police officers, had shouted "Jack the Ripper".

V

SOMEONE, somewhere, shared Jack the Ripper's guilty secret. Of this I am tolerably certain.

The man lived somewhere. Each time there was a murder[366] he must have returned home in the early hours of the morning. His clothing must have been bespattered with blood.

These facts alone ought to have been sufficient to arouse suspicion, and to cause a statement to be made to the police.

Suspicion, I have no doubt, was aroused, but that statement to the police was never made.

Why should anyone seek to shield such a monster?

Well, my experience has taught me that the person who remained silent may have been actuated by any one of a number of motives.

It might have been sentiment. It is asking a lot of a wife to give

366   "On the night of each of the murders" in *STWN*, 16 February 1935.

away her husband when she knows in advance that she is handing him over to the gallows. That also applies to a mother.

The motive which prevented the words of betrayal from being spoken might also have been fear. There were many simple-minded people living in the East End of London at this time, who, with the knowledge which would have led to the Ripper being caught and convicted in their possession, would have been afraid to use it. The very terror the murderer inspired might well have been his own safety valve.

Quite apart from these two possibilities it is an established fact that many law-abiding folk are reluctant to communicate valuable information to the authorities in murder and other serious cases.

And this, despite the fact that their silence renders them liable to severe punishment as accessories either before or after the fact.

Some people take the view–Why should I say anything?

If I do I have to go to the police court, hang about there in a musty room waiting to give evidence: my name and perhaps my photograph will be published in all the newspapers. Then I shall have to give evidence again at the Old Bailey or the Assize Court as the case may be.

Another man hangs back because of a skeleton in his cupboard. He is frightened of cross-examination and what might be revealed.

I myself have stood in criminal courts and listened to the cross-examination of witnesses until I have been led almost to wonder whether the witness has not been mistaken for the prisoner.

The plain fact is that few people court the publicity which is bound to follow a person's close association with a sensational trial.

Over and over again I have had the greatest difficulty in persuading people who have been the victims of extensive robberies to attend the police court. They have told me bluntly that they would rather lose their property than face such an ordeal.

My sympathy has often been with them, although as a police officer I was only doing my duty in using my utmost endeavours to get them to come forward.[367]

Women, as a rule, are more shy than men. Can you wonder at it? It is not nice for a woman to have to hang around for days in a

---

367   These previous three paragraphs were not in *STWN*.

place like the Old Bailey and listen to the sordid stories which are told there.

The police of to-day are handicapped by the same reluctance that was shown in the days of Jack the Ripper.[368]

Jack the Ripper worked alone. Therefore there was never any hope of his being given away by a fellow-criminal.

We hoped for a long time that one day information pointing to the monster would be volunteered. We were disappointed.[369]

Of information there was plenty. We were flooded with volunteered statements and anonymous letters after the murder of Annie[370] in Hanbury Street. But not a single clue resulted.

Senseless criticism of so-called police inefficiency broke out again when it became obvious that the Hanbury Street crime would have to be relegated to the "unsolved" list, and it was probably the distrust thus engendered that caused the formation of a Vigilant Committee. The members of this committee–all men–took upon themselves to patrol the streets at night in the hope that they would succeed where the police had failed.

The motive was praiseworthy enough, but the organization turned out to be more of a handicap than a help. It had no official recognition, and the only result, so far as I could see, was that the task of the police was doubled. The fewer people using the streets at night the better the chance of the police in checking the movements of any suspicious person!

A sigh of relief went up throughout the East End of London when news came which seemed to indicate that Jack the Ripper had appeared in the north of England.

Near Gateshead-on-Tyne, a young woman was found lying, murdered and mutilated, in a ditch.

So strong were the indications that this was a Ripper crime that I believe[371] Dr. Phillips, who by this time had become a specialist on the Whitechapel mutilations, and Scotland Yard officers journeyed north. At first both the doctor and the police were deceived and gave it as their opinion that the girl had been a Ripper victim.

368   This sentence was not in *STWN*.
369   This sentence was not in *STWN*.
370   "Annie Chapman" in *TWN*, 16 February 1935.
371   "I believe" was not in *TWN*.

Panic spread to the industrial north and even into Scotland, whence it was rumoured the fiend had gone, until later developments proved that the girl had been killed by her own sweetheart. It was an imitative crime.[372]

And so the public attention became focused once more on Whitechapel, where, in fearful expectancy the people waited for the next blow to fall.

Rumours of all kinds became rife. People allowed their imaginations to run riot. There was talk of black magic and of vampires, especially among the superstitious foreigners.[373]

Other criminals made capital out of the police concentration on the greater evil. Ordinary crime not only continued unabated, but actually increased. Every day people were robbed and assaulted, and the knife was freely used.

One would have thought that in the circumstances,[374] these lesser criminals would have joined in the fight against the common enemy. Unfortunately for the hard-pressed police they did not do so.

We *were* hard pressed. Sometimes, as I went wearily about my work, ever seeking the elusive clue that would bring the Killer to justice, I became sick at heart as I wondered how much longer those nightmares were to continue.

Now, as I sit quietly in my home on the Sussex coast[375] and hark back in my mind to those racking days, my greatest wonder is that the man we were so zealously hunting escaped again and again the watchful eyes of hundreds of policemen nightly on the look out for him.

It was soon after the Hanbury Street murder that strange messages began to be chalked up on the walls in the vicinity of the crime. On a wall in a passage running off Hanbury Street this terrible prophecy was read with awe by thousands of people:

---

372   The murder was that of Jane Beadmore by William Waddle on 22 September 1888. Waddle was executed on 18 December 1888.

373   These last two sentences were not in *STWN*.

374   "in the presence of such a menace as the Ripper had become" in *TWN*, 16 February 1935.

375   Upon retiring as a private detective Dew left London and moved to 10 Beaumont Road, Worthing, West Sussex. The bungalow was called "The Wee Hoose" when Dew bought it in 1928 and he retained the name. It is now called "Dew Cottage" in his honour.

"THIS IS THE FOURTH. I WILL MURDER 16 MORE AND THEN GIVE MYSELF UP."

The public, ready by this time to believe anything, assumed that this message and others similar could have been written by the man who inspired their dread.

They may have been, but I very much doubt it. Far more likely that the writing was the work of mischievous-minded people who obtained some grim pleasure in adding to the fears of an already demented people.

Unfortunately, the "Ripper" messages were read by children as well as adults. Many of them became so nervous that they were afraid to go to school. Jack the Ripper became the children's bogey man.

It is not easy to understand the mentality of a person who at such a time deliberately sets out to add to the general panic by chalking the walls with bogus messages. It is equally hard to explain the large number of anonymous letters received by the police purporting to have been written by the murderer.

Those letters received by the police were not made public, but some which were sent to other people were widely published in the press. One such letter, posted in the East End of London, was sent to a news agency. It had been written in red ink, and had apparently been smeared with blood. This was the letter:

"Dear Boss,–I keep on hearing the police have caught me, but they won't fix me yet. I have laughed when they look so clever, and talk about being on the right track. Great joke about Leather Apron. Gave me real fits. I am down on women and I shan't give up my work until I get buckled. Grand job the last was. I gave the lady no time to squeal. How can they catch me? I love my work, and want to start again. You will soon hear of me again with my funny little games. Ha! ha! ha![376] The next job I shall do I shall clip the lady's ears and send them to the police. Keep this letter until[377] I do another job, and then send it out straight. (Signed) Jack the Ripper."

That letter did not deceive me for one moment. I am ready to

---

376 Just "Ha! Ha!" in *TWN*, 16 February 1935. The original letter had "ha.ha."
377 "Keep this letter back until" in *STWN*, 16 February 1935.

stake my reputation that it was never penned by the man whom the signature was supposed to represent.

The man who wrote that letter was illiterate. If you accept it at its face value you must rule out at once the theory widely held at the time, and accepted in many quarters to-day that Jack the Ripper was a man of education and culture.

One of the strongest rumours at the time was that the Terror was a medical student or a doctor, support being supposedly lent to this suggestion by a certain anatomical skill shown in the mutilations.

I did not see all the murdered women, but I saw most of them,[378] and all I can say is that if the wounds they sustained are representative of a doctor's skill with the knife, it is a very simple matter to become a surgeon. This is certainly true of the case of Marie Kelly, whose poor body had been hacked about in a manner far more suggestive of a maniac than a man with knowledge of surgery.

The doubts I cast upon the letter I have quoted are prompted by a different consideration. Jack the Ripper, whoever and whatever he may have been was obviously a man of cunning.

The mental picture I have formed of him cannot by any stretch of the imagination be reconciled with the writer of such a crude and childish letter.

If he had written a letter, it would, I am sure, have been just as clever, calculating and cunning as his crimes and his escapes.

We had scarcely recovered our breath after the horror of Hanbury Street, when the Ripper came once more from his hiding place to eclipse in cunning, speed and silence all his previous crimes.

Three days only had elapsed since the death of Annie Chapman— the date was 30th September, 1888—[379]when the whole country was horrified beyond measure by the news that not only one ghastly crime had been discovered, but two.

The first body was found under an archway leading to some stables in Berners Street, off Commercial Road, the second in Mitre Square, a quiet little spot in the City of London, not far from

---

378 Dew repeated this in *ICC* (p. 146), saying "I had seen most of the other remains." In his retirement he wrote a letter to a newspaper saying: "I still retain the awful memory of seeing each of the victims." (*Sunday Express*, 3 October 1943).

379 Clearly a mistake as Chapman's death had taken place on 8 September.

Aldgate, and close to the scenes of all the other murders.

That two such crimes should have been committed in such circumstances seemed incredible alike to police and public.

Never in the history of the East End of London had such elaborate precautions been taken to prevent the very thing which had not only been done, but repeated.

Hundreds of police, in uniform, in plain-clothes and in all manner of disguises–some even dressed as women–patrolled every yard of every street in the "danger zone" every few minutes.

The most obscure corners were periodically visited. All suspicious characters were stopped and questioned.

Knowing all of these precautions and knowing how determined were the police, I would have staked my life almost that the Ripper, or any other human being, could not have penetrated that area and got away again.

Even now I am completely mystified as to how the terrible events of that night could have happened. What courage the man must have had, and what cunning to walk into so carefully prepared a trap and to get out again without anyone having the slightest suspicion that he was abroad.

It seemed as though the fiend set out deliberately to prove that he could defeat every effort to capture him. He killed one woman in Berners Street. With that he was not satisfied. Before the body of his first victim was cold he went to Mitre Square and took the life of a second.

In both cases the Ripper must have been within an ace of capture.

Perhaps in Berners Street he had his narrowest escape of all, for he did not stay to mutilate the body.[380] Perhaps it was this which sealed the fate of the second woman. His blood lust was not satisfied.

No one saw him, or at any rate no one associated him with the crime, as he made his way from Berners Street to Mitre Square, passing presumably along Commercial Road, through Butcher's Row, Whitechapel, Aldgate, and various side streets.

And again no one saw him as he passed away from the scene of that second tragedy to the shelter of his own home.

The Ripper's escape that night was little short of a miracle.

---

380   "mutilate the victim." in *STWN*, 16 February 1935.

Small wonder, when it became known, that there were many among the public ready to ascribe to him powers gained from supernatural sources!

It is believed that the Berners Street murder was discovered less than five minutes after the fatal blow had been struck. The alarm was immediately given. A cordon was thrown round the district. But it is probable that by this time the Ripper was well on his way to Aldgate and his second crime, which is believed to have taken place within half an hour of the first. Mitre Square was left unguarded for fourteen minutes. That was long enough for the man who worked so stealthily and swiftly.

Berners Street had been reformed. Formerly it had been known as Tigers' Bay and had been the refuge of many of the most desperate criminals of the East End. But the police had combed and cleaned it, with the result that it had become a comparatively decent street in which to live.

Some distance along the street was a dark, narrow court, leading to Commercial Road. The court was closed at night by two large wooden gates, in one of which there was a small wicket gate for the use of residents when the larger ones were closed. It was through this wicket gate that the Ripper and the first of his two victims that night passed.

The court had no lamps and was in darkness. On one side were cottages occupied mostly by cigarette-makers and tailors. The whole length of the other side was taken up by the rear of a social club known as The Working Men's Educational Club.[381] A back entrance linked the building with the court and was in fairly frequent use.

The club had a good name.[382] Its members were nearly all foreigners–Russians, Germans, Poles and Continental Jews. That night there happened to be a special function at the club, and a good many men[383] were in the building from 8.30 p.m. till past eleven o'clock. It was a wet night. The rain beat mercilessly on the windows of the room.

Not a single suspicious sound was heard by any of the men

---

381   Its correct title was the International Working Men's Educational Club.
382   "The club had quite a good name." in *STWN*, 16 February 1935.
383   "something like two hundred men" in *TWN*, 16 February 1935. *STWN* had: "special function at the club, and this was going on from 8.30 p.m. till past eleven o'clock"

inside the building, but it is more than probable that a woman living in one of the cottages on the other side of the court was the only person ever to see the Ripper in the vicinity of one of his crimes.

This woman was a Mrs. Mortimer. After the main meeting at the clubhouse had broken up some thirty or forty members who formed the choir, remained behind to sing. Mrs. Mortimer, as she had done on many previous occasions, came out to her gate the better to hear them. For ten minutes she remained there, seeing and hearing nothing which made her at all suspicious.

Just as she was about to re-enter her cottage the woman heard the approach of a pony and cart. She knew this would be Lewis Dienshitz,[384] the steward of the club. He went every Saturday to the market, returning about this hour of the early morning.

At the same moment Mrs. Mortimer observed something else, silent and sinister. A man, whom she judged to be about thirty, dressed in black, and carrying a small, shiny black bag, hurried furtively along the opposite side of the court.

The woman was a little startled. The man's movements had been so quiet that she had not seen him until he was abreast of her. His head was turned away, as though he did not wish to be seen. A second later he had vanished round the corner leading to Commercial Road.

It was left to Mr. Dienschitz to make the discovery that that court had been chosen by the Ripper for the dispatch of yet another unfortunate.[385]

The shying of the steward's pony led him to investigate a huddled mass against the wall. It was the body of a woman.

VI

IT will never be known just what were the powers of fascination Jack the Ripper held over women.

There must have been something about him which inspired immediate confidence in those he selected as his victims.

These poor women knew better than anyone else the grave risks they ran in associating at this time with strange men. This danger to

---

384   Named variously as Dienschitz or Diemschitz in *TWN*.
385   "another poor unfortunate." in *TWN*, 16 February 1935.

themselves must ever have been uppermost in their minds. Yet they accepted the man's advances seemingly without question.[386]

How was he able so readily to allay their fears?

Is the explanation the more simple one[387] that the man in appearance and conduct was entirely different from the popular conception of him?

Take the Berners Street victim. She knew that only three days before Annie Chapman had been lured by the enemy of her kind into that little backyard in Hanbury Street to a swift and relentless death.[388] Her sense of personal danger must in consequence have been acute.

In spite of this she allowed herself to be taken by the man whose coming she dreaded more than anything else in the world into that Berners Street court in which she met her own fate.

It is this aspect of the murders which suggests to one's mind that Jack the Ripper might have been a real-life counterpart of the villain of the murder mystery novel. Is it not feasible that there was something about him which placed him above suspicion?

Let us assume for a moment he was a man of prominence and good repute locally. Against such a man, in the absence of direct evidence, it is too much to expect that local police officers would hold such a terrible suspicion.

And, assuming this to be the case, the man's amazing immunity can be the more readily explained. The same qualities which silenced the suspicions of his women victims would keep him right with the police officers who knew and respected him.

I am not putting this forward as anything more than a reasonable deduction from the facts as they are known. It is merely one of the many possibilities, though, I must say, far more likely than some of the wild theories that have been advanced.

I cannot conceive any woman at that time accompanying any man of whom she entertained the slightest suspicion into that dark and dismal court off Berners Street into which Mr. Lewis Dienschitz drove his pony and cart just a few minutes too late.

I have told you that Mrs. Mortimer, one of the women who lived

386 "Yet they seemingly went with this man without question." in *STWN*, 23 February 1935.
387 "the more simple one" was not in *STWN*.
388 Dew repeats his error. It had been just over three weeks.

in the court, had, while standing at her gate, watched the furtive figure of a man steal away in the darkness. She then went indoors. The cosmopolitan choir in the club-room across the way was still singing lustily.

The pony swung through the familiar gateway without checking its pace, but it had proceeded only a few yards along the court when it stopped so suddenly that Mr. Dienschitz was nearly thrown to the ground!

The driver was amazed. The pony was quiet and not in the habit of shying. He got down from the cart and, taking the animal's head, endeavoured to lead it forward, but it edged nervously over to the left.[389]

Realizing now that there must be something to account for the animal's strange behaviour, Mr. Dienschitz strained his eyes in an effort to penetrate the inky darkness.

What was that against the wall on the right?

All he could see was an indefinable mass, but he was certain it had not been there when he had left the court earlier in the day. He moved forward, prodded the object with his stick. Something about the feel of the thing made him shudder. He struck a match. The flickering glare showed up a woman lying in a pool of blood.

"The Ripper!" was Mr. Dienschitz's instinctive cry, as he hurried towards the rear entrance to the Working Men's Club calling for help.[390]

His cries caused the singing to cease, and a moment later one of the men, bolder than his fellows, came out with a lighted candle. Together the men stooped over the body as it lay face downwards, the head lying in the little gutter which ran close to the wall. The woman's throat had been deeply gashed.

There had been no mutilation. The explanation seems simple. Jack the Ripper had been disturbed by the arrival of the steward. He had heard the coming of the pony and cart, when he had had time

---

389 "But the pony refused to be coaxed. Throwing up its head and showing the whites of its eyes, it edged nervously over to the left." in *TWN*, 23 February 1935.

390 In reality, the light of the match only allowed him to see that it was a woman lying there. Diemschitz then went into the club and told his wife and some club members that there was a woman lying in the yard, but he did not know if she was drunk or dead. It was not until he looked again with a candle that he saw blood and went to look for a police officer.

only to kill, and so, observed, but unsuspected by Mrs. Mortimer, he slunk away in the darkness later to claim another life.[391]

In less time than it takes to tell the court was a mass of frightened, gesticulating foreigners from the club, augmented by white-faced men and women from the cottages.

"It's the Ripper. The Ripper's been here," were the cries in a babel of tongues.

The police were quickly on the spot. They had, in fact, never been far away. Then came Dr. Phillips. He found the body quite warm.

Poor, pathetic thing! Just another unfortunate of the streets whose pinched face and shabby clothing spoke plainly enough of struggling poverty.

The woman's check scarf had been pulled tightly around her neck, while pinned to her black dress was a faded white rose. In one hand she was holding a little bag.

Traces of prettiness remained in her face, and there must have been a time when she had been exceedingly proud of her curly black hair.

The police lost no time in beginning their investigations. Immediately every member of the club who had been present that night was sought out and questioned. Statements, were taken too, from all the residents of the little cottages which lined one side of the court. In this way there came to light the experience of Mrs. Mortimer, which showed how narrow on that occasion had been the Terror's escape.

Hundreds of police then began one of the most intensive man-hunts ever known, but even as this force was being marshalled, the Ripper, with mocking nonchalance, was striking again. The second murder that night in Mitre Square was the boldest thing he ever did.

Think of the circumstances. The man had been disturbed–almost caught–in Berners Street. The ordinary criminal would have been intent only on getting safely to his own home.

Not so the Whitechapel murderer.

Instead he made his way to Mitre Square which stands just

---

391   A man named Leon Goldstein told the police that he was the man seen by Fanny Mortimer.
       He had passed that way after leaving a coffee house and his bag contained empty cigarette
       packets. Dew was either unaware of this or had forgotten it.

inside the City of London boundary, at the back of Katherine Free Church–[392]a walk of some eight minutes–to find another victim.

Mitre Square is small as a square, but very much larger in area than the court in Berners Street. Moreover, even in those days, it was well lit. On three sides it was flanked by large warehouses, and on the fourth by two dwelling-houses.

Ironically enough, a police officer lived in one of the houses. He had gone to bed at midnight, worn out by a long day of Ripper hunting, and was doubtless fast asleep by the time the murder was committed, almost under his own window.[393]

The square lies close to Aldgate and Houndsditch, and is fairly near both Middlesex Street (Petticoat Lane) and Dorset Street.

I suppose Mitre Square is very little different to-day from what it was in 1888, I do not know, for since I left Whitechapel I have avoided the scenes of the Ripper murders as I would a plague. Enough of those terrible scenes remain in my memory without seeking to recall any incident which may have been forgotten.

Even in the early hours of Sunday morning the neighbourhood was by no means deserted. Traders were already preparing for the Sunday market in Petticoat Lane and using the short cut through the square to the city. But it was a police officer and not a market worker who discovered the crime.

P.C. Watkins' beat compelled him to pass through Mitre Square every fourteen minutes. At 1.30 he saw nothing abnormal. He stayed a moment or so to talk to George Norris, a night watchman at one of the warehouses, and it was from Norris that he learned that police whistles had been sounded "up Whitechapel way".

"Must be the Ripper," conjectured Norris, as the constable went on his way.

Fourteen minutes later P.C. Watkins was back in the square again. This time his eyes caught the dim outline of something against the wall near the carriage way entrance. He turned his lantern on to the strange object, his blood turning cold at the fearful sight his lamp rays revealed.

Dashing to the door of the warehouse at which Norris was on

392   Dew meant St. Katherine Cree Church in Leadenhall Street.
393   This was Constable Richard Pearce of the City of London Police who lived at 3 Mitre Square. He slept as the murder took place within view from his bedroom window.

duty, he cried:

"For God's sake, mate, come to my assistance."[394]

Norris came, and was sickened by what he saw.

Next day London awoke to the staggering news that Jack the Ripper, in a district infested with police officers, had come to claim two victims and make yet another sensational escape.

The Mitre Square crime brought the City of London police more actively into the hunt, for the square came within their jurisdiction. It was, to date, the most shocking tragedy of all. The mutilations were frightful. The face was terribly disfigured by wounds.[395]

This victim was just as shabbily dressed as her fellow in Berners Street.

She had been wearing a black apron.[396] Part of this was missing. The torn portion was found later by a police constable on the steps of a block of buildings in Goulston Street, nearby. It was covered with blood, and had obviously been used by the woman's assailant to wipe his blood-stained hands as he ran away.

On a wall close by this message had been written: "The Jews are the men who will not be blamed for nothing."

This message was rubbed out by someone.[397]

Its destruction was certainly unfortunate. We could not afford to lose even the slenderest of clues. But I doubt if it made a lot of difference anyway. There was no reason, so far as I can see, why this particular message should have proved more useful than many others which Jack the Ripper was supposed to have written.

As I have said before, it is questionable whether these messages were the work of the murderer at all. Why should he fool around chalking things on walls when his life was imperilled by every minute he loitered?

Murderers do foolish things, I know, but such an action does not fit into the mental picture I have formed of the character of Jack the

---

394   The night watchman's name was George Morris, not Norris as *ICC* and *TWN* had it. Watkins did say to him "For God's sake, mate, come to my assistance." However, the "Must be the Ripper" quote appears to have been invented.

395   Just "terribly disfigured." in *STWN*, 23 February 1935.

396   The police list of her possessions described it as "1 Piece of old White Apron."

397   It was rubbed out by the police with a wet sponge. The message spelled Jews as "Juwes".

Ripper.[398]

A criticism levelled at the police at this time was that following the Mitre Square murder there was little or no co-operation between the City and the Metropolitan police forces. This is sheer nonsense. The two forces worked amicably together in this as in thousands of other cases.

There was never the remotest reason for one body of police to be jealous of the other.[399]

Speaking from my own experience, I can only say that I always found both the detective and uniformed branches of the City police ready and willing to help. Their main purpose, as ours, was to prevent and detect crime.

Of the two women who died that Saturday night–or rather Sunday morning–the Mitre Square victim was the first to be identified. She was found to be a woman in the early forties, named Catherine Eddowes.

A strange thing is, I understand,[400] that, less than half an hour before her fateful encounter with the Ripper in Mitre Square, Mrs. Eddowes was safely locked in a cell at Bishopsgate police station.

Earlier that day she had returned with a man from a hop-picking expedition, pawned some boots and spent the money in public-houses with the result that she was "taken inside" by a constable.

At one o'clock in the morning, by which time she had become normal once more, the gaoler set her free until such time as she would be required to appear before the magistrate on a "drunk and disorderly charge".

"Good night,"[401] she called back to the gaoler, as she passed out into the deserted street and started to walk in the direction of Houndsditch.

Somewhere on that walk, presumably in the region of Mitre Square, she came face to face with the demon who was making his furtive escape from his crime at Berners Street.

Even when running away from a murder a few minutes old, Jack the Ripper stopped, spoke to the woman, gained her confidence,

---

398   These previous two sentences were not in *STWN*.
399   This sentence was not in *STWN*.
400   "I understand" was not in *TWN*.
401   "Good-night, old sport" in *TWN*, 23 February 1935.

and a few seconds later had made possible a sixth notch on the handle of his knife.

More difficulty was experienced in establishing the identity of the Berners Street victim. She was claimed to be a widow named Elizabeth Stride, aged thirty-seven, a Swede who had married an English carpenter.

Mrs. Stride was a woman with a tragic history. She had sunk low socially after her husband and two children had (so it was said)[402] been drowned in the Thames disaster when the pleasure boat, *Princess Alice*, returning from a trip to Margate, collided with a collier off Blackwall, and sank with the loss of several hundred lives.[403]

The police were satisfied, but on the Sunday evening there was a surprise development. Another claimant came forward, this time a woman. She pleaded tearfully to be allowed to see the body in the mortuary. Permission was given and, between hysterical outbursts, the woman declared emphatically that the dead woman was her sister.

Every Saturday, this woman said, she and her sister had been in the habit of meeting in Chancery Lane. The sister had been in impoverished circumstances, she said, and she used to give her two shillings every Saturday.

On this Saturday the sister had not kept the appointment, and this fact, coupled with a strange dream premonition, had made the woman suspicious that the murdered woman was her sister.

This story, which sounded plausible enough, was repeated to the Coroner at the inquest, with the result that there was the unprecedented situation of the dead woman being doubly identified. The problem remained unsolved when the inquest was adjourned.

But inquiries subsequently made by the police proved beyond all question of doubt that this second woman's convincing story was nothing but a tissue of lies.

The victim was undoubtedly Mrs. Stride.[404]

---

402   "(so it was said)" was not in *TWN*.

403   The *Princess Alice* paddle steamer sank on 3 September 1878 with the loss of over 600 lives. Stride's family were not among the dead.

404   "But inquiries subsequently made by the police proved beyond all question of doubt that the victim was undoubtedly Mrs. Stride." in *STWN*, 23 February 1935.

On the Monday morning following the double murder, another postcard, purporting to have been written by the Ripper, was received. It ran:

"I was not codding, dear old boss, when I gave you the tip. You'll hear about saucy Jack's work to-morrow. Double event this time.[405] Couldn't finish straight off. Had not time to get ears for the police. Thanks for keeping letter back till I got to work again.

Jack the Ripper."

Two murders in a single night!

Panic became more widespread. Rumours became wilder. We worked harder than ever, but except for the fearful evidences of his coming the Ripper remained as phantom-like as ever.

VII

ALTHOUGH in Jack the Ripper times I was only a young detective, I succeeded by industry and keenness in gaining the confidence of my superiors, with the result that I was trusted with many delicate inquiries which, in other circumstances, would have been given to an officer of higher rank.

One of my chief assets then–and, indeed, through the whole of my police career–was a splendid memory. I made notes, of course, sometimes lengthy ones as to what prisoners said on arrest, but it was rarely indeed that I made use of my notebook when giving evidence.

I have known police officers who would never dream of going into the witness-box in any important case without producing that bugbear to judges and counsel alike–the pocket-book.

Unfortunately, my dream as a young detective one day to stand in the witness-box and give evidence against Jack the Ripper, was never realized.

Once or twice my hopes were raised, only to be dashed, when the clue I was pursuing was falsified.

The Berners Street murder yielded a clue which, for a time, raised

---

405   "No. 1 squealed a bit." appeared here in *TWN*, 23 February 1935; "number one squealed a bit" in the original postcard.

the hopes of us all. Our inquiries brought to light the important fact that a few minutes–or at any rate a very short time before her death, Elizabeth Stride, or "Long Liz", as she was known to her intimates, had actually been seen in the company of a man.

This evidence was supplied by a man who kept a small fruit shop in Berners Street.[406] His story was that in the early hours of that Sunday morning he had sold the couple some grapes.

The real value of the fruit vendor's information lay in the fact that he swore he had seen the woman's companion before and would recognize him if he saw him again.

Unfortunately his story was backed by a description of the man which could only be described as vague.[407] It might have applied equally to thousands of men.

Then came dramatic corroboration of his story. In the little Berners Street court, quite close to the spot where the body was found, detectives searching every inch of the ground came upon a number of grape skins and stones.

The obvious deduction was that these were the remains of the grapes which "Long Liz's" companion had bought at the fruit shop, and that she had probably been eating them right up to the moment of her death.

The only alternative–which hardly seemed feasible–was that at that time of night–or early morning–Mrs. Stride had got rid of one man and sought the companionship of another.

And now comes what to every police officer engaged on the case was the most maddening incident of the whole Ripper mystery.

A few days after the murder the shopkeeper actually saw the man to whom he had sold the grapes pass his shop.

He knew that this man was suspected of being Jack the Ripper.

Tragedy of tragedies, he let the opportunity of catching him slip by. He made no attempt to follow the suspect. He did not even have the presence of mind to dash with the information to the nearest constable. There he stood in his shop, while the mystery man boarded a tramcar and disappeared.

There was another man in the shop. To him he mentioned his

---

406   This was Matthew Packer (1831-1907).

407   Packer described the man as aged between twenty-five and thirty, about 5 ft. 7 in. tall with rather broad shoulders and a rough voice. He wore a long black coat and a soft felt hat.

suspicions when it was too late.

The shopkeeper said afterwards that he was afraid to leave his shop.

The moment the shopman's story reached the ears of the police, scores of officers were immediately put on the new scent. It was too late. Jack the Ripper, if indeed it was he, had once more vanished into thin air.

But was he Jack the Ripper? This is a question none can now answer. One can, however, ask how it came about that a man, who had shown himself to be a master of cunning, should have fallen into the elementary error of risking recognition by passing so soon again along that street and exposing himself to the view of a man whom he must have known linked him with one of his crimes.

It might also be asked why, on that occasion, the Ripper should have departed so far from custom as to purchase fruit for one of his intended victims?

Although it has never been seriously suggested that the Berners Street murder was not a Ripper crime.[408] I confess I am puzzled. Frankly, I cannot reconcile the buying of those grapes in the company of the woman he was about to kill, and his reappearance a few days later in the same street, with the undoubted cleverness of the Ripper.

At that I must leave it, with the comment that if the shopkeeper was right in his second identification it was about the worst piece of luck the police could possibly have had. This was not the only bad luck we had. I used to feel at times that the fates were conspiring against us and doing everything to assist the man behind the problem which was daily deepening in horrifying mystery.

The police at this time[409] were terribly buffeted. In some cases they did not receive the support they had a right to expect.

Let me tell a little story in this connexion. In an East End police court the magistrate was for some reason, lenient to all offenders charged with assaulting the police. He seemed to think that police evidence in such cases was coloured. His punishment was, almost without exception, a fine.

---

408   Full stop here in *ICC*. *TWN* had a comma.
409   "The poor police at this time" in *TWN*, 2 March 1935.

At length he was persuaded to pay two or three nightly visits in the company of police officers to some of the most vicious haunts in his judicial area. What he saw changed his views. There were no more fines in police assault cases, but imprisonment without the option.

I wish some of those other critics of the police at the time of the Ripper could have been compelled to spend a few nights in the districts in which it was our unenviable job to try to keep law and order. They, too, would have changed their opinions.

And now I approach a phase of the Ripper story which I would give a great deal even now to have expunged from my memory,

As my thoughts go back to Miller's Court, and what happened there, the old nausea, indignation and horror overwhelm me still.

The thing of which I am about to write happened nearly fifty years ago.[410] Yet my mental picture of it remains as shockingly clear as though it were but yesterday.

It is all before me now. Jack the Ripper at his most devilish. No savage could have been more barbaric. No wild animal could have done anything so horrifying.

If I remember rightly it was between ten and eleven o'clock in the morning that I looked in at Commercial Street police station to get into touch with my superiors. I was chatting with Inspector Beck,[411] who was in charge of the station, when a young fellow, his eyes bulging out of his head, came panting into the police station.[412] The poor fellow was so frightened that for a time he was unable to utter a single intelligible word.[413]

At last he managed to stammer out something about "Another one. Jack the Ripper. Awful. Jack McCarthy sent me."

Mr. McCarthy was well-known to us as a common lodging-house proprietor.[414]

"Come along, Dew," said Inspector Beck, and gathering from the terrorized messenger that Dorset Street was the scene of

---

410 "happened 46 years ago." in *TWN*, 2 March 1935, suggesting this part of the text was written in 1934.

411 Inspector Walter Beck (1852-1927). He joined the Metropolitan Police in 1871 and retired in 1896. (PRO, MEPO 21/25).

412 This was Thomas Bowyer, an army pensioner, known as "Indian Harry."

413 "a single word." in *STWN*, 2 March 1935.

414 "a lodging-house proprietor." in *STWN*, 2 March 1935.

whatever had happened, we made him our pilot, as we rushed in that direction, collecting as many constables as we could on the way.

The youth led us a few yards down Dorset Street from Commercial Street, until we came to a court approached by an arched passage, three feet wide and unlighted, in which there were two entrances[415] to houses which fronted on Dorset Street. The place was known as Miller's Court.

Leaving the constables to block Dorset Street and to prevent anyone from leaving the court itself, Inspector Beck and I proceeded through the narrow archway into what might be described as a small square. It was a cul-de-sac, flanked on all four sides by a few mean houses.

The house on the left of the passage was kept by McCarthy as a chandler's shop, while one room of the houses on the right was rented by a girl named Marie Kelly.

McCarthy's messenger was by this time able to tell a more or less coherent story. He told us that some of the neighbours had become alarmed at the non-appearance that morning of Kelly. They had spoken about it to McCarthy, and he had sent the youth to find her.

The door of her room was locked, but the lad looked through a broken pane of glass in the only window in the room which faced the wider part of the court, and had seen something which froze the blood in his veins and sent him helter-skelter to the police station.

The room was pointed out to me. I tried the door. It would not yield. So I moved to the window, over which, on the inside, an old coat was hanging to act as a curtain and to block the draught from the hole in the glass.

Inspector Beck pushed the coat to one side and peered through the aperture. A moment later he staggered back with his face as white as a sheet.

"For God's sake, Dew," he cried. "Don't look."

I ignored the order, and took my place at the window.

When my eyes had become accustomed to the dim light I saw a sight which I shall never forget to my dying day.

---

415 "two side entrances" in *STWN*, 2 March 1935.

The whole horror of that room will only be known to those of us whose duty it was to enter it. The full details are unprintable.

There was a table just beneath the window. On the bed, which was drawn obliquely across the small room, was all that remained of a good-looking and buxom young woman.[416]

There was little left of her, not much more than a skeleton.[417] Her face was terribly scarred and mutilated.

All this was horrifying enough, but the mental picture of that sight which remains most vividly with me is the poor woman's eyes. They were wide open, and seemed to be staring straight at me with a look of terror.

Inspector Beck quickly recovered from his shock and sent messages to the chief station by quick-running constables. From there the messages were promptly relayed by telegraph to Scotland Yard.

Obviously nothing could be done for the woman, but Dr. Phillips was sent for as a matter of form and was soon on the spot.

Officers were sent in all directions to make inquiries and interrogate any and every person likely to be able to give information.

No attempt was made by us to break into the room. It was deemed advisable to wait until the higher-placed officers arrived on the scene before anything was touched. This was essential if bloodhounds were to be used, although how bloodhounds could be expected to track a criminal in a place like London, I have never been able to understand.

However that may be, the Commissioner of Police and other high officers were soon on the spot,[418] and one of the first decisions was that bloodhounds should be tried.

They never were, however, for the owner of the hounds decided that it would be utterly futile. That one can readily understand, considering that by this time thousands of people had used the adjoining thoroughfares. Moreover, it was a drizzling morning.

Again the critics of the police seized upon this to castigate the officers in charge of the case. It was said that bloodhounds should

---

416   "a good-looking young woman." in *STWN*, 2 March 1935.
417   This sentence was not in *STWN*. *ETWN*, 2 March 1935, had "the skeleton."
418   "the big guns from the Yard were soon on the spot" in *TWN*, 2 March 1935.

have been used and that there was unnecessary delay.

I flatly contradict the suggestion of delay. There was none, and the only reason for not using the bloodhounds was that they could not possibly have helped.

It would have been a different matter if bloodhounds had been available, and could have been put immediately on the trail.[419] The experiment would then have been worth trying, though I doubt if it would have met with any success, as the crime was already several hours old.

There are differences of opinion as to the actual time of the Marie Kelly murder, but I have always inclined to the view that it took place somewhere between midnight and 2 a.m.

As soon as the chief officers arrived they decided to force the door which, if I remember rightly, had an automatic lock.

I followed the others into the room. The sight that confronted us was indescribable, infinitely more horrifying than what I had seen when peeping through the broken pane of glass into the room's semi-darkness.

I had seen most of the other remains. They were sickening enough in all conscience. But none of the others approached for bestial brutality the treatment of the body of poor Marie Kelly,[420] whom I had known well by sight as a pretty, buxom girl.

The effect on me as I entered that room was as if someone had given me a tremendous blow in the stomach. Never in my life have I funked a police duty so much as I funked this one.

Whatever the state of the killer's mind when he committed the other murders, there cannot be the slightest doubt that in that room in Miller's Court he became a frenzied, raving madman.

With the state of that room in my mind, I cannot see how the murderer[421] could have avoided being covered from head to foot with blood.

Some of these traces must have remained when he reached

---

419 "It would have been a different matter if Mr McCarthy had had bloodhounds at his disposal, and could have put them immediately on the trail." in *STWN*, 2 March 1935. Although the Metropolitan Police had obtained two bloodhounds to try to track the Whitechapel murderer, they had been returned to their owner by the time of the Kelly murder and were unavailable.

420 "the treatment of poor Marie Kelly" in *STWN*, 2 March 1935.

421 "the Ripper" in *TWN*, 2 March 1935.

his home or his lodgings. Yet no one came forward to voice the suspicions which such a spectacle must have aroused. Proof positive to my mind that the Ripper was shielded by someone.

The room was on the ground floor and about 12 ft. by 10 ft. It was self-contained. A sort of one-room flat. The only door in use was that by which we had entered. There was another, leading to the upper part of the house, but this had been nailed up. So that the murderer could only have entered and retreated by that narrow archway leading from Dorset Street.

There was very little furniture, a bed, a table, a chair or two, all in a bad state of repair.

But Marie could scarcely have expected more. The rent worked out at only 6*d*. a night. Even this sum had proved too much for her. She was several weeks in arrears.

The atmosphere of the room was stifling, and this in spite of the broken window.

There was no fire in the grate, but there were signs that there had been a big blaze. For one thing, the kettle standing on the burnt-out fire had melted at the spout. Candles which had been used to light the room had been burned right down.[422]

The girl's clothing had nearly all been cut from her body in the mad process of mutilation.

All these things I saw after I had slipped and fallen on the awfulness of that floor.[423]

VIII

I HAVE told you about the eyes of Marie Kelly, wide-open and staring in death.

To someone, those eyes suggested a possible clue.

There was at the time a wide-spread superstition that the retina of a murdered person's eyes would, if photographed, give a picture of the last person upon whom the victim looked.

I do not for a moment think that the police ever seriously expected the photograph of the murderer to materialize, but it was

---

422 At the inquest Inspector Abberline agreed with the melted spout theory, but said the fire was used to light the room as there was only one piece of candle in the room.

423 These last two sentences were not it *STWN*.

decided to try the experiment.

Several photographs of the eyes were taken by expert photographers with the latest type cameras.[424]

The result was negative.

But the very fact that this forlorn hope was tried shows that the police, in their eagerness to catch the murderer, were ready to follow any clue and to adopt any suggestion, even at the risk of being made to look absurd.

The public, I fear, knows little of the many-sided activities of the police in bringing criminals to justice. It is impossible for them to know. So much that is done behind the scenes can never be revealed to the public.

Many get their ideas of police procedure from reading thrilling detective stories in which the criminal is always traced. And they overlook the fact that it is easy to unravel a plot which you yourself have created–a different matter altogether from starting, as the police have to do, the other way round.

It was very much a case of the other way round in the hunt for Jack the Ripper.

When, for instance, he left Miller's Court in the early hours of November 9th which way did he go?

There were several possibilities. He could have turned abruptly into Commercial Street and, crossing the road, soon found himself in a veritable maze of streets and courts. He could have made his way towards Aldgate, or he could, on leaving the court, have turned right, making for Wentworth Street and Petticoat Lane, and thence to the City.

It is idle now to speculate as to which direction he chose. The miracle is that he ran the gauntlet successfully, and escaped.

I have already referred briefly to the theory held in some quarters that the Ripper might have been a man so well known to the police, either because of his profession or his standing locally, that his immunity even from suspicion was assured.

This is a very plausible explanation–one of the most plausible

---

424 "latest cameras." in *STWN*, 9 March 1935. Just as there is no independent corroboration that Dew was the first detective to arrive at Miller's Court, nobody else involved in the investigation claimed that Mary Kelly's eyes were photographed. Dew repeated the claim in a 1943 letter to the *Sunday Express*. (See Appendix 1).

of all–until one sets out to analyze it.

The big point which this suggestion overlooks is that hundreds of policemen of all ranks had been drafted to the East End from all parts of London. Local celebrities cut no ice with them, and would have been arrested just as promptly as anyone else had their actions been at all suspicious.

Constables going on duty had very definite instructions. They were told to pull up and search any man whose actions raised the slightest doubt in their minds, and, if the answer given were not satisfactory, to bring such men to the police station while inquiries about them were made.[425]

Since 1888, many people have written on the subject of the Ripper's uncanny escapes, some of them putting forward their own theories. I am less presumptuous.

I was on the spot, actively engaged throughout the whole series of crimes. I ought to know something about it. Yet I have to confess I am as mystified now as I was then by the man's amazing elusiveness.

England had never known anything like it before; I pray she never will again.

Equally mystifying was the man's power to quell the natural fear in the minds of women, and especially of the type to whom his coming meant an unspeakable death.[426]

There was no woman in the whole of Whitechapel more frightened of Jack the Ripper than Marie Kelly.

The day of her death was the Lord Mayor's Show, London's greatest pageant of the year. She had planned to see it and was looking forward to the spectacle with all the enthusiasm of a girl born and bred in the country.

Just the night before, Marie had been fearfully discussing the killer of her kind with Lizzie Albrook, a nineteen-years-old friend.[427]

"This will be the last Lord Mayor's Show I shall see," said Marie tearfully. "I can't stand it any longer. This Jack the Ripper business is getting on my nerves. I have made up my mind to go home to my mother. It is safer there."

---

425   This paragraph was not in *STWN*.
426   This sentence was not in *STWN*.
427   "with a nineteen-year-old girl friend." in *STWN*, 16 March 1935.

Marie was Irish born, but her mother at this time was living in Wales.

Poor Marie!

When the Lord Mayor's Show swept through the streets of the City the next day, she was lying in that little back room in Miller's Court.

News of this fresh Ripper visitation came to the crowds cheering the Lord Mayor's Show. The cheers died in their throats; the smiles left their faces.

"Have you heard the news?" one whispered to the other. "The Ripper's been again. Dorset Street, they say."

Thousands forgot the Lord Mayor's Show and flocked with morbid curiosity to Dorset Street, but this time they were doomed to disappointment. Past experiences had forewarned the police and barricades at each end of the street prevented the mob from close approach to the scene of the Ripper's first indoor murder.

Meanwhile, in Miller's Court itself, there was something approaching panic. Marie had been well-known to every resident and, sunny of nature, had been very popular.

Here was a crime different from the others. The circumstances of it held out bright possibilities. Surely someone must have seen the girl and her companion in a little court in which every person knew the other's business. At last it seemed likely that we should get some information pointing to the identity, or at any rate, to the appearance of the man we had hunted so long.

There was no lack of information, but as so often happens, when the various statements had been sorted and sifted they were so contradictory as to be well-nigh valueless.

Of Marie Kelly herself, very few intimate details were known. She had occupied her room, which she rented from John McCarthy, the chandler, for ten months. During the greater part of that time she had been very friendly with a young man.[428]

A short time previously the couple had had a tiff, all because Marie, in a fit of Irish generosity, had allowed an unfortunate to use her room. This upset with her boy friend may have to some extent

---

428   This was Joseph Barnett (1858-1926), an unemployed fish porter who had lived with Kelly for eighteen months.

accounted for the girl's despondency on the eve of her death.

That evening, as I have said, Lizzie Albrook found her in tears.[429] After that she remained in her room for two hours and then, as though to drown her sorrows, went drinking in the local public-houses. This was unusual, for normally Marie was a sober girl.[430]

The first information led the police to believe the girl was last seen alive, except by her slayer, at midnight, when she was seen by a neighbour, Mary Cox, walking in the direction of her home.

Marie was not alone. With her was a man described by Mary Cox as "short, stout, bearded, shabbily dressed in a longish coat and billycock hat, and carrying a pot of ale in one hand".

Mrs. Cox followed the couple through the passage leading to the court and called out: "Good night, Marie," as they were about to enter Kelly's room.

The girl looked round, recognized Mary Cox, and called back, "Good night. I am going to have a little song." Both then disappeared through the doorway.

Was the man in the billycock hat Jack the Ripper?

In spite of contradictory evidence which came to light later, and in spite of a departure from his method of swift and sudden attack, I think he was, always providing Mary Cox was correct in what she said.

A little later, more than one neighbour heard Marie singing blithely, if a little unsteadily. The singing continued for fully an hour.

Then came silence, a silence which synchronized, if my theory is correct, with the transformation of the quiet-looking bearded man who had mysteriously won the girl's confidence, into the inhuman devil his previous deeds had shown him to be.

Marie Kelly died swiftly then, but not, if the story of terror in her eyes is accepted, before she had realized who her visitor was.

The description given by Mary Cox was circulated immediately. This information gave us for the first time something really tangible to work upon. We knew what the man we were after looked like. We knew the kind of clothes he wore and, most important of all, we

---

429 "her girl friend found her in tears." in *STWN*, 9 March 1935.
430 Although it was reported that "the deceased woman was somewhat addicted to drink" in *The Times*, 10 November 1888.

knew that he was bearded.

Hopes ran higher than they had done at any time since the first visitation. The police were inspired to even greater efforts and the public, buoyed up with the expectancy of an early arrest, forgot their fears.

The people of the East End were horrified by such revolting details of the crime as were revealed, but hope had taken the place of panic as the prevailing emotion–hope that at long last the district would be freed from its mystifying terror.

Alas, this was not to be.

Within a short time, other information was obtained by the police which seemed to blow sky high the theories they had based upon the evidence of Mary Cox.

The new evidence was supplied by another woman, named Mrs. Caroline Maxwell, wife of the deputy at No. 14 Dorset Street, which adjoined Miller's Court. She claimed to know Marie Kelly well, and to have seen her alive only two hours before her body was discovered.

Imagine the sensation this story caused. If true it put an entirely new complexion upon the whole case.

If Mrs. Maxwell had been a sensation-seeker–one of those women who live for the limelight–it would have been easy to discredit her story. She was not. She seemed a sane and sensible woman, and her reputation was excellent.

She stated that at eight o'clock on the Friday morning she was going into Mr. McCarthy's chandler's shop, when she saw Marie standing in the passage leading to the court. The girl looked ill, and Mrs. Maxwell went over to her and asked if anything was the matter.

"I feel bad," she quoted Marie as saying. "I was drinking last night. It has made me ill."

She then asked Mrs. Maxwell if she could suggest anything she could take to make her feel better. The women exchanged a few more words; then the girl re-entered her room.

Mrs. Maxwell repeated this evidence at the inquest, and told her story with conviction.

In one way at least her version fitted into the facts as known. We knew that Marie had been drinking the previous night, and, as this was not a habit of hers, illness the next morning was just what might have been expected.

Then followed other information which further shook the police reconstruction of the crime.

The informant this time was a young man named George Hutchinson, who declared that he had seen Kelly at 2 a.m. in Dorset Street. She had been drinking. He spoke to her, and she confessed that she was "broke".

A few minutes later he saw her again. This time she was in the company of a man, and the two were walking in the direction of Miller's Court.

This man had no billycock hat and no beard. He was in fact the exact opposite in appearance of the man seen by Mrs. Cox.

Hutchinson described him as well-dressed, wearing a felt hat, a long, dark astrakhan collared coat and dark spats. A turned-up black moustache gave him a foreign appearance.

But I know from my experience that many people, with the best of intentions,[431] are often mistaken, not necessarily as to a person, but as to date and time. And I can see no other explanation in this case than that Mrs. Maxwell and George Hutchinson were wrong.[432]

Indeed, if the medical evidence is accepted, Mrs. Maxwell could not have been right. The doctors were unable, because of the terrible mutilations,[433] to say with any certainty just when death took place, but they were very emphatic that the girl could not have been alive at eight o'clock that morning.

And if Mrs. Maxwell was mistaken, is it not probable that George Hutchinson erred also? This, without reflecting in any way on either witness, is my considered view. I believe that the man of the billycock hat and beard was the last person to enter Marie Kelly's room that night and was her killer. Always assuming that Mrs. Cox ever had seen her with a man.[434]

The days passed. Jack the Ripper remained as mythical as ever so far as the police were concerned.[435] The only certain evidence of

---

431 "that witnesses with the best of intentions" in *TWN*, 9 March 1935.

432 "Mrs Maxwell and George Hutchinson had, though they were perfectly genuine in their beliefs, made a mistake." in *STWN*, 9 March 1935.

433 "the mutilations" in *STWN*, 9 March 1935.

434 This last sentence was not in *TWN*.

435 After the Kelly murder Dew gave evidence at Worship Street Magistrates' Court against

his existence was his fearful crimes.[436]

The Miller's Court murder made it more obvious than ever that the murderer was being shielded. This time, as I have indicated, he must have returned to his home or his lodgings with the evidences of his handiwork still upon him.

In order to allay the fears of those who may have possessed knowledge, but were afraid to come forward with it, the officers in charge of the investigations took an unusual step. This striking notice was posted up outside every police station:

PARDON.–Whereas on November 8 or 9 in Miller's Court, Dorset Street, Spitalfields, Marie Janet Kelly was murdered by some person or persons unknown, the Secretary of State will advise the granting of Her Majesty's pardon to any accomplice (not being a person who contrived or actually committed the murder) who shall give such information as shall lead to the discovery and conviction of the person or persons who committed the murder. (Signed). Charles Warren.

This offer was construed by many people into a confession of failure. It was nothing of the kind. The step was taken after careful consideration with the definite object of securing vital information which the police were convinced existed.

The effort failed, like all the others, but it was none the less commendable for that.[437]

Swede Nikaner Benelius who had been charged with entering a dwelling house for an unlawful purpose. He had previously been arrested and questioned over the Elizabeth Stride murder. Benelius was cleared of any involvement in the murders. (*The Star*, 19 November 1888; *The Times*, 19 November 1888).

436   These previous two sentences were not in *STWN*.
437   Additional text here in *TWN*, 9 March 1935:

"Towards the end of September [sic], Jack the Ripper may, or may not, have appeared again. There was an attempt at murder in George Street, which certainly had the Ripper touch about it and which remained a mystery.

It was about nine-thirty in the morning that the cry of murder went up from one of the lodging-houses in the street. Several people were about.

Suddenly a man of foreign appearance, dark moustache, medium build, well-dressed, emerged from a passage into the street. In his hand he held a small knife.

Some of the men in the street made bold to close with the runaway until the screams of a woman were heard–"Hold him. It's Jack the Ripper," she cried.

At the sound of that dread name the men's courage left them, and the foreigner continued on his way with no serious attempt made to hinder him until he disappeared through some courts.

IX

A LTHOUGH many people may not agree with me, I believe that the Miller's Court outrage was the last murder ever committed by Jack the Ripper.

There were, I know, other baffling East End murder mysteries which remained unsolved, but I have never been satisfied that they were the handiwork of the demon Jack.

People in those days had what may be described as the Jack the Ripper complex. Immediately a murder and mutilation was reported, whether in Whitechapel or in any other part of the country, they jumped to the conclusion that he was the culprit.

In other parts of the country, there was always the subconscious fear that sooner or later Jack the Ripper would leave Whitechapel and pay a visit to their particular neighbourhood.

The police were never misled by alarms elsewhere.[438] In Whitechapel our inquiries went on and on. The chiefs from Scotland Yard continued to make their headquarters at Leman Street Police Station, battling with their problem long after the public had

Meanwhile the police had entered the house from which the cries had come. Here they found a middle-aged woman suffering from a slight wound in the throat. The woman was under the influence of drink, and it was not until much later in the day that she was able to make a helpful statement.

The story she then told was strange. The previous evening, she said, she had been accosted by the stranger, and they had spent the evening together. She drank a lot, but the man scarcely at all.

In the morning something disturbed her, and she felt the prick of a knife in her throat. She screamed. The man, who was already dressed, ran out of the house.

The doctors stated it was a miracle the woman, who had been attacked from behind, had not been murdered. The sudden movement of her head had saved her life.

Here again the police did not get the help they were entitled to expect. The woman was virtually useless. She was unable even to give a description of the man. Other people in the lodging-house had scarcely seen him.

People, who had been standing in the street and might have given useful information, were too ashamed of their inaction to come forward.

So once again we were up against the inevitable blank wall."

This referred to an attack on prostitute Annie Farmer on 21 November 1888. Again, Dew got the date wrong, but given that the tale appeared after Dew's account of Mary Kelly's murder, it could have been *TWN*'s typographical error that gave the date as September.

438 Yet Dew had previously stated that after the Gateshead-on-Tyne murder: "At first both the doctor and the police were deceived and gave it as their opinion that the girl had been a Ripper victim." (*ICC*, p. 125).

assumed that all hope of catching the fiend had been abandoned.

One of the strongest inferences to be deduced from the crimes was that the man we were hunting was probably a sexual maniac. This angle of investigation was pursued relentlessly. Inquiries were made at asylums all over the country, including the Criminal Lunatic Asylum at Broadmoor, with the object of discovering whether a homicidal lunatic had been released as cured about the time the Ripper crimes commenced. No useful evidence was obtained.

Anonymous letters and postcards continued to roll in, magnifying our work without providing a single valuable clue.

One such letter, bearing the Portsmouth postmark, received by Mr. Saunders, the magistrate of the Thames Police Court, was typical. It ran:

"Dear Boss,–It is no use for you to look for me in London because I'm not there. Don't trouble yourself about me until I return, which will not be very long. I like the work too well to leave it alone. Oh, it was such a jolly job the last one. I had plenty of time to do it properly in. Ha, ha, ha. You think it is a man with a black moustache. Ha, ha, ha. When I have done another one you can try and catch me again. So good-bye, dear boss, till I return.

Yours,

Jack the Ripper."

Curiously enough, a few days after the receipt of this letter a boy was attacked and murdered in the Portsmouth district. A clasp knife was found near the body. The dead boy's companions stated that they had been accosted by a tall dark man. The others ran away, leaving the victim with the stranger.

This crime, as may be expected, following so swiftly upon the letter, created a real Ripper scare in the neighbourhood.

Scotland Yard officers went down and quickly satisfied themselves that the crime had no connexion at all with the Whitechapel horrors. But it was not so easy to convince the public, especially as the mystery remained unsolved.[439]

About the same time, too, a little girl was outraged and murdered in Somerset.[440] Again Jack the Ripper was blamed, rumour even

439   This was the murder of eight-year-old Percy Searle at Havant on 26 November 1888.
440   "near Yeovil, in Somerset." in *TWN*, 16 March 1935.

going so far as to suggest that he had left Whitechapel for a murder and mutilation of the country.[441]

All this panic was unnecessary. The murderer was caught and executed.[442]

Then came a Ripper scare in the north of England,[443] where a boy of eight years of age died as a result of a number of vicious knife wounds.

The boy's unclothed body was found near some stables, his clothes in a bundle close by. He had been missing two days.

The police were able to rule Jack the Ripper out at once on the ground that the man who committed the crime must have had an intimate knowledge of the district. The boy had been killed elsewhere and the body deposited at the spot where it was found by a policeman on his beat, several hours after death.[444]

Murders continued to take place in London. In December, 1888, a woman was found dead in strange circumstances in Poplar, and for a time Ripper fears were needlessly revived in the East End.[445]

Later there was some doubt as to whether this was a murder at all. It was first assumed that the woman had been strangled, but there was afterwards a conflict of opinion on this, one doctor declaring that the woman had died a natural death.

In any case, the only relation the mystery bore to the Whitechapel horrors was the fact that the woman was of the unfortunate class.

She had actually been driven out of Whitechapel by her dread of Jack the Ripper.

The trouble was that people's minds were so dominated by Jack the Ripper thoughts and fears, that they sought to fasten upon him every murder no matter how, where or when it was committed.

441 "a murder and mutilation tour of the country." in *TWN*, 16 March 1935.
442 "The Yeovil murderer was caught and executed." in *TWN*, 16 March 1935. This was Samuel Reyland who murdered nine-year-old Emma Davies on 2 February, 1889. He was executed on 13 March, 1889.
443 "at Bradford" in *TWN*, 16 March 1935.
444 "This murder also remained a mystery." appeared at the end of the paragraph in *TWN*, 16 March 1935. The victim was John Gill who had been murdered and mutilated on 27 or 28 December, 1888.
445 This was Rose Mylett who died on 19 December, 1888. Dew had been transferred to F Division (Paddington) in December 1888, so he must have maintained an interest in the Whitechapel murders to be able to write about these later cases, or referred to other sources for his information.

Many diabolical murders were committed in the Whitechapel district after the Miller's Court drama. Several of these are still ascribed to the Ripper. People seem to forget that there were plenty of similar crimes in Whitechapel long before Jack the Ripper was ever heard of.

One of these so-called Ripper murders took place on 17th July, 1889, nearly a year after hapless Marie Kelly met her death. The scene of the tragedy was Castle Alley, a notorious place just off the "Haymarket", Whitechapel High Street, and quite close to Dorset Street.

The victim was Alice Mackenzie, a charwoman, who had come to the East End of London from Peterborough, and lived in a common lodging-house.

Castle Alley was well lighted, but it was nevertheless just such a place as Jack the Ripper himself might have chosen. The place was little frequented, and many of the houses were partly demolished and fronted by hoardings.

About 12.30 (midnight)[446] a constable patrolling his beat found the woman lying near a lamp-post. Thinking she was the worse for drink, he shook her. It was then he discovered that she was dead. Her throat had been cut, and, more significant as a pointer to the Ripper, her clothing had been disarranged.

Dr. Phillips was sent for and came to the conclusion that the fatal wound had been inflicted from behind.

To explain the absence of mutilation, it was suggested that the man had been disturbed and had decamped.

Underneath the body was found a brightly polished farthing. This in the dim light might easily have been mistaken for a half-sovereign, and the theory held was that Mackenzie had been lured to her death by the offer of a gold coin.

This was probably the true explanation, for another woman came forward to say that the offer of a similar coin had been made to her, but she had discovered the trick and had run away. Her description of the man was "a dark foreigner, speaking good English".

Jack the Ripper had never been in the habit of decoying his victims with bright farthings. Nor had he ever made the mistake of

---

446   "Just after midnight" in *TWN*, 16 March 1935.

allowing one of his intended victims to escape.

It is true that this murderer succeeded in getting away, but so have many others.

I do not think this was a Jack the Ripper crime any more than I think he had anything to do with the murder of another woman whose body was found in the foundations of a huge new building on the Thames Embankment, now known as New Scotland Yard.[447] The site was chosen originally for an opera house, but plans were changed, and the building became the headquarters of the Metropolitan Police and the C.I.D.

One other East End crime which comes within the category of Ripper possibilities I will touch briefly upon.

In February, 1891, the body of a woman was found in Swallow Gardens, a place of evil repute not far from Leman Street Police Station. Close by ran the arches of the old London, Tilbury and Southend Railway. The arches were used as warehouses. On the other side of the street were ramshackle houses tenanted by people of very doubtful character.

Badly lighted, it was indeed a place best avoided, though it was frequently used by perfectly respectable railwaymen.

A constable found the woman dying from throat injuries. A few minutes later she breathed her last. The alarm was given. The place was surrounded. Every house was searched.

The man had worked swiftly. Swallow Gardens had been patrolled a few minutes previously and nothing then was seen, either of him or of his victim. Again there was disarrangement of the clothing without mutilation, and again those who attributed the crime to the Ripper argued that he must have been disturbed.

The victim was later identified as Frances Coles, young and not bad looking, an unfortunate who lived in one of the many common lodging-houses in Spitalfields.

A man in whose company the woman had been seen was questioned and detained. He was released after he had satisfied the police that he had nothing to do with the crime.[448]

There was great excitement. Ripper panic was revived. My view is that this was a false alarm. There was a tendency–and a natural

447   The woman's torso was discovered on 2 October, 1888.
448   This was James Thomas Sadler, a ship's fireman.

enough tendency–for years for any violent murder which was not followed by a conviction to be laid at the Ripper's door.

One big question remains to be asked, but, I am afraid, not to be answered.

Who was Jack the Ripper?

I was closely associated with most of the murders. Yet I hesitate to express a definite opinion as to who or what the man may have been.[449]

He may have been a doctor. He may have been a medical student. He may have been a foreigner. He may even have been a slaughterman, and so on.[450]

Such speculation is little more than childish, for there is no evidence to support one view any more than another.

But this, I think, can safely be said. The man at times must have been quite mad. There can be no other explanation of those wicked mutilations. It may have been sex mania, blood lust, or some other form of insanity, but madness there certainly was.

Yet it is quite possible that Jack the Ripper was quite sane at all other times. There have been plenty of instances of this. Seemingly clever, cultured and normal people can be found in any lunatic asylum–even in Broadmoor–but they are none the less dangerous for that.

The late Dr. Forbes Winslow, an authority on mental diseases, gave it as his view that by the morning, the frenzy of insanity having passed, Jack the Ripper might not have been able to remember what he had done.[451]

With all due respect to the late doctor, I cannot agree with him. There is a big stumbling block to the acceptance of his theory. It

---

449   Dew briefly held suspicions against one man. In January 1889 Harry Fife was tried at the Old Bailey for his part in a series of silk thefts within the Whitechapel Division. Fife's alibi was that on the night of one of the robberies he was at Commercial Street Police Station accusing a man of being Jack the Ripper. Dew's colleague Thomas Stacey told the court that when the man was brought in he was behaving "in such a strange manner that Dew thought he might be the Whitechapel murderer." (PRO, CRIM 10/79).

450   "He may even have been a police officer." in *TWN*, 16 March 1935, instead of slaughterman.

451   Dr. Lyttleton Stewart Forbes Winslow (1844-1913). See Whittington-Egan, *Doctor Forbes Winslow Defender of the Insane* (2000), pp. 166-218, for a detailed examination of Winslow's views on the case. Ironically Winslow boasted at a magistrates' court in 1910: "I think I am more likely to catch "Jack the Ripper" than they [the police] are to catch Crippen." (*The Morning Advertiser*, 27 July 1910). The opposite proved to be the case.

is that the man who committed the Whitechapel murders had with him when he met his victims the weapon–and no ordinary weapon– with which the deeds were done. This surely suggests premeditation and indicates when he set out on his evil excursions it was with deliberate intent.

There was, too, more method about the Ripper than one would have expected of a man of the type described by Dr. Winslow. He always returned to the same locality; and on each occasion he chose his victim from the same class of women.

Various men who were hanged for subsequent murders, notably Neil Cream,[452] came under the suspicion of the public, but there were never any real grounds for believing that any one of them had had anything to do with the Whitechapel crimes.

Many other theories have been held. Far be it from me to ridicule the most improbable of them. I saw so much that was uncanny during the reign of Ripper terror that it would be in keeping with the whole case were the most unlikely solution to be the correct one.[453]

I cannot, however, refrain from asking why so many people, even to this day, cling to the opinion that the murderer must have been a doctor or a medical student.

I never thought he was.

There are many people besides doctors expert in the use of the knife. Why not a butcher, or a slaughteman, or even the proprietor of an East End stall?[454]

Not even the rudiments of surgical skill were needed to cause the mutilations I saw.

But there was one thing about the mutilations which seems to have escaped general notice. They showed a graduating ferocity.

All of them were terrible, but the second was worse than the first

---

452   Dr. Thomas Neill Cream (1850-1892), executed for the fatal poisoning of four prostitutes in London. It has been alleged that his last words, spoken on the scaffold, were "I am Jack the…"

453   There had already been many theories about the Ripper's identity by the time Dew wrote his memoirs. His magnanimous attitude towards them is in sharp contrast to his easily taking offence at what he felt were false perceptions about the Crippen case. This was probably because that he was in charge of the Crippen investigation and took the criticisms personally and because he honestly had no idea who Jack the Ripper was.

454   "an East End eel stall?" in *TWN*, 16 March 1935.

and the third worse than the second, until the climax was reached in that terrible room in Miller's Court.

And with that crime, or so it seems to me, even that seemingly insatiable monster was satisfied. He came back no more.

There is little doubt now that Jack the Ripper is dead. I often wonder what sort of an end he met—whether it was peaceful or whether he did develop into the stark, raving maniac he must have appeared at the moment of striking his victims down. Somehow I cannot picture such a man on a peaceful death bed.

One word more.

I took pleasure in nearly all my work as a police officer. Sometimes it was possible to find even a touch of humour.

There was neither pleasure nor humour in the part I played in the greatest crime drama of all time—the mystery of Jack the Ripper.

Leopold Buildings, Bethnal Green. Dew's home in 1888.
(Author's collection)

Above: Osborn Street, Whitechapel,
the scene of Emma Smith's attack.
(Living London)

Left: Dew's H Division colleagues;
Johnny Upright, Teddy Reid and Tommy
Roundhead, (William Thick, Edmund Reid
and Eli Caunter).
(Stewart P. Evans)

Right: Detective Inspector
Frederick Abberline.
(Toby)

John Reeves discovers Martha Tabram's corpse.
(Thomson's Weekly News)

Charles Cross and Robert Paul in Buck's Row.
(Thomson's Weekly News)

Dew and Thomas Stacey in pursuit of
George "Squibby" Squibb.
(Thomson's Weekly News)

Fanny Mortimer sees a suspicious character.
(Thomson's Weekly News)

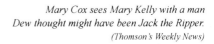

Leman Street, Whitechapel.
(Living London)

Goulston Street, Whitechapel.
(Living London)

Dorset Street, Spitalfields.
(Living London)

FROM PITCH AND TOSS
TO MURDER

FROM PITCH AND TOSS
TO MURDER[455]

I

IT is not always the most sensational case which gives the biggest kick to the detective.

I admit I was proud of the capture of Crippen, but there were many less spectacular feats from which I got just as much satisfaction.

In telling you of these cases of mine, I shall show you, as far as I can, just how the C.I.D. man works.

The first thing I want to say is that the real detective is by no means like the detective of fiction, who is always successful–in the end. Hard thinking is necessary. But with hard thinking must go hard graft as well.

Dogged perseverance has brought far more criminals to book than flashes of genius.

As I sit and think over the past, my mind goes back to the now distant days when I was a young, enthusiastic and ambitious detective-sergeant stationed at Notting Hill.[456]

Periodically each police station in the Metropolitan district received from headquarters a circular headed "Persons Wanted". It was part of our job to digest the contents of the circular, and keep

---

455 *ETWN*, 4 July 1936 had the following introduction:

"EX-CHIEF INSPECTOR WALTER DEW is known throughout the country as the man who tracked down Crippen.

In his long experience at Scotland Yard, he has met with every kind of crime–"from pitch and toss to murder," as they used to say in the old days.

Here, in telling of his most interesting cases, he takes you behind the scenes and shows just how the C.I.D. man works." *STWN*, 27 June 1936 had an almost identical introduction. In this section *TWN* footnotes have been given the publication dates of the English edition.

456 Dew had been promoted to sergeant (3rd class) on 14 December, 1889. (PRO, MEPO 21/39). The events in this case took place in February 1891.

a weather eye open for any of the offenders, big or small, who had thus qualified for arrest.

Appearing in the list of "persons wanted" one day was a woman who had committed a series of thefts in various parts of London. Her method was to call at good-class houses in response to advertisements for cooks or housemaids.

She had no intention of taking the situation. All she wanted was to be left alone for a few minutes–long enough in fact, to permit her to grab anything of value and make off with it.

Her description was given, but this was so vague that it might have applied to hundreds of women walking about the streets of London at that time. Her age was given as about 30, and her height about 5 ft. 6 in. or 5 ft. 7 in., and it was stated that she generally wore a long dark coat. There may have been one or two more details, which I have now forgotten, but if there were they were no more helpful than the others.

As a keen young officer should, I always studied the "persons wanted" list very carefully, on the off chance that during my wanderings about the Notting Hill district I might have the luck to recognize someone appearing in it.

My diligence was rewarded. One evening I was strolling along High Street, Notting Hill Gate, when my attention was attracted– goodness knows why–to two women sauntering past me.[457] One was taller than the other, and something about her stirred a chord of memory. Had I seen her before? For a moment I was puzzled.

Then I knew what it was that had caused me to pay her more attention than the dozens of other women passing by. From the description which I had memorized, she might have been the woman thief mentioned in the "Persons Wanted" circular.

But the "might" was so big that I dare not even think of arresting the woman. There is no more certain way for a police officer to get into trouble than by arresting people upon evidence as vague as that I now had to go upon. It was nothing more than a fancy.

Having nothing very important on, however, I decided to follow the women–just to see where they went. They led me to a small, respectable house just at the back of Notting Hill Gate Station, and

457   "who sauntered past me." in *TWN*, 4 July 1936.

disappeared within doors.

Well, I thought, that's that. Looks as though my fancy has misled me this time. Probably two perfectly respectable women. In any case, it seemed a little too much to hope for. Coincidences of this kind do not play a big part in the work of the real detective.

Throughout the remainder of that day I was very busy on other inquiries, and the matter of the mystery woman passed out of my mind.

Next day it came back with a bound. Round about midday I was passing almost the identical spot at which I had seen the two women the previous evening, when the taller of them–the one who had set me thinking of that "Persons Wanted" description–emerged leisurely from Clanricarde Gardens.

This time she was alone. Under her arm she was carrying a very good lady's umbrella. It was not raining.

The previous night, I recalled, when, if not actually raining, showers threatened, the woman had not been carrying an umbrella at all. This didn't seem right, somehow. I decided to follow her again.

She led me along the High Street, turned into Pembridge Road, and entered a pawnbroker's shop.

I followed her into the shop, and entered the next compartment.

"I want to pledge this umbrella," I heard her say to the assistant. "Only for a few days, I hope. My allowance hasn't come this week. Very embarrassing."

Before the assistant could complete the transaction I had managed to attract his attention.

"I'm a police officer," I whispered. "Don't take it. Hand it back."

Thereupon, to the surprise of his client, the assistant made some sort of excuse for not accepting the umbrella, and the woman, with a look of disappointment on her face, walked out of the shop.

Before she had gone a dozen paces I had overtaken her.

I told her I was a police officer, and said, quite politely, that I should be obliged if she would tell me how the umbrella she had just tried to pawn came into her possession.

My word, what a show of indignation.

How dare I question her like that? The umbrella was her own property! Of course it was. She had bought and paid for it.

The woman's protests were almost convincing, but away in the back of my mind was the description in the "Persons Wanted" circular, and, having gone so far, I was determined to make quite sure.

I felt I was justified in taking the chance, and so ignoring the violent protestations, I said it was my duty to take her into custody on a charge of unlawful possession.

That did it. Indignation turned to wild-eyed anger. She talked glibly about consulting her solicitor, and prophesied for me the most alarming consequences.[458] She continued to talk in this strain until we had reached the police station. Here I asked for her name and address. With a free use of adjectives, none of which were complimentary to myself, she flatly refused to give any information.

"Very well, then," I said. "If you refuse to give me the information I want, I shall have to see what I can find out at So-and-So," mentioning the house I had seen her entering the previous evening.

I saw at once that I had struck home. First surprise, and then fear were registered on her face. I knew then that I had not made a mistake.

Having seen the woman installed comfortably in a cell, I made my way to the address I had mentioned. The door was opened by the landlady, none other than the companion of the previous evening. A few questions and answers satisfied me that this woman was straight enough, and I told her why I had called.

She said that her lodger had been with her only a few days, and that, beyond the fact that she was a servant girl out of a situation, she knew nothing whatever about her. The name she had given was Mary ——.[459]

At my request the landlady showed me into the comfortably furnished room which Mary had occupied. Here I made a search, finding confirmation of my suspicions in the shape of a number of pawn tickets relating to umbrellas, silver salvers, clothing and other articles.

Feeling very pleased with myself, I returned to the police

---

458   Dew told the West London Magistrates' Court that she had said: "You are making a mistake, old boy; I will make you pay for it." (*The Times*, 23 February 1891).

459   Her name was Mary Reynolds.

station, arriving there just in time to hear a voluble and excited servant girl describing to the inspector in charge the theft from her mistress's house of a valuable umbrella. A woman, she said, had called at the house in reply to an advertisement for a cook. She had been left alone in the hall for a few minutes, and had disappeared. The umbrella was missed immediately afterwards.

I chipped in to ask the girl the address of her mistress's house.

"No. — Clanricarde Gardens," was the reply.

I produced the umbrella. The girl recognized it at once. She was delighted, for the umbrella proved to have been a present from her master to her mistress, and she had been blamed for leaving the thief alone in the hall.

The case against the woman I had arrested was complete.

A little later I confronted Mary with the facts. As she listened the fight went out of her. But she was curious to know how I had discovered her name and where she lived. As there was no reason why she should not know, I told her.

Her reply was a compliment.

"You jolly well deserve a better job than the one you've got," she said.

Of course, Mary was the woman described in the "Persons Wanted" circular. She was soon identified in connexion with a large number of cases, and I was able to recover and restore to the rightful owners many pounds worth of stolen property.[460]

She appeared on several remands before the late Sir Curtis Bennett (then Mr. Curtis Bennett) at the Marylebone Police Court. Sir Henry Curtis Bennett, now also dead, was a son of the former Metropolitan Magistrate.[461] In those days he was a slim lad, who used to regard it as a treat to be allowed to sit beside his father on the Bench.

After he had sentenced Mary to twelve months' hard labour,[462]

---

460   There were still thirty umbrellas which Dew could not find owners for indicating how prolific a thief Reynolds had been. (*The Times*, 2 March 1891).

461   "The present Sir Henry Curtis Bennett is a son of the former Metropolitan Magistrate." in *TWN*, 4 July 1936. When Dew wrote this Sir Henry Curtis Bennett (a barrister and M.P.) was still alive. He died on 2 November 1936, which suggests Dew had proof-read his original manuscript and made this update for the book. Bennett senior was knighted and died in 1913.

462   Bennett described Reynolds as "one of those pests who went about stealing from house to house." (*The Daily News* (London), 2 March 1891).

Sir Curtis complimented me highly on my conduct of the case, and this was supplemented later by a pat on the back from the Commissioner, and congratulatory letters from the people whose stolen property had been restored.

Mary was not an old hand in the sense that she had been previously convicted. Up to a few months previously she had been a steady, hard-working cook employed by good families. Then for no apparent reason, she had taken the wrong turning, and developed into a cunning thief.

I wish I could say that Mary profited by this lesson. She did not. No sooner was she out of prison than she started her tricks all over again. Several times she was caught and sentenced, and on each of these occasions it was my sad duty to attend at the London Sessions and prove her "record". Finally, as was inevitable, she was sent to penal servitude.

Mary bore me no malice. Whenever I saw her I talked to her, and tried to persuade her to lead an honest life.

"I know you're right, Mr. Dew," she would say. "Of course, it doesn't pay. It's rotten, but I just can't help it. I guess I'll never be any different now."

What was the explanation? Just one simple word–drink!

A detective officer never knows what mystery is going to confront him when he arrives at his office in the morning.

I remember when I was in charge of Hammersmith, or "T" Division,[463] I looked like having a very heavy day before me, and arrived especially early at the office. Here all my plans were upset by the news that the body of a little girl, aged about 2½ years, had been found under a hedge in a field not far from Kew Bridge.[464]

It looked like a case of murder.

In a case of such seriousness I should, in the ordinary way, have proceeded at once to the spot and taken personal charge of the investigations. But on this particular morning I was due at ten o'clock at the Central Criminal Court, where I was the principal witness in two cases, involving in all 95 witnesses.[465]

---

463   Dew held this position from February 1900-September 1903.
464   This happened on 10 March 1903. The girl's name was Edith May Kersley.
465   It is not clear what case Dew was referring to here. The Old Bailey had been in session since 9 March 1903, and it continued in session until 19 March, hearing dozens of cases. In

The situation was annoying.

If it was murder, delay, as I well knew, might mean the missing of a valuable clue, which would make all the difference between failure and success.

But there was no getting out of going to the Old Bailey, and the only thing I could do was to put Detective-Sergeant Lambert, my second-in-command, in charge of the supposed murder inquiries, and leave him to carry on until such time as I myself was free.

At the Old Bailey I was lucky enough, after the expending of a good deal of energy, to get my cases immediately before the Grand Jury, and to make arrangements for them not to be taken for a day or two.

Then post haste to Brentford.

My first call was at the mortuary, where I saw the body. The little girl–so pretty–had all the appearance of being in a comfortable sleep. There was no sign of external injury. Only a post-mortem examination, I was told by the medical man, could establish the cause of death.

Leaving it at that for the moment, I started to find out what was known.

A constable passing along a lane in the early morning had seen a bundle lying close to the hedge in a field. He went to see what the bundle was, and found it to be the body of a little girl.

I went to the field, where I made a thorough examination without finding a scrap of anything likely to help me.

Who was the little girl? That was the first problem. Was she a local child? Or had she been brought from a distance.

The doctors were able to say she had been dead several hours.

I discovered that a band of gipsies, who had been in the neighbourhood several days, had left the night before. They were traced, and were soon able to satisfy us that they had nothing to do with it.

A description of the child was circulated to every district in

---

none of them did Dew appear as a material witness, let alone "the principal witness", although he could have been the prosecutor in one or both of the two cases which appear as if they may have derived from T Division: those against Edward Chuter and John Ernest O'Brien. Each man was charged with forging and uttering postal orders, and with burglary. Chuter was found guilty on the evidence of eight witnesses, and O'Brien was found not guilty on the evidence of nine witnesses–not even nearly ninety-five.

London and the Home Counties. No one came forward to claim it.

What did this mean? So far as I could see at the time, it could only mean one thing–that someone closely connected with the child–in all probability the mother–knew the answers to the questions I was eager to ask.

Throughout the rest of the day I had all the officers I could muster making a house-to-house canvass of the district. I joined in the hunt myself. Late at night I called a halt until the following day. We had learned nothing. So far as we could discover no child was missing from that district.

Early the following morning I was back again at Brentford. I decided to continue with the house-to-house inquiry, and mapped out a district for each officer to cover. I also took one myself. I was still of the opinion that the solution lay locally, probably within a radius of a mile or two of the spot where the body was found.

At each house we visited[466] we asked if the people in it knew a child about the age of the dead girl. If they did, we made certain that the child was still at home. It was a heart-breaking business. Endless knocking at doors, incessant questioning, receiving in many cases answers which were misleading, and in others replies which were far from civil.

On this second day of the inquiry I had personally called at scores and scores of houses without result. I decided to try a new district, and resumed my door-knocking in a neighbourhood which I think is known as ———, a Green near Gunnersby Station.[467]

In those days there were a number of quite small houses facing the green. I commenced at the one nearest the lane where the body had been found.

For a time I got no satisfaction. Then, at one house, my knock was answered by a typical working-class woman. I put my questions. She replied that she was afraid she could not help me.

There was something about the woman's manner which told me that she was keeping something back. I persevered, gained the woman's confidence, and got my first real clue.

"I don't want to say anything," she said. "You know what it is,

---

466   "at which we called" in *STWN*, 27 June 1936.
467   Named as "Kew Green" in *TWN*, 4 July 1936; "a Green near Gunnersby Station" was not in *TWN*. Dew meant "Gunnersbury Station".

sir. A respectable woman don't want to get mixed up in no murder mysteries. But perhaps I'd better tell you. Mrs. ——, who lives a few doors along has two children–a boy and a girl.[468] She told me yesterday that the little girl had gone away for a few days. A lady had taken her, she said, to give her (the mother) a rest. So far as I know it's true. You'll be able to find out, but, for goodness' sake, don't bring me into it."

"That's all right, Mother," I assured her. "I shan't bring you into it unless I can't help it. Thank you very much."

I went straight to the house the woman had indicated and knocked at the door.[469] Frankly I expected nothing to come of it. After all the disappointments I had had, such a stroke of luck seemed too much to expect.

Such were my thoughts as I waited for the door to open. My first knock brought no response. Neither did the second. But at the third time of asking the door was opened by a somewhat untidy woman, whose age I guessed to be anything between 30 and 35.

I told her I understood she had two children. She agreed.

"May I see them?" I asked, having explained that I was a police officer making inquiries.

The woman immediately produced an infant of from 12 to 18 months old.

"It's the little girl I'm chiefly interested in," I then said.

"Oh, you can't see her," the mother replied. "She's not at home."

A strange look came into the woman's eyes–half fear and half defiance.

When I asked where the little girl was I was told that a lady was minding her for a few days, but when I demanded to know who the lady was, and where she lived, she made the amazing reply: "I don't know the lady's name. I've forgotten it."

"Do you mean to tell me," I challenged, "that you have placed your little girl in the charge of a lady whose name you don't even know?"

"Well, what of it?"

"What about the address? Surely you must know that?"

---

468   This was Edith Kersley. She was unmarried with a five-year-old son and twin daughters.
469   No. 93, Strand-on-the-Green.

The woman then gave me the name of a road some distance away but said she couldn't remember the number.

I knew by this time that she was lying, and that, if I had not actually found the mother of the dead child, I had come upon a woman with a secret to hide.

I now told her the whole purpose of my inquiries, watching her face closely. But the woman betrayed nothing.

"If you have not seen your child for a day or two," I said, "it is possible that the dead girl is yours. I think the best thing for you to do is to come along to the mortuary and see the body."

"I'll come if you want me," she said, "but I am quite sure it isn't mine."

I had no intention of letting the woman out of my sight now, so telling her to put on her hat and coat, I took her to the mortuary in High Street, Brentford.

As long as I live, I shall never forget that experience. This woman entered the mortuary with me, and, without betraying a trace of emotion, gazed on the peaceful face of the little victim.

She took one of the cold little hands in hers as she said: "Poor little dear. It is not my child. I have never seen her before."[470]

I began to think I must have made a mistake. Surely no mother in the world could look on the face of her dead child without showing some sign of agitation or distress. This woman was completely unmoved. Even her "Poor little dear" was said without real feeling.

But I had to be certain.

As we left the mortuary I turned to her and said: "I am glad it is not your little girl. But I am afraid I must ask you to take me now to the woman who is looking after your child."

The woman agreed without comment. We retraced our steps to the Green, passed her own house, and came eventually to a road with good-class houses.

When we reached the centre of the road she pointed to a house and said: "That's the place."[471] Together we mounted the steps to the front door. I rang the bell. An elderly woman came to the door.

---

470   In the Old Bailey trial transcript it was Detective Sergeant William Hailstone who first spoke to Edith Kersley and took her to the mortuary. He then spoke to Dew about what had happened.

471   No. 16, Cambridge Cottages.

"That's the woman," said my companion. "She's got my little girl."

The elderly woman looked aghast.

"Whatever does she mean?" she asked, turning to me.

I explained, and, as I did so, the woman to whom I was talking became more and more indignant.

"How dare you?" she finally burst out. "You wicked woman! I have never seen your child."

And I knew at once that it was not she but the woman at my side who had lied.

My companion apologized.

"I am very sorry," she said. "I have made a mistake in the house. It is farther up the road."

Making my apologies to the lady of the house, who was still looking daggers at my companion, we left and tried a second house. The same farce was gone through. A third produced a like result.

Then I got tired of it.

"Whether the child at the mortuary is yours or not," I said, "I am satisfied that you are not speaking the truth, and I am going to take you to Brentford Police Station and detain you while I make further inquiries."

We walked some distance in silence. Then the woman looked up at me and said: "I don't think it's any use telling any more lies. That is my little girl in the mortuary. I put her in the field."

At that I cautioned her and said she would probably be charged with causing the death of the child.

At the police station she made a statement. She said she was a single woman, and both the dead child and the one at the house were illegitimate. She had found it hard to make ends meet, and decided to get rid of the little girl.[472]

"Late at night," she said, "I wrapped her up and carried her fast asleep to the lane. I pushed her through a hole in the hedge and left her there."

That, unbelievable though it may seem, was the gist of her story.

The cause of death being still undecided, she was charged with

---

472   She had been an inmate at Brentford Workhouse along with her daughters from 4 July 1901–23 February 1903.

causing the death of the child by means unknown, and upon this charge appeared at Brentford. She was remanded for a week.

In the meantime a post-mortem examination was made without definite results. Nothing could be found to account for the child's death, and the only conclusion the doctors could reach was that the little one had died from shock–in other words, that she had been frightened to death.[473]

The mother was eventually tried at the Central Criminal Court, found guilty of manslaughter, and sentenced to a long term of imprisonment.[474]

I never saw or heard of her again, and although it may have been another case of a woman paying the price, I could never feel any pity for her. I had seen that mother in the mortuary gazing unfeelingly on the body of the child whose death she had caused.

For my part in this case–in which I was ably assisted by many other officers–I was complimented by the Brentford Bench, the Grand Jury at the Central Criminal Court, and finally, the Commissioner himself.

II

MY capture of the "man with the funnily-shaped hat"[475] was one of my best as a young officer.[476]

The end of the case, I remember, brought me a lot of pleasure, not only because my work attracted the notice of my superiors, but because this particular criminal was a proper scamp.

It happened this way. A woman reported to the Paddington police that a man whom she had invited to her flat in Maida Vale had left hurriedly. Shortly afterwards she discovered that two valuable bracelets were missing.

Although at the time I was a uniformed officer, Inspector Morgan, who then had charge of the Criminal Investigation Department of the Paddington Division, frequently detailed me for plain-clothes duty.[477]

473 Dr. Henry Bott told the court she had died of exposure.

474 The jury strongly recommended mercy and she received a fifteen-month sentence.

475 "funny-shaped hat" in STWN, 4 July 1936.

476 This case took place in July 1886.

477 On Dew's retirement a journalist wrote that when it came to Inspector Daniel Morgan, Dew,

When the theft of the bracelets was reported, he sent for me, and said something like this: "Here you are, young Dew. A chance to distinguish yourself."

He then gave me the details, and dismissed me with a smile, which I took to mean that his hopes of my success were not at all high.

Having got all the additional particulars I could from the station officer, I decided that my best course was to go and see the woman who had laid the complaint. So I hied myself to her flat.

I was shown into the flat by a demure and neatly-dressed maid, and received by the owner of the missing bracelets, a woman of considerable attraction and charm, whose age I judged to be round about forty.

The flat was a comfortable apartment, most tastefully furnished. Its owner was obviously a woman of some means.

It was necessary to my inquiries to find out something about the woman herself. She told her story quite frankly. Her name, which I already knew, she gave as Amelie ———,[478] but it was news to me that she was an American. Her husband, she said, was away in the States. Consequently she was left very much alone. This she stressed, doubtless to prepare the way for the indiscretion to which she was about to confess.

"A few evenings ago,"[479] she went on, "I was walking along the Edgeware Road on my way home–it would be about nine o'clock– when a strange man spoke to me. In the ordinary way I would never have dreamed of speaking to a man in such circumstances, but he spoke in an American accent, and professed to know me.

"We talked for a time. I found that he knew friends of mine in Boston, U.S.A., and I was naturally interested. He walked with me as far as my flat. Then he left me. I thought I had met a real American gentleman.

"Nothing was said about a further meeting, but on the following Saturday he called at my flat. What was I to do? The man seemed

"cannot speak highly enough, considering him the finest detective he had ever known, and brimful of confidence." (*Police Review and Parade Gossip*, 30 December 1910). Morgan was born in Wales on 18 May 1845 and joined the Metropolitan Police on his twenty-third birthday. He retired in 1894. (PRO, MEPO 21/24).

478   It was Amelia Hughes.

479   On 8 July 1886.

all right. Although I didn't feel quite happy about it, I invited him in.

"On this occasion he told me about himself, giving the name of the West End hotel at which he was supposed to be staying,[480] and saying that he was over in this country studying law.

"Next day he came again, although I had not asked him to do so. We talked for a time. Then he complained of feeling unwell, and asked me if I could get him a little brandy. Without being in the least suspicious, I went to the kitchen to fetch the brandy, leaving my visitor in the sitting-room.

"My dressing-room adjoins the sitting-room. The door was open, and it is quite probable that from where he was sitting the man could see the two bracelets on the dressing-table.

"I was out of the room no more than a minute or so, but it was long enough. My American friend drank the brandy, thanking me profusely, and apologizing for giving me so much trouble. Then, a few minutes later, he said he felt better and left."

A short time later she went into her dressing-room and discovered the theft.

I believed the woman's story, though I doubted very much whether the thief was anything like so well acquainted as he professed with the lady's Boston friends.

It looked very much to me as though the man had set out deliberately to cultivate the American woman's acquaintance.

Only police officers know how hard it is to get a good description of a person. This case was no exception.

Amelie did her best. She said the man was well-dressed, tall, very gentlemanly, and undoubtedly an American.

Perhaps the man was slightly coloured. She wasn't sure. Certainly he was not a negro. Yes, his hair was very dark and inclined to curl. He might have had a moustache. If so, it was a dark one.

I tried hard to get something more definite and distinctive, but this woman, evidently not an observant person, could give me nothing more.

Yet, vague though the description was, I had a feeling at once that somewhere and at some time I had seen a man who answered

480 The Langham.

it. I racked my brains to try and "place" him. It was useless. The recollection wouldn't come. Still I badgered the victim, hoping that by persistence I should get her to say something which would link my memory man with her handsome stranger.

But the clue, when it came, was not supplied by the woman.

It suddenly flashed through my mind that the man of whom I had been thinking had one peculiarity in his dress, and doubtless, it was this which had attracted my attention to him. He wore a black, hard felt hat, with a perfectly flat brim, instead of the usual curled one.

At the same moment I recalled where I had seen him. He had passed me several times when I had been on patrol duty in Westbourne Grove. The hat had first caught my eye. Then my mind had registered the man's dark handsomeness. He was, however, so very dark that I had put him down as a half-caste.

Mrs. ——— had already described her visitor as having worn a black felt hat.

"Was it by any chance," I now asked, "a hat of peculiar shape? Had it a flat brim?"

"Why, of course," she agreed. "How silly of me! I might have remembered that before. I took particular notice of it the first time he came. It was hanging in the hall. It did have a flat brim."

It had taken a full hour to get from the woman this tiny, but as it turned out, vital clue,[481] but I didn't mind that. I came away from the flat feeling very pleased with myself.

I was no longer on the look out for a man of mystery, but for a definite person whom, if I saw him again, I should be certain to recognize.

While it was still not certain that I was on the right track, it seemed unlikely that there would be two dark, handsome men wearing the same peculiarly-shaped hat.

If only Mrs. ——— had been curious enough about the hat to have looked inside it, and find out the name of the firm which had made it! Unfortunately, she had not.

My first call after leaving her was at the West End hotel at which the supposed thief had claimed to be staying. As I already half-

---

481   "vital fact" in *TWN*, 11 July 1936. It was said that Dew had a "flair for getting precisely what he wanted when he interviewed people." (*The Worthing Herald*, 10 June 1938).

suspected, he was not known there.

Next I took Mrs. —— with me to Scotland Yard, and introduced her to the "rogues gallery", where thousands of photographs of crooks are filed. Her man, so far as she could say, was not among them.

So I was thrown back on the clue of the hat. Bowler hats with flat brims were not on general sale. This meant that the man who had worn it must have had it made specially. I made a round of the best-class shops in the West End of London. For a long time I had no luck at all.

Then came a turn of the tide. After disclosing my identity and explaining my quest at a big shop in Oxford Street, I was ushered by the assistant into the presence of the proprietor, whose name all the hats made by the firm bore. He promised to help me all he could. The assistants were interviewed one by one, until we came at last to one who recalled having received an order for such a hat from "a very dark gentleman".

I almost gave a whoop of joy.

Books were searched. These revealed that the name of the man who had ordered the flat-brimmed bowler was J——,[482] with an address in Hatherley Grove, Westbourne Grove.

After thanking the big hatmaker for his assistance, I hurried off to the address given. Here my hopes were dashed. The landlady, whom I discreetly approached, agreed that Mr. J —— had stayed there, but he had left ten days previously, and she had no idea where he had gone. He left no address for the forwarding of letters.

No, he did not have a cab. He walked out, carrying his luggage. She would like to get into touch with him. The dark gentleman had omitted to pay his last week's rent.

Up against a blank wall. I was very disappointed. It had looked as though I was at the end of the journey. Now I had to start all over again. To make matters worse, the Maida Vale lady was beginning to get anxious about her bracelets, while at the police stations[483] questions were being asked as to when I was going to put on my uniform again and do a bit of "real police duty".

I went to see Inspector Dan Morgan, told him the exact position,

---

482   Archibald Johnstone, 26, a law student from America.
483   "the police station" in *TWN* 11 July 1936.

and asked permission to carry on. He wasn't too hopeful. Said it was rather like looking for a needle in a haystack. But I got what I wanted–a permit to continue for a few days longer in plain clothes.

In the meantime a full description of the man and the jewellery had been circulated in every division through the Metropolis, and every jeweller and pawnbroker had received a full description of the missing bracelets.

During the days that followed I haunted Edgware Road, Oxford Street, and surrounding district. It all seemed dreadfully futile. I spent hours making inquiries at apartment houses. It looked as though the man had vanished completely from that neighbourhood.

I was handicapped through not at this time being a member of the Criminal Investigation Department. Certain members of the C.I.D. looked at me askance. Though they did not say so in so many words, I felt they resented my attempting to do what was really their work. I was worried, too, by the knowledge that the uniformed branch wanted me back.

Even Dan Morgan could not keep me indefinitely on plain-clothes duty. He gave me a quiet hint to this effect.

It began to look as though, in spite of my promising start, that I had failed in this, one of my earliest efforts as a sleuth.

As a sort of last desperate throw, I called again on the landlady in Hatherley Grove. This time I pressed her to try and remember any scraps of conversation she may have had with her former lodger, and especially any reference he may have made to a locality he had been in the habit of visiting.

At first her face was a blank, but, after thinking for a while, she brightened up and said: "Oh, yes, I do remember something. Mr. J ——— did say that he liked walking in Regent's Park, and spoke once or twice about Albany Street."

Like a drowning man clutching at a straw, I seized upon this clue, and transferred my inquiries to the neighbourhood of Regent's Park. It was not long before I had picked up the trail. The dark handsome man with the funny-shaped hat had certainly been seen in the vicinity.[484]

There was nothing for it but to make a round of the apartment houses in this district. I met with many rebuffs until I came to a

484   "the vicinity of Park Street." in *STWN*, 4 July 1936.

street called Park Place. Here, after saying my little piece to the landlady, giving J———'s name, and describing his appearance, the woman replied: "No, he does not live here, but there is a gentleman exactly like that living next door but one."

I went at once to the house indicated. A servant answered the door. I asked for Mr. J ———, and was told that he occupied the front room on the first floor, and was in.

To the amazement of the girl, I pushed past her, dashed up the stairs, and, without waiting to knock, walked into the room.

A tall man was standing at a mirror with a razor in his hand. He turned round as I entered and though his face was half-hidden by a copious covering of lather, I recognized him at once as the gentleman I had formerly seen in the Westbourne Grove district.

With an open razor in his hand, and his powerful athletic build– he was much bigger than I was–looked a formidable customer.[485] If he cut up rough, I thought to myself, I am going to have a job. I had not even my truncheon with me.

But I put on a bold front, and spoke as authoritatively as it is possible for a young policeman to do. I told him who I was, and said I should arrest him for the theft of Mrs. ———'s bracelets.

My quarry tried a bluff. He said he knew nothing whatever about the matter. As soon, however, as he realized that I had no intention of wavering in my decision to arrest him, he changed his story.

He admitted knowing Mrs. ———, but alleged that the charge of theft had been trumped up because he would not give her a cheque for £55.

"I picked up with her in Oxford Street a fortnight ago," he said. "I went home with her, stayed the night at her flat, and paid her £5. Altogether, I have seen her three times. I will make her pay for this."

To my great relief, he offered no resistance, and I placed him in a cab and took him to Harrow Road police station, where he was seen and identified by Mrs. ———.

On being charged and placed in the cells, he said: "When the case is disposed of I will start. It is because I would not live with her."

---

485 "he looked a formidable customer." in *TWN*, 11 July 1936. Both Dew and Johnstone were 5 ft. 9 in. tall. (PRO, MEPO 21/39; Hertfordshire Archives and Local Studies, HPF/H/21).

At J——'s apartment I found several pawn tickets, none of which, however, related to the missing bracelets. I also found a lady's gold watch which, it came out later, had been stolen from a woman in circumstances exactly similar to those described by Mrs. ——.[486]

The pawn tickets enabled me to trace and recover a good deal of property stolen from ladies in various parts of London. These came forward to identify their property, and, incidentally, the tall, handsome man who had so easily gained their confidence.

His methods never varied. Either he accosted his victims or they accosted him. A visit to the woman's flat would follow. He would then wait a favourable opportunity to decamp with all the jewellery he could lay his hands on, and dispose of it at once through the medium of the convenient pawnbroker.

You might wonder why he had not been laid by the heels before. The explanation is quite simple. The majority of women he robbed preferred not to complain to the police. They imagined–quite wrongly–that because of their mode of living they were not likely to get any assistance from the police.[487]

Many came forward when the newspapers published reports of the man's arrest, but it was not necessary to call more than three or four of them for the purpose of proving the case against him.

It was part of my job now to find all I could about J——'s past. He had never been convicted before, this explaining why the Maida Vale victim failed to pick him out in the Rogues' Gallery, but he had a pretty lurid history all the same.

He was an American half-caste–negroid. Well educated and of good address, he had been in England for a year or so, representing himself as a Trinity College, Oxford, undergraduate.[488] He was nothing of the kind.

---

486 Johnstone would also be charged with the theft of jewellery from Charlotte George at Marylebone on 17 July.

487 A convict register stated that Johnstone "Robs prostitutes." (Hertfordshire Archives and Local Studies, HPF/H/21). This might explain Dew's subtle reference to the victims' "mode of living." The suggestion that they wrongly believed the police wouldn't help them because of their occupation is similar to what he said about the victims of Jack the Ripper: "The very nature of their livelihood precluded them from appealing for protection to the police, though this would have been given readily enough in the case of a known danger." (*ICC*, p. 109).

488 Oxford was not named in *TWN*, 11 July 1936.

His name had certainly been registered as a student at one of the halls,[489] but on the Vice-Chancellor discovering his true character his name had been expunged.

For a considerable time he had lived in Oxford, where he swindled many hotel-keepers.

One of his dirtiest tricks was to steal money and a gold watch from a governess, and then threaten to accuse her of immorality if she exposed him. He never paid his landladies, and on one occasion he had behaved indecently towards his landlady's daughter.

Only once had he found his way into the dock. Then he was acquitted on a charge of indecent assault.[490]

All these unpleasant details were related to Sir Peter Edlin, K.C., at the Middlesex Sessions, where, after a lengthy trial throughout which he denied all the charges, the man with the funnily-shaped hat[491] was found guilty, and sentenced to six years' penal servitude.

He continued to behave like the cad he was, declaring that he had been convicted on perjured evidence.

I was more than repaid for the hard work I had put in on this case by high praise from the judge, and commendations from the Grand Jury and the Chief Commissioner.

There was only one fly in the ointment. The missing bracelets had not been found.

This was rectified, curiously enough by J —— himself after he had been some time a convict at Parkhurst. A communication was received by the authorities asking if I might visit J —— in prison.

Inspector Morgan accompanied me to Parkhurst, where, after some demur, J—— gave us the address of a pawnbroker in Kensington, where we should find the bracelets he had stolen. They were there all right. They had been pledged for £20.

There was a little difficulty with the pawnbroker. I had to get a magistrate's summons before he could be induced to hand the bracelets over without payment.

---

489 "at St Mary's Hall" in *TWN*, 11 Jul 1936.
490 This was at the Oxford Assizes in April 1881 when he stood trial for committing an indecent assault against Alice Richardson in February, (the charge of rape had been abandoned). The trial was reported in *Jackson's Oxford Journal*, 30 April 1881.
491 "funny shaped hat" in *STWN*, 4 Jul 1936.

III

IF a foreigner who masqueraded under the name of Henry Clifford[492] had not bought a watch carrying a guarantee from a London jeweller, I might never have had the pleasure–and it was a real pleasure–of bringing to justice one of the cleverest swindlers I struck throughout my police career.[493]

The watch went wrong. Clifford, under the terms of the guarantee, took it back to the jeweller. In doing so he fell right into the trap we had prepared for him.

The case was one of the most difficult I have ever tackled. For a long time it looked pretty hopeless. All the information indicated that our man had fled the country.

So he had. But he made the mistake of coming back. That was when we got him.

My introduction to this case followed a report to Scotland Yard by the head officer[494] of Parr's Bank that their Notting Hill branch had been swindled out of £1700 by means of a forged draft. The draft had been made payable to a Mr. Henry Clifford.

It did not take me long to make up my mind that I was up against a criminal of "class". In the conception and execution of the fraud great ingenuity and daring had been shown.

The facts, in so far as I was able to obtain them from the head office of Parr's Bank, showed that the London agents of a big American banking corporation had received through the bank register a draft for £1700 in favour of Mr. Henry Clifford, who, it was stated in a covering letter, had an account at the Notting Hill branch of Parr's Bank.

The document had every appearance of being genuine. The signature of the New York Bank official who had signed it was compared with the sample signature and found to tally.

The next step was the receipt by the Notting Hill branch of Parr's Bank of a letter from Clifford, written from America, requesting them to "collect" from the agents. This they did, and all that now

---

492 Unusually, Dew gives the name of someone in a case. However, Henry Clifford was the alias of Conrad Harms.

493 This case took place in June 1909.

494 "head office" in *TWN*, 18 Jul 1936.

remained was for the swindler to draw out the money.

A short time later Clifford sent a cable to Notting Hill asking that £100 be sent to him in America. This was done, and with the money Clifford booked his passage to England.

On reaching London he promptly appeared at the Notting Hill branch in person, and presented a cheque for the whole–or practically the whole–of the £1600 balance.

The signature on the cheque was carefully scrutinized. A few questions were asked to confirm the man's identity, and Clifford walked out with the cash, mostly in Bank of England notes of large denominations.

That the whole transaction was a swindle was not discovered until Parr's Bank, in the ordinary course of business, sought to recover from America the £1700 they had paid out on the draft.

Then it was found that the American bank knew nothing at all about it, and that the money had been obtained as a result of a clever scheme.

This was the position when I was called into the case.

I was frankly pessimistic. Unless the man was a fool–which it was pretty obvious he was not–he would long since have crossed the Channel to the Continent.

But the fact that the case looked hopeless didn't stop me from working hard upon it.

The first thing to be done was to get the numbers of the Bank of England notes which Clifford had fraudulently obtained. Having done this, I went back to the Yard and circulated the wanted man's description throughout the country generally, and particularly to every seaport.

As it looked like being a longish job, I got Sergeant Berrett (later Chief-Inspector Berrett) to assist me.[495]

Now, Sergeant Berrett was a splendid chap to have as an assistant. He was always exceedingly painstaking, and never minded how many hours he put in on a job. I am afraid no other sort of man would have suited me.

---

495   James Berrett (1871-1940). Berrett joined the Metropolitan Police in 1893 and retired in 1931 as a chief inspector at Scotland Yard. (PRO, MEPO 21/65). In his memoirs Berrett wrote that, at the time of this case, "Dew was then at the height of his brilliant career." (Berrett, *When I Was at Scotland Yard*, p. 40).

We quickly traced some of the bank-notes. They had been returned to the banks by money changers. These people were traced and interviewed. They told us that the notes had been changed into foreign currencies, this confirming my suspicion that our man had in all probability gone abroad.

I am not going to weary you with details of all the hard work put in by Berrett and myself, in which we were ably helped by Sergeant Ferrier, who finished up with the rank of inspector.[496] It is enough to give the results.

We discovered, for instance, that Henry Clifford was not the swindler's real name. He was of Russian birth.

Before going to America he had been employed for some time in London, and it was then he had opened the account—in the name of Clifford—at the Notting Hill branch of Parr's Bank.

Why did he keep that account open after he had left London for New York. Did this mean that he had thought out the details of the fraud before leaving for America? It rather looked that way.

In New York he obtained employment with a big banking corporation,[497] and did well. The man was clever, and, among other accomplishments, was an excellent linguist. He rose to a position of trust, and it was because of his apparent dependability that he was able to carry through his scheme without arousing suspicion.

During our London inquiries we made a call at a celebrated jeweller's and money-changer's in Victoria Street.[498] Here we got news of Clifford. He had changed two £100 notes there into French and Austrian notes and gold.

Berrett, who was on excellent terms with the assistant at this establishment,[499] picked up another piece of information which proved the turning-point in the whole case.

He learned that while in the shop Clifford had produced a watch, mentioning casually that he had purchased it at a jeweller's in the Strand. Clifford, it seems, was none too pleased with his bargain, and he was advised by the assistant with whom he discussed the

---

496   John Ferrier (b. 1875), from Dundee, joined the Metropolitan Police in 1896 and retired in 1924 as the local inspector for the Wandsworth Division. (PRO, MEPO 21/55).

497   J.S. Bache & Co.

498   T.M. Sutton.

499   "the assistants at this establishment" in *TWN*, 18 July 1935.

matter that, if he felt that way about it, his best course was to take the watch back. It carried the usual guarantee.

Berrett hastened back to me with the news, and all efforts were then concentrated on tracing the Strand jeweller.[500] We found him all right. He had no difficulty in recalling Clifford from the description we were able to give, and told us that his customer had paid £20 for the watch. So far he had not been back with it.

"I don't suppose he will now," the jeweller added. "The purchase was made several weeks ago."

"Perhaps you are right," I agreed, "but if by any chance he does bring that watch back I want you to be quite clear as to what you are to do. You must try and keep the man in the shop while you get into touch with Bow Street police station. If you can't do this, you must do your level best to get the man's address."

The jeweller readily promised, and there the matter was left.

I had little real hope of any such development, though I felt that the jeweller would play his part all right if given an opportunity to do so.

Berrett and I continued for a time to hunt around for other clues. We succeeded in tracing several more of the missing notes, but not as much as a hint could we get as to our man's present whereabouts.

I was, in fact, on point of abandoning the inquiry when the miracle happened.

The Strand jeweller clue had come up trumps after all. A telephone message was received at Bow Street. The man who had bought the watch had come back. He had left the watch, and was to call back for it in two days' time.[501] The jeweller was also able to give us his address.

I cannot now definitely remember[502] if I arrested him myself or not; but it was a pretty dangerous business.

My recollection is that Berrett and I arrested him at an hotel in Northumberland Avenue, where he was staying with his young wife.[503]

---

500   John Chisholm.
501   According to the trial transcript he was asked to come back in half-an-hour, but didn't return for two-and-a-quarter hours.
502   "I cannot now remember" in *TWN*, 18 July 1936.
503   Sergeant Crutchett and Constable Bishop arrested him at the jeweller's on 26 June 1909, and it doesn't appear to have been dangerous. Harms was staying in Room 442 at the Grand

He certainly had a loaded automatic in his possession, and was a particularly ill-tempered and dangerous subject.[504]

But this is one of those instances when one cannot remember an important detail, of thirty years ago, and so, to be on the safe side, raise the doubt, as I don't wish to claim credit for something I have not done.[505]

The lady, obviously a foreigner, was both young and pretty. We thought she was the man's wife. She thought so, too, until we were able to prove that there was a predecessor still alive.

They were taken to Bow Street police station. The "wife" was dreadfully agitated. She knew little English, but it was clear from her demeanour that she understood enough of the conversation to realize that something terrible was happening to her "husband".

It was not for this that she had travelled with him from Vienna to London.

At Bow Street our suspect was placed among a dozen other men resembling him, and promptly picked out by officials of Parr's Bank, who had at once been sent for. Later there were other identifications, equally emphatic.

Now, when a wanted person is so overwhelmingly identified as this man was, he or she generally gives in and tries to find some defence other than an alibi.

Not so Mr. Henry Clifford. He maintained from the first that a mistake had been made, and he stuck to it right to the bitter end.

In a way I admired him for it. The dice were loaded heavily against him, but he put up a stout fight.

Hotel in Northumberland Avenue with his wife Frieda Braun, who he had bigamously married two days previously at Dover. He had married her under the name of Henry Clifford.

504 Crutchett made no mention of this when giving evidence at Harms' trial.

505 These three paragraphs were extensively rewritten from *TWN*, 18 July 1936, which had:

"Detectives called at the hotel where he was staying, and were told that "Mr Clifford and his wife" were in.

So there was a woman in the case. The couple, we were told, occupied rooms on the second floor.

The detectives' visit, as you may guess, was unannounced. They found both the man and the woman in the sitting-room. The man rose challengingly as the boys announced themselves and why they wanted to see him.

"Mr Clifford" became defiant. He might easily have become dangerous had not Berrett, quick to sum up the situation, slipped to his side, and extracted a loaded automatic from his hip pocket."

As soon as Clifford was safely under lock and key, and his weeping "wife" had been placed in charge of a police matron at a comfortable hotel, Berrett and I returned to his hotel to search for any evidence the arrested man's rooms or luggage might contain.

We found little apart from a goodly supply of money–and a small key. The key was responsible for my later making a trip to Vienna.

Now that the big job of catching the man was over, I was able to devote more time to delving into his past history, and into tracing his movements after he had brought off his £1700 coup.

His method of getting the New York bank chief's signature to the draft was very neat. He worked in the bank in a secretarial capacity, and part of his duties each day was to take documents to the head for signature.

He realized after a while that, with so many documents to be signed, it was a physical impossibility for the chief to read them all thoroughly.

And in this way one day the manager unwittingly signed a document which had been concocted by Clifford himself, and which later was to enrich him to the tune of £1700.

From what I know of this dark-visaged, sharp-featured little man, he would not have turned a hair as he waited by his chief's side with his fate hanging in the balance. He was a cool customer, if ever there was one.

Having secured the signature to the bogus document, his one desire was to free himself from the shackles of the bank which employed him and to be off to England. This he accomplished quite simply by behaving in such a way that the bank had no option but to demand his resignation. His employers may have been surprised at the sudden change in the character of so perfect a servant, but they could never for a moment have guessed the reason behind it.

It has always puzzled me that a man so astute in every other way should have been guilty of such a cardinal mistake as to return–at any rate so soon–to England.

He lost no time after drawing the money in changing it into foreign currency and bolting to the Continent. He was safe in Vienna. Why did he come back?

The answer is–a woman.

He met her in Vienna. She was very charming. He made violent love to her. She responded. He was eager for a quick marriage. She was more than ready.[506]

But the marriage laws of Austria made things difficult. They found they could not get married for several weeks.

Then it was Clifford had his brain-wave. Let the girl travel with him to England. It would be only necessary to go as far as Dover. They could be married at once at the register office there.

This, in those days, was indeed the case, and I have always understood that it was largely as a result of the representation I made, following this case, that the marriage laws were tightened up.

They came to Dover. The marriage, or what purported to be a marriage, took place. But instead of returning at once to Austria, they continued their journey to London.

Surely it wasn't Clifford's misbehaving watch which caused him to change his mind. No, I don't think he was quite such a fool as that. But when he was in London he couldn't resist the temptation of taking the watch back to the jeweller and complaining about it.

The consequences you know.

It was a bad miscalculation. Seems as though he underestimated the memory of Scotland Yard. Of course, he did not know that, while he was love-making in Vienna, Berrett and I were working early and late in our efforts to trace him and to recover the stolen money.

Our inquiries after the arrest brought to light something which came as an even bigger shock than the arrest to the pretty little girl from Vienna.

When he met her Clifford was a married man. His wife was still alive. Long before, he had ingratiated himself into a good-class family, and made love to a charming girl, and married her.[507]

The romance was short-lived. He deserted his wife soon after the wedding, and was not heard of again until we had caught him for the bank forgery.

---

506 Harms had told her that he was a mining engineer and promised to open a shop for her to run.

507 Harms' legal wife was Edith Kate Garman, a doctor's daughter, whom he married at Kensington Register Office on 1 December 1906. She divorced him on 1 May 1911 on grounds of adultery and bigamy. (PRO, J 77/996/235).

Whether this was his first venture into the troubled waters of matrimony I never found out. What we had discovered was enough for our purpose.

He was brought face to face with the woman he had previously married. She identified him immediately. He looked her fully in the eyes and declared: "I have never seen that woman before in my life."[508]

Nothing could shake him.

In order to complete an already strong case against him, I travelled to Vienna, armed with the little key of which I have already told you. His bigamous wife had told us about a mysterious little box he kept in the home of her people. The key fitted that box.

The opening of the box was in some ways a disappointment. It contained nothing sensational. But in it was a considerable sum of money, which I brought back with me to be returned to the rightful owners. The trip was fruitful in others[509] for, if any doubt had remained as to his guilt, it was dispelled by the evidence I got of stolen notes he had changed in the gay city.

And so to the Old Bailey, where, in spite of his continued denials, Clifford was found guilty of both bigamy and forgery, and sentenced to seven years' penal servitude.[510]

IV

I WONDER if the general public realizes the dangers run by the police officers[511] in the execution of their duty.

Of the two branches the members of the Criminal Investigation Department run the greater risk. They lose prestige by being in plain clothes.

Often when making an arrest they are mistaken for the culprit, and on other occasions the struggle—when resistance is offered—is thought to be between two civilians.

On more than one occasion I was attacked by law-abiding

---

508   Since his arrest Harms had insisted he was Henry Clifford, Harms' identical cousin. He maintained this deceit throughout his trial.

509   "in other ways" in *TWN*, 18 July 1936.

510   Actually six years with a recommendation that he should be deported at the end of his sentence. Richard Muir appeared for the prosecution.

511   "run by police officers" in *TWN*, 25 July 1935.

citizens, who were under the impression that I was the aggressor.

Once, when I was struggling with a prisoner, a pail of dirty water was thrown over me. I couldn't blame the servant-girl who did this, as at the time I was disguised as a rag-and-bone man, and looked far more unprepossessing than the man I was trying to arrest.

But far more serious things than these happen to police officers.

During one case of mine I had two extraordinary experiences. In both, though in an extremely different way, I was lucky to escape with my life.

In the first the menace was a would-be murderer. All one Sunday afternoon I walked about with death at my elbow.

I had been sent to one of our great naval ports to carry out a secret investigation into the loss of large quantities of marine stores.[512]

You might think this a simple enough inquiry. It was anything but that.

It is difficult to convey to the ordinary mind the enormous amount of work entailed by such an investigation, and the heartbreaking disappointments one met with before obtaining a clue, if ever one was found.

In those days–I am writing of thirty years ago–many people resident in seaport towns did not regard it as a serious thing to annex Government property, or to buy it for next to nothing. Therefore any member of the public almost might have been the guilty party.

On this particular inquiry I worked hard for several weeks before obtaining my first slight clue. This led me to a shop in a busy thoroughfare–a sort of general store at which all kinds of things were sold.[513]

The proprietor whom I will call L———, had lived many years in the town, was highly respected, and generally looked upon as a good citizen.[514]

These facts did not lessen my difficulties.

I kept the shop under discreet observation for several days. But

---

512 This investigation took place in 1907 at Portsmouth, although the thefts had been taking place since 1906. (*The Evening News* (Portsmouth), 28 May 1907).

513 41 Arundel Street.

514 This was Walter Lewis, aged forty-seven, who had been in business for twenty-seven years. Contemporary newspapers described him as a fishmonger, but the contents of his shop were more in keeping with Dew's description.

I was not discreet enough. It became clear to me that I had been "spotted". Quick action then became necessary if the evidence was to be obtained.

By this time I was quite satisfied that a visit to the shop would disclose goods that had never seen an invoice. So I obtained a search warrant, and, accompanied by an officer of the local police,[515] called on Mr. L——— at his shop.

When I told the man who we were and what our business was he gave me an ugly look, to which I paid little attention at the time, but which sensational events afterwards brought vividly back to my mind.

In our search at the premises I found ample reward for the hard work I had put in. The place abounded in naval stores. Broom heads, paint brushes, and other articles used in the dockyard and on board ship, as well as a large quantity of "prick tobacco",[516] came to light.

We also found a number of second-hand revolvers and many cartridges.[517] The total haul was valued at a pretty considerable figure.

During the search I kept close to Mr. L———, whose face throughout wore a threatening scowl. "This man is a nasty piece of work," I thought.

The man's arrest was automatic the moment we had found stolen Government property in his possession. We took him to the local police station, where he was duly charged with stealing and receiving the goods.

Later he would also have been charged[518] in respect of other property found at his shop. This was discovered to have been the proceeds of local robberies.[519]

When Mr. L——— appeared before the local Bench the follow-

515   Chief Inspector Moore of the Portsmouth Borough Police.

516   A naval term for a tightly-rolled length of tobacco, wrapped in canvas and tied with tarred twine.

517   Two colour-sergeant instructors from the Hampshire Regiment stood trial for the theft of the cartridges at a military court martial at which Dew gave evidence. (*The Evening News* (Portsmouth), 14-16 August 1907).

518   "Later he was also charged" in *TWN*, 25 July 1936.

519   These robberies had been committed by members of staff at Sir George Edwin Couzins' shop and Messrs. Bowerman Bros. in neighbouring Southsea. They sold the stolen goods to Lewis. (*The Evening News* (Portsmouth), 11 & 17 June 1907).

ing morning he was remanded for a week.

I strongly opposed bail, pointing out that a serious view was taken of the case, and that the Director of Public Prosecutions would take over its conduct. Probably because of Mr. L ——'s previous good character my protest was ignored, and bail, though in a substantial amount, allowed.[520]

After a trip to London for a consultation at the office of the Director of Public Prosecutions, I returned to the seaport on the following Saturday.

Sunday was a nice day. I fancied a walk in the country, and, persuading a gentleman[521] engaged in the case to accompany me, set out to enjoy the afternoon sunshine.

We had left the town behind us, and were strolling along a country lane, when the incident happened. On one side the lane was flanked by a low hedge. Presently an uncanny feeling came over me. There seemed something sinister about that hedge. I got the impression that we were being followed.

Now, I have never been subject to delusions or to other tricks of the imagination, and I could not understand it at all.

For a time I resisted the temptation to leave my companion's side and see for myself whether there was anyone behind the hedge or not, but the feeling persisted, and at last I yielded to it.

There was something! Nothing definite. A mere shadow. I called out. There was no reply. We continued our walk without any further mental disturbance on my part. That evening I spent quietly at my hotel. The incident of the shadow behind the hedge passed from my mind.

Next morning about nine o'clock I was having breakfast, when the waitress told me I was wanted on the telephone. A little surprised at a call at that time of the morning, I went to the instrument. The voice at the other end I recognized as the local inspector.

"Is that you, Mr. Dew?" he asked.

"Yes," I told him. "Anything wrong?"

"Very much so," came back over the wire. "L —— has just committed suicide. Blown his brains out."

---

520   Bail was set at £200 plus two £100 sureties. (*Ibid.*, 24 June 1907).
521   "another gentleman" in *TWN*, 25 July 1936.

"Where?" I queried.

"At the shop."[522]

This was staggering news, but as I dashed to the shop I recalled the moroseness of the man, and realized that such a sequel was not so surprising after all.

The police were in charge of the premises. I was taken to the bedroom–the living-rooms were over the shop–and saw all that was left of L———. He was lying on the bed with a mirror at its foot, presumably to help him in the firing of the fatal shot.

"I must congratulate you, Mr. Dew." The speaker was the senior local police officer.

"Congratulate me!" I cried. "Whatever for? It's your sympathy I want. I don't like losing my prisoners in this way."

Then the officer explained. His congratulations were not official, but personal. I had had a narrow escape of losing my life.

The dead man had left a note. In this he had blamed me for all his troubles, and added that he had followed me about the previous afternoon with the intention of shooting me before taking his own life. His excuse for failure was that he had "not been able to get near enough to me."

Later this note was produced at the Coroner's inquest, at which other people gave evidence of threats the dead man had uttered against me.[523]

The shadow behind the hedge was explained. It must have been the would-be murderer's shadow I saw when I shouted out. It had been a close call.[524]

---

522 Actually at his sister's house at 73 Londesborough Road, Southsea on 24 June 1907, the day he was due to appear at the magistrates' court. Dew had correctly remembered that this had taken place on a Monday. (*The Evening News* (Portsmouth), 24 June 1907).

523 Lewis had spent three weeks on remand at Kingston Gaol before he was granted bail. In a letter written to the coroner Lewis wrote: "I attribute this rash act to the cruel action of the police in compelling me to serve three weeks in gaol before trial. It has broken my heart and I have no wish to live." His sister told the inquest that Lewis had a "complete dread" of his forthcoming appearance at the magistrates' court. Lewis told an acquaintance that "the way and manner of the police when they came to his place so preyed upon his mind that, if he had a loaded revolver, he would not have hesitated to have used it against the police." (*Ibid.*, 25 June 1907).

524 Dew told the coroner's inquest a different story. He said that on the Sunday in question he was at Brockhurst [sic-Brockenhurst] "and saw Lewis on the platform. On looking round he saw the man following him, but on turning sharply the deceased walked away." (*Ibid.*).

I can to some extent understand L——'s animosity. His guilt was plain. He was faced by ruin. But I still cannot understand his feeling so deeply about it as to want to kill me. After all, the man must have known that I had done only what was my duty.

Those magistrates who granted bail must have been almost as relieved as I was.[525]

Now for my second adventure. In the course of my inquiries in this same case it became necessary to interview two or three bluejackets, who, I hoped, would be able to give me useful information. But the cruiser on which they were serving had left the seaport, and was on gun-firing practice in Bantry Bay, Ireland.

I travelled to Rosslare, and thence to Cork, where I stayed the night, completing the journey to Bantry the following morning.

The Head Constable of that splendid body of men, the Royal Irish Constabulary–now, alas! superseded–gave me a warm welcome, and was eager to help.

Of warships, however, there was no sign. Then I realized that Bantry Bay was not a small bay like, say, Weymouth, but extended many miles out to sea. The cruiser I wanted was away out there. How was I going to reach her?

I made inquiries as to whether it was expected boats would put in there from the fleet. Not for some time, I was told. The best chance of this was at Glengariff, a few miles down the coast.

Owing to an important case pending in London, my time was limited. So, rather than wait at Bantry, I boarded a small coasting steamer for Glengariff. Still the warships for which I was searching were invisible.

As I haunted the seafront the weather changed ominously. Clouds began to gather, and a high wind whipped the sea into angry life.

My patience was at last rewarded. A small sailing-boat put in. She turned out to be from one of H.M.s ships in the bay, in charge of one of the smallest midshipmen I have ever seen.

When I presented myself to the little "middy", produced my credentials from the Admiralty, and explained my mission, he

---

525   Additional sentence here in *TWN*, 25 July 1936: "My death would have been on their consciences if things had turned out the way L—— had wished and willed."

readily agreed to take me out to the cruiser I was so anxious to visit.

Thus, as soon as the officer had completed his errand ashore, I boarded the vessel, and we cast off on the choppy sea.

This was one of the occasions when I was made to suffer for my conscientiousness. By this time the howling wind was accompanied by heavy rain. Although fortified with an overcoat, I was soon drenched to the skin. The little boat pitched and tossed.

We seemed to have travelled well out to sea before the battleships loomed up in the hazy distance. The journey was nearly over, but our real adventures had not yet begun.

First, our sail went overboard. By a superhuman effort the crew rescued it. Then began the battle between these fine lads and the elements as they tried to get our small vessel alongside the great cruiser.

To me this seemed an impossible task. The little midshipman took it all as part of his day's work. He sat there calm and unperturbed, giving his orders and seeing that they were obeyed.

Through megaphones, directions were shouted by officers on the cruiser as one attempt after another was made to get our little vessel in position. One moment we would be alongside, in danger, it seemed to me, of being smashed to matchwood against the warship's huge bulk. The next we seemed to be a furlong away.

Throughout all this I was none too happy, and I should have been far less so but for the confidence I had in the sailors who were handling the boat.

What worried me was how I was going to board the cruiser even if we succeeded in getting alongside her. Looking up from our little craft, her sides seemed as unscalable as the walls of St. Paul's. She was, in fact, one of our largest cruisers of those days, having a complement of over 1000 men.

The midshipman shouted me instructions during lulls in the storm. If and when we got alongside I was to jump to the wooden ladder which ran down the big ship's side, and so climb to her decks.

Frankly, I didn't like the prospect. Being neither a sailor nor a steeplejack, I had little stomach for the climb and less for the jump. In fact, encumbered as I was by soaking clothing and a leather attaché-case, I doubted very much if I could do it.

And if I failed–well, it looked as though the sea would

accomplish what Mr. L——'s revolver had failed to do. I couldn't live minutes in that sea.

Had it not been for the sake of the dignity of the force I represented and that little imp within me which hates to be beaten, I should never have taken what seemed to me at the time to be far less than an even money chance.

It required every ounce of effort to fight back the protest which my lips were so eager to make. But I did fight it back and when seamanship had conquered those tempestuous seas and loud voices called on me to "Jump! Jump!"–well, I just set my teeth and sprang.

By some miracle I got one hand and one foot to the ship's ladder. It was just as well, for already there was a wide space between the boat and the cruiser.

Having accomplished the jump I was faced by the climb. There seemed to be millions of rungs before hefty hands seized me and hauled me on to the deck.

With a feeling of intense relief, I gathered myself together, and a few minutes later was restoring my lost nerves with a stiff drink of brandy in the captain's cabin.

Then I discovered that all my efforts had been for nothing. The sailor I wanted had been transferred to the flagship, many miles down the bay.

For a fleeting moment I had visions of another desperate jump and another ship's ladder climb. But this was not necessary. I was conveyed to the Admiral's ship in a torpedo-boat destroyer, boarding it by means of a gangway.

Admiral Sir Curzon Howe,[526] one of the finest officers who has ever walked a ship's bridge, was kindness itself. He placed one of the officer's cabins at my disposal, gave me a change of clothing, and insisted on my dining with him and his chief officers.

After dinner I talked with the sailors I had come to see, getting from them information which assisted me greatly in my subsequent inquiries.

Next morning I made the return journey to Bantry, not in a small storm-tossed boat, but in a destroyer, and, having been lent a waterproof and a sou'-wester by the kindly Admiral, I was able to

---

526   Admiral Sir Assheton Gore Curzon-Howe (1850-1911).

stay on the bridge with the officer in charge.

All's well that ends well, but I never, even now, think of Bantry Bay without a cold shiver.

V

ONLY a few weeks after I was sent to take charge of the C.I.D. of the Hammersmith Division[527] I found myself up against one of the coolest and cleverest swindlers I have ever struck.[528]

It beats me to know how so many really brainy people turn to crime when I am perfectly certain they could be successful in a business or profession.

You may wonder why crooks of the calibre of this one are allowed to carry on for long periods with impunity. Well, the blame, in most cases at any rate, has to be laid at the door of the public rather than of the police.

So many people are shy of having anything to do with the police and the police court. They prefer to lose their money in silence to hearing their friends say, "How could you have been such a fool?"

Arrest is delayed in other cases because the frauds are so ingenious that it is very difficult indeed to get the evidence necessary for a conviction.

Both these reasons applied in the case of the "gentleman" with whose exploits I am about to deal. He had been defrauding the public both in this country and on the Continent for about twenty years, operating nearly all the time from a succession of addresses in London.

Unfortunately for him, and equally fortunately for his many victims, he had just before my transfer to Hammersmith taken a big house in this district,[529] which he used both as a residence and business premises. A large number of clerks, both English and foreign, were employed there.

---

527   Dew took up the appointment in February 1900, and this case took place over a year—rather than "only a few weeks"—later.

528   Dew had similarly described Conrad Harms/Henry Clifford as "one of the cleverest swindlers I struck throughout my police career." (*ICC*, p.189).

529   "a big house at Gunnersbury" in *STWN*, 25 July 1936. Just "a big house" in *ETWN*, 1 August 1936. The house was called "Longcott."

In addition he had a printing works,[530] and ran an advertising agency.[531]

The first complaint, which reached me via Scotland Yard, was from a person in the provinces who alleged that he had had certain dealings with Mr. Blank,[532] let us call him, and had been cheated out of a few shillings,

But attached to this complaint was a dossier showing that many other complaints had[533] been received previously and so far as one could see, little had been done about it.

Such a state of affairs I regarded as a blot on my district, and I made up my mind at once that if Blank was a swindler, I would make it very uncomfortable for him.

The division was a huge one, carrying with it big responsibilities and an enormous amount of work, but as this seemed to be a case out of the ordinary I decided to have a cut at it myself.

Having studied all the documentary evidence furnished by the letters of complaint, I made a few discreet inquiries. From these I learned that Blank was an advertiser on a very large scale, both in this country and abroad.

The advertisements were passed through his agency to newspapers all over the world. I also discovered that he himself controlled a woman's journal in which he took up most of the advertising space.[534]

One thing in particular was advertised. It was what was called an "ornithological contest", for which valuable prizes, such as clocks and rings, were offered to successful solvers.[535]

The advertisements of this contest made it clear that a board of arbitrators had been set up to judge the efforts of competitors and make the awards.

This seemed all very nice and fair. But if this was so, why all the complaints? I made up my mind to find out, and realizing that

---

530   "a printing works at Brentford" in *STWN*, 25 July 1936. This was the Imperial Type Foundry, 9 High Street, Brentford.

531   The European & Colonial Advertisement Company, 144 Fleet Street, London.

532   Mr. Blank was John Nicholson, aged forty-seven.

533   "many others complaints concerning the man" in *TWN*, 1 August 1936.

534   The journal was called *Woman's World*.

535   "successful solutionists." in *TWN*, 1 August 1936.

I was letting myself in for a lot of work, I looked round for a likely assistant. My choice fell on Sergeant Fowler, a very intelligent and capable officer, who subsequently became a chief-inspector.[536]

"It'll mean a lot of hard work, Fowler," I told him, "but I am going to put my back into it, and I want you to do the same."

Such advice was unnecessary, for Sergeant Fowler was as keen as mustard to get to the bottom of the mystery.

Some of the complaints went back many years. Fowler and I spent hours, days and weeks over them, and worked so hard generally that there were times when I wished I had left the inquiry to a subordinate.

But at length I was perfectly satisfied in my own mind that the thing was a swindle from beginning to end.

The problem was to prove it.

Of the scores of people we interviewed who alleged that they had been victimized, not one showed any real eagerness to come forward and give evidence, and unwilling witnesses were of no use to me.

So I decided to become a competitor in the "ornithological contest" myself, and try in that way to get a line on the elusive Blank.

The idea of the competition was quite simple. All the entrant had to do was to send in a list of the names of birds. The longest list, providing, of course, that it was accurate, was supposed to be the winner.[537]

My list was very long, but it was far from accurate, for I made no attempt to confine it to birds. I deliberately slipped in such names as "elephant, camel, walrus, and whale."[538]

Fowler and two of our women folk sent in similar bogus entries.[539]

---

536 Possibly Henry John Fowler (b. 1870) who joined the Metropolitan Police in 1890 and retired in 1919 as a chief inspector at Scotland Yard. (PRO, MEPO 21/46).

537 The list had to contain at least twenty-five names, not using the letters j, x, y or z. (*St. James's Gazette*, 22 July 1901).

538 Dew only sent nineteen names, including "sticklebacks", "dromedaries" and "midgets." Others sent in lists of 4,000 names. (*Ibid.*).

539 According to the trial transcript Fowler submitted his list under the name of "Miss Fowler." Fowler said he "did not go to a treatise on natural history for his list", which included "canary, starlight, foxglove and sturgeon." (*The Times*, 22 July 1901).

The ruse worked beautifully. About a week later all four of us received a long typewritten letter[540] on imposing notepaper announcing that the arbitrators had carefully studied our efforts and had awarded us prizes in each case, a "diamond ring".

To be quite fair, the word diamond was qualified by a lot of other adjectives, but the whole letter had been so phrased as to convey to the unlearned that they had in fact, won a valuable prize.

As to this, I may say here that at a later date, I visited the business house which supplied the rings, and discovered that their actual cost to Blank was from four to five shillings a gross. In other words, they were of no more value than the sort of thing you get in a Christmas cracker.

Now comes the swindle. There was a condition attached to the sending of the prize. The letter stated that on receipt of a year's subscription to the woman's periodical I have already mentioned the ring would be forwarded.

Fowler and I at once sent the sum demanded, and by return of post our "diamond" rings. We had no need to take them to an expert to judge their approximate worth.[541]

At last we had some real evidence that Mr. Blank was a twister. Our experiences had demonstrated clearly enough that lists sent in were not scrutinized by anyone, much less a board of arbitrators. If they had been, our elephants, camels, &c., would never have got by.

The whole scheme was a trick to get a yearly subscription for Blank's worthless periodical.

We were encouraged now to further efforts, and in the end I succeeded in getting several people to make signed statements alleging frauds, and, better still, got some of them to consent to give evidence if required.

I then placed the mass of evidence I had collected before the Director of Public Prosecutions, who ultimately decided there was sufficient evidence to institute criminal proceedings.

Information was sworn before the justices at Brentford police court, and I at once obtained a warrant against the man.

---

540   "long type-written letters" in *STWN*, 25 July 1936. Dew told the court it was a printed letter made to look like it had been typed.

541   The cost of the subscription was 5*s*. 10*d*. Dew received a brass ring set with glass worth 3*d*. (*St. James's Gazette*, 22 July 1901).

When I went to Blank's house[542] armed with my warrant I took Fowler with me. The place was double-fronted and quite imposing—a mansion, I estimated, of anything from fifteen to twenty rooms.

By good fortune our man was in.

This was the first time I had seen Mr. Blank. He was a middle-aged man, say between forty-five and fifty, shortish, dapper, well-built, and immaculately dressed in a grey frock-coat, top hat, &c. His speech left no doubt that he was an American.

On telling him who we were and what our errand was he expressed first surprise and then indignation, in which he was joined by his charming lady secretary.

"Such a suggestion was preposterous." "He had never heard of such a thing." "His business was perfectly legitimate," and so on.

He threatened me with all sorts of dire penalties if I arrested him, but when he realized that my purpose would not be changed by anything he could say he calmed down and came quietly with us to the police station. There he was formally charged.

My next job was to get back to the big house, search it thoroughly, and interview the large number of clerks, male and female, English and foreign, employed there. It was soon quite clear that the employees had no knowledge that they were taking part in a swindle, and firmly believed the business to be genuine.

Of documents we made such a huge haul, a small van was required to remove them. We also got a mass of correspondence from the advertising and printing premises.

We came across numberless answers to the "ornithological contest". Some of these were very crude, but others were works of art. In some cases the names of the birds had been worked in beautifully coloured silk; in others they had been finely painted and lithographed.

The letters were from all parts of the world, from Pekin to Peru and Greenland to the South Seas.

Some of them were very pathetic. One, I remember, was from a child in New Zealand, in which she said she hoped she would get a prize, as she had been saving up her pennies for the entrance fee.

Another, which came from abroad, was obviously from a man

---

542   On 12 July 1901.

in poor circumstances because he wrote: "If I win a clock, please don't send me a grandfather one as my cottage is too small to stand it in."

At this I had to smile.

Poor old chap. He need not have worried. The clocks sent out were small tin things which cost 1s. or less.

When Blank appeared at the Brentford police court on remand a representative of the Director of Public Prosecutions took charge, and Blank was defended by that fine old barrister, the late Mr. J. P. Grain.[543] Many witnesses were called from London and the provinces, and eventually the prisoner was sent for trial at the Old Bailey.

The trial was a long one. The judge was the then Common Serjeant of the Central Criminal Court, and Blank was here represented by the late Lord Coleridge, then a barrister.

In spite of a great fight on his behalf, both at the lower court and the Old Bailey, the jury made no mistake. The verdict was "guilty".

My evidence as to the names I had sent in was greeted with loud laughter, in which Blank himself joined.

Before passing sentence, the judge called me forward, and asked me to tell him anything I could about the accused man's history. I had got as far as saying that he was a highly educated man and had been carrying on this class of fraud for twenty years, when Lord Coleridge jumped to his feet with the comment: "Then it does not redound to your credit to have allowed it to go on so long."

"As to that," I retorted, "I would like to say that I have been engaged on this case for exactly six months."

In passing sentence of eighteen months' imprisonment,[544] the judge probably took into consideration the fact that there were no previous convictions.

Fowler and I were commended by the judge and jury, and later by the Commissioner himself.

When Blank was taken below I assumed, not without relief, that that would be the last I should see of him. This, however, was not

---

543 At an earlier hearing Nicholson was defended by Travers Humphreys and Richard Muir prosecuted. In another similarity to the Crippen case, Nicholson described himself as an aural specialist who sold deafness cures, as did Crippen.

544 With hard labour.

so.

After he had been in prison some months the German authorities got busy and decided that they, too, had a little account to square with the bird contest man. Many people in that country had been tricked by him.

So, on completion of his sentence, he was promptly re-arrested and charged at Bow Street under an extradition warrant with his German frauds.

After the customary proceedings, he was committed for extradition to Germany, and in due course conveyed to Hamburg, and handed over to the German police.

Again I thought that was the last I should see of him. Once more I was wrong.

A month or so later the German Government made a request that I should be allowed to proceed to Hagen, in Westphalia, and give evidence against Blank at his trial there.

Permission was given, and off I went to that lovely Prussian town. When Blank spotted me in court his face betrayed surprise and consternation. But he recovered himself quickly, and was afterwards as debonair as ever.

The procedure in the German criminal courts is very different from ours. Before the case had been heard the three judges called upon me to tell them all I could about the man's career. This I proceeded to do to his obvious disgust.

During the course of the afternoon it was announced that the case would have to be adjourned for several days. The judges had to proceed to another part of Germany.

Through an interpreter Blank was asked if it was his desire that I should remain.

His reply was most emphatic.

"No," he cried, adding, "I never want to set eyes on him again."

His wish was fulfilled. I have never seen him since, though some time later I heard the result of the German trial. He was sent to prison for twelve months.

He deserved every day of it, as you would agree had you read with me some of the pathetic letters written by his victims.[545]

---

545 Dew mentioned this case when giving evidence to the House of Commons Joint Select
     Committee on Lotteries and Indecent Advertisements in 1908, saying "If the law had been

VI

IN a sense, I suppose it is true that the successful detective is born, not made.

Most men, when they join the police force, dream dreams of one day holding a responsible position at Scotland Yard. With the majority of them, this remains a dream, for the simple reason that they have not the temperament or the talent to succeed as detectives.

I was luckier than most, for I was chosen for plain-clothes work soon after I had joined the force.

In those days the life of the young policeman was anything but pleasant. In certain localities it was the custom of the toughs to "blood" the youngster in blue. Often he was attacked.

I did not escape such attention, but I always regarded it as part of the price to be paid, and never rested until I had squared accounts with the men who had molested me.

I cannot say I got any pleasure as a young constable at Paddington out on my all-night hunts in plain clothes for sheep-stealers at Harrow and Sudbury. Gangs of these sheep-stealers were making raids at night, say between 8 p.m. and 2 a.m. on flocks of sheep in these districts, killing large numbers of them, carrying off[546] the prime joints, and making away with their booty in vehicles drawn by fast-trotting horses.

We patrolled in couples, armed only with small wooden truncheons as against the sharp butchers' knives which the raiders carried and, from all accounts, would not have hesitated to use.

---

different, we could have stopped an immense amount of harm which he did for some considerable time." He explained to the committee that newspaper competitions, such as filling in missing words and writing limericks, "inculcate the spirit of gambling in the young, and not only young but old people." They often led to people buying multiple copies of newspapers and journals to obtain more entry coupons for the competitions, which generally required a postal order being sent also. Dew said "there is nothing to prevent young lads sending in 200 or 300 coupons, and I say that is an inducement to them to steal money." He argued that the volume of entries these competitions received, along with the arbitrary way the winners were chosen, eliminated any element of skill on the part of the competitors, thus making them games of chance or a lottery, adding "it is obvious that while there is any element of skill shown we shall never be able to get a prosecution against these people. Wherever they can show an element of skill we fail." (*Report From the Joint Select Committee on Lotteries and Indecent Advertisements*, 1908, pp. 45-48).

546   "carving off" in *TWN*, 8 August 1936.

"From pitch and toss to manslaughter" is a saying sometimes used to illustrate the limits of crime.

As far as my own career is concerned, it is more accurate to say "Pitch and toss to murder", for at one time and another I have arrested persons for every offence it is possible to commit under the criminal law.

Coming right down the scale, as a young constable I often arrested young children sent out to beg to provide their drunken parents with money for still more drink.

It was not my eagerness to get a case or my love for making arrests which caused me to charge these poor kiddies. I arrested them for their own sakes.

It was good to see their faces–these little mites–when at the police station I sent them down to the single men's quarters where they got a good feed and hot coffee. Many of them were half-starved.

I have always held there are two ways of effecting an arrest–a pleasant way and an unpleasant way. Whenever possible I have adopted the former, always forcing myself to remember that an arrested person is innocent until proved guilty.

I was human enough, too, to feel that the poor devil had enough to put up with without circumstances being made deliberately worse for them.

I have been assaulted over and over again, but this was almost without exception when I was arresting a violent prisoner. The police officer expects that.

Take a district like Saffron Hill, or "Little Italy", as it is commonly called. This area came within my jurisdiction when I was in charge of Bow Street.[547]

In the main the members of this Italian colony in London were a law-abiding community, respectful of the police.

The minority, as is often the case, caused the trouble. Feuds among these were frequent, ending too often in the use of the knife and sometimes the revolver. Murder was by no means unknown.

If the murder was committed in this locality and the assailant was not caught red-handed, the police were right up against it.

---

547   Dew had charge of this district from October 1903-October 1906.

Not a vestige of information would be given by any of the wanted man's compatriots. Their creed seemed to be "Never mind about the dead. Look after the living," and it didn't matter to them if the "living" had taken a human life.

An Italian was shot dead in Saffron Hill.[548] Uniformed police were on the spot almost immediately, but no information as to the dead man's assailant could be traced.

I was communicated with and was quickly in "Little Italy" with several members of my staff from Gray's Inn Road Police Station. What a babel of excitement I found. I couldn't speak Italian. Few of the Italians understood English.

However, we did the best we could with the assistance of an interpreter, though the house-to-house search and other inquiries yielded nothing.

Later, however, after several hours' hard work, I got information which satisfied me as to the identity of the murderer.[549] He was by this time missing. His description was circulated throughout the country. Every Italian colony in the country was combed. Railway stations and ports were watched. All without result.

It was the old story of a vendetta between two Italian families.[550]

Passports in those days were not necessary. Therefore it was much easier for a wanted man to leave the country than it is to-day. At the same time, I felt that with the precautions we had so promptly taken, it was impossible for the fugitive to have got away.

Weeks passed without news. During this time a description of the wanted man was circulated to other countries, including Italy, and a close watch was kept on his relatives in London in the hope that they might furnish a clue. All was unavailing, and at length I was driven to the conclusion that the murderer, after all, must have

548 Paolino Amato was fatally stabbed in Warner Street on 15 May 1904. Shots were also fired at him, but a surgeon at the Royal Free Hospital stated: "the deceased was not shot at all. He bore, however, eight wounds about his face and body caused by stabs." (*The Illustrated Police News*, 28 May 1904).

549 This is another example of Dew's memory lapsing. There were two killers; Andrea Peretta and Guiseppe Jovino. Peretta had previously served an eighteen-month sentence for shooting a man.

550 Amato had been paying unwelcome attention to a married Italian woman, Carmela Caccavello, for two years. A vendetta was declared against him and Carmela identified Amato to his killers by saying, "Here comes the pig." (*The Illustrated Police News*, 28 May; 11 June 1904).

been smuggled out of the country.

At long last I was rewarded. After a lot of hard work, and a little luck, I established beyond all doubt that our man had indeed reached Italy and was living in Genoa. I got into touch with the Italian police, and derived a lot of personal satisfaction from the news, which came a short time later, that they had effected the arrest.

I should like very much to tell you about the small chance which led to my tracing of the man, but this is a secret which I shared only with my late honoured chief, Sir Melville Macnaughton, and I do not feel justified even now in divulging it.

Unfortunately all our work was wasted. The crime went unavenged.

There is no capital punishment in Italy. Therefore, if an Italian guilty of murder in this country, succeeds in making his way to Italy, as this one did, he is quite safe so far as hanging is concerned. There is logic in this, for the surrender of the man would mean that he would receive a punishment unrecognized in his own land.

What happened in this case was that the Italian authorities offered to try the man themselves. Conviction would have meant imprisonment for life.

A mass of evidence which had already been collected was sworn before the Chief Magistrate of Bow Street Police Court, and in due course transmitted to the Italian authorities. There were also protracted negotiations as to the witnesses who should travel from London to Genoa.

All this time the man was kept in prison. But the prisoner was never brought to trial. On some pretext or other–the actual reason I cannot recall–this man was set at liberty.

In a sense that was a disappointment, though I personally had the satisfaction of solving the case, and could in no way be held to blame for what the Italian authorities did.

There is one crime almost even worse than murder–blackmail.[551]

Happily, blackmail is less prevalent than it used to be. One reason for this is that nowadays it is the practice to keep the names of prosecutor's secret.

---

551   "even worse than murder–blackmail." in *TWN*, 8 August 1936.

Formerly this was not so, and it wanted a really brave man to face the ordeal of publicity.

Let me quote you a case from my own experience.

About ten o'clock one morning, a young man came rushing into Scotland Yard in a state of great excitement.[552] I saw him, and he told me a story which, had I not known that such things did happen, might have seemed incredible.

The young man said that on leaving his West End club[553] at 1 a.m. he was accosted in the street by a young foreigner[554] who told him a pitiful story of a sick mother in Germany whom he was anxious to visit, but had not the funds for the journey.

Mr. X. was, of course, foolish to talk to a stranger at that time of night, but he did so, and was so impressed that he gave the young foreigner ten shillings and invited him to his flat for a drink.

There they sat for some time drinking, smoking and talking.

Then came the shock. The youth, who had professed to be so concerned about his sick mother, revealed himself in his true colours–that of a blackmailer. He made accusations against Mr. X., alleging indecent conduct, and demanded a sum of money.

Mr. X. took the right line then. He used a stick on his nocturnal guest and drove him out of the house.

But soon after nine o'clock the same morning there was a development. His visitor of the night before came back. This time he was not alone, but was accompanied by a hefty German a few years older who claimed to be his brother.[555] The charges were repeated.

Mr. X. became alarmed and, although entirely innocent of the conduct alleged against him, gave the man a cheque for £5 and an I.O.U. for £15 to get rid of them.

The men then left, taking with them a sovereign and a silver cigarette case which they had brazenly lifted from the dressing-table.

Mr. X. went on to tell me that the I.O.U. was to be redeemed at

552 This happened on 29 May 1897. The man was law student John Arthur Bleackley of 91 Victoria Street.

553 The New Lyric Club.

554 Paul Ullrich, aged eighteen.

555 Arthur Manzal, aged twenty-two.

2 p.m. the following Sunday. He had arranged to meet the two men with the money in Dover Street, Piccadilly.[556]

The first thing to be done was to try and intercept the men at the bank when they appeared to cash the £5 cheque. Chief-Inspector Froest and I jumped into a cab–there were no telephones in those days at the Yard–and dashed to the bank. We were too late. The cheque had already been presented.

Our hope now lay in the Dover Street appointment. Would the two blackmailers turn up? Froest and I hardly expected that they would do so, though we both knew from experience that avarice will drive men to take foolish risks.

In good time for the two o'clock meeting, Froest and I took up our position in the Green Park, from which we could keep the proposed rendezvous under observation.[557]

Presently two men, who looked promising, turned up and loitered aimlessly about.

Mr. X. appeared. The two men we had been watching immediately approached him. Froest and I were on their heels and got close enough to hear the elder of the two men say they "had to have the money".

We pounced on them, and after a bit of a struggle overpowered them both. The elder man dropped a paper. I picked it up and found it to be to Mr. X.s I.O.U.[558]

Both were waiters of German nationality.

On one we found a number of visiting cards bearing the name of a lieutenant in the German Navy,[559] a stamped envelope bearing the name of Mr. X. with particulars of the £5 cheque and the place and time of the Dover Street appointment.

Thus we had overwhelming evidence against them.

In due course the prisoners were committed for trial to the Central Criminal Court. The judge, unfortunately for them, was Sir Henry Hawkins (later Lord Brampton), a holy terror to all violent criminals and blackmailers.

---

556 Down Street is named in contemporary newspaper reports.

557 Dover Street cannot be easily observed from Green Park, whereas Down Street can be.

558 "Mr X's I O U." in *ETWN*, 8 August 1936; "Mr X's I.O.U." in *STWN*, 1 August 1936.

559 "German Army" in *TWN*, 8 August 1936. The name was Lieutenant Paul von Rubenstein. (*The Times*, 9 June 1897).

The verdict was "Guilty". The elder was sentenced to ten years' penal servitude and the other to eight years.[560] The distinction was made solely because of the youth of the second man.

By a curious coincidence three other men who had been put back after conviction received heavy sentences on the same day and in the same court for obtaining money by menaces.

This is what Mr. Justice Hawkins had to say about this bright trio:

"You have been guilty of a series of most cruel and abominable crimes, and by your system of almost unexampled terrorism, carried on for a period of not less than five years, have extorted on countless occasions sums of money amounting in the aggregate to £1500. Within my memory such an offence was punishable by death.

"I am satisfied that you belong to a gang of miscreants who for years have traded in this way.[561] For five years you have pursued Mr. M. (the prosecutor)[562] with relentless cruelty. You have not allowed him in that time a moment's peace of mind. You had neither remorse nor pity. Not even the pleadings, the piteous pleadings of the prosecutor's sister, had any influence in turning you from your wicked purpose. I cannot imagine a worse case.

"I shall sentence G —— and C —— to penal servitude for the term of their natural lives. T —— will go to penal servitude for fifteen years."[563]

Neither before nor since have I heard such a series of terrible sentences passed in a few minutes.

But they were richly deserved.

These blackmail cases are depressing. Here is a case that will give you a laugh. It concerns raids on gambling dens.

I was spurred on in this work by the tragic letters which

---

560 Both were known to have previously attempted similar crimes and Ullrich had previous convictions for theft and forgery.

561 Dew had told the court at the trial of Ullrich and Manzal that there were a number of blackmailers "who infested the West-end and carried on their business in female attire." (*The Morning Post* (London), 5 July 1897). It is not known if these three men fell into that category.

562 Joseph Stanley Matheson.

563 The three blackmailers were Arthur Grant, Herbert Coulton and Archibald Thorpe. Paul Ullrich lived with Grant and Coulton.

sometimes came to us from the wives of men who frequented these places, dissipating their earnings and leaving their families poverty stricken.

One such letter, anonymous, of course, called me to account for allowing a ready-money betting office to carry on business over a shop in the Strand. I had not known of the existence of the place, but I was quick to act upon the information.

After a lot of hard work had been put in by Police Constables Henry and Stephens, two of my best workers, I got the evidence I wanted and applied for a warrant.

We visited the premises and found the principal and two or three clerks hard at work. So far as could be seen, the business was lawful.

Presently, however, a man entered and after passing the time of day, produced a betting slip and handed it with a sum of money to the principal. I took it and asked the visitor to wait. Other men came in and the same procedure was followed.

All the men were detained, taken to Bow Street and charged. They were then allowed out on bail. As the offenders were signing the bail book, I was struck by the peculiar hand-writing of one of them. Unless I was very much mistaken it was the same as that on the anonymous letter which had laid the information about the betting house.

I asked this man to stay behind, invited him into my office. Then I produced the anonymous letter and asked him point-blank if the writing was his.

He burst out laughing.

"Yes," he promptly agreed. "I wrote it. I did it out of pique. Got a bit annoyed over a betting transaction."

I laughed too.

"But you didn't expect to get caught yourself?" I said.

"You're right there. I was never more surprised in my life than when I walked into my own trap."

A case of the "biter being bit".

When the cases came before the magistrate the principal was fined £100 and £20 costs. The frequenters were bound over.[564]

---

564   Dew was involved in several investigations into illegal gambling operations. This one may have been the raid at 434 Strand on 5 May 1905 when eleven arrests were made. The

VII

THE making and uttering of counterfeit coins is one of the meanest of crimes. Poor people are nearly always the sufferers.

I have had several cases of this sort, one of the first when I was a young uniformed constable in the X Division.[565] One day[566] I was on duty at the police station, when a man rushed in and excitedly reported to the inspector that he had been tendered a bad half-crown at the sub-post office run in conjunction with his small shop some quarter of a mile away.[567]

The fact that the coin was counterfeit had been discovered by the postmaster immediately the man had left, and he had at once followed the suspect. Outside the shop his quarry[568] had been joined by a second man,[569] and together, he said, they had passed the front entrance of the police station.

I had overheard the conversation, and the inspector, a man of action, turned quickly to me and said: "Get on the job, Dew."

I rushed to the single men's quarters, slipped off my tunic, grabbed the first coat and hat I could find, and in a matter of seconds had joined the informant and taken up the trail.

A few minutes later we caught sight of the two men, and almost immediately one of them crossed the road and entered a small grocer's shop to which was attached a sub-post office.[570] Their game was obvious. Quick action was necessary.

I dashed up to the man who had been left outside, seized him by the scruff of the neck and hauled him across the road and into the shop which his companion had entered. I banged the door after me.

The first man was just leaving the postal counter.

"Place the money this man has passed on one side," I called out

following week at Bow Street Magistrates' Court William Scott and John Shepherd were found guilty of keeping and assisting in the management of two rooms on the first floor at 434 Strand for the purposes of betting and fined £52 with £5 7s. costs. (*The Daily News* (London), 6 & 12 May 1905).

565 Dew served in the Paddington Division from June 1882 until his transfer to H Division, Whitechapel, in June 1887.

566 It was 1 June 1887, Dew's last day at Paddington before his transfer to Whitechapel.

567 A stationer's in Goldburn Road.

568 George Kirk, aged fifty-two.

569 George Macey, aged thirty-one.

570 Run by Henry Barnard at 38 Chippenham Terrace.

to the girl behind the counter.

The man who had made the purchase, as I suspected with bad money, was now only intent on getting past me into the street. He did his best, but I got the better of the scuffle and managed to push him into a large case of lemons standing on the floor.[571] In the meantime other people in the shop had had the presence of mind to lock the door and send to the Harrow Road Police station for assistance.[572]

I told the two men who I was, and why I had butted so unceremoniously into their business. They not only hotly disputed the charge, but stoutly denied all knowledge of one another.

But within a short time a uniformed constable had arrived,[573] and with his assistance both men were searched. This, by the way, is one of the offences in which the police are empowered to search on the spot. Any doubts to which the men's protestations might have given rise were set at rest by what we found. On the man I had dragged into the shop we found a large number of counterfeit half-crowns done up in rolls.

When searching the second man we found nothing suspicious— at first. There was nothing incriminating on him. But a search of the lemons into which he had fallen revealed several bad half-crowns, and it was quite obvious that he had tried to get rid of the evidence.

I should not have been surprised had the man who first entered the shop had no more bad money on him. As a rule, the person actually passing bad money takes with him only the coin or coins he is about to utter, leaving the bulk of the counterfeit stuff with the carrier outside. This is so that in the event of his being challenged nothing incriminating will be found upon him.

Both men were charged with uttering, and eventually sent for trial at the Old Bailey, where they were found guilty.[574]

---

571 At the trial Dew said: "he then slipped down on to a basket of lemons which was standing on the floor–I had not got hold of him then; it was an action of his own."

572 "and to ring the Harrow Road Police Station for assistance." in *TWN*, 15 August 1936. Dew had said in the 1897 blackmailing case that Scotland Yard did not have telephones at that date so it is unlikely that a police station would have had them in 1887, although *TWN*, 2 March 1935 included a modern drawing with one on the wall of Commercial Street Police Station in 1888.

573 P.C. Joseph Collinett.

574 Kirk's sentence was respited until the next sessions, but he was eventually received four months' imprisonment without hard labour. Macey received fifteen months' hard labour.

In those days there was no finger-print identification in England–[575]China had practised the method a thousand years before–and the police had been unable to find anything against either man. They would probably have been dealt with as first offenders had not a chief warder chanced to enter the court.

"Have those two been identified?" he asked me.

"'No," I replied. "Nobody knows anything about them."

"Oh, don't they?" the warder then said. "Get your counsel to put me in the witness-box."

This was done, to the consternation of the prisoners, and particularly one of them. The chief identified one of the prisoners as an old convict, though he was not at the moment in a position to prove the previous conviction.

The case was adjourned to the next Sessions, and then it was revealed that whereas little was known against one of the men, his companion had been sentenced to terms of imprisonment totalling something like forty years.

And as a direct result of this case certain action was taken–as a young constable I had no part in this–which resulted in the breaking up of a clever gang of base coiners who were all sent to long terms of imprisonment. One man, known as "Little Johnny", was sent to penal servitude for twenty years.

Although our joint action had resulted in the uprooting of this gang, neither the sub-postmaster nor myself received the slightest recognition. I have always felt a bit sore about this. The inspector in charge of the case might, it seemed to me, have put in a word for a young officer.[576] But in the long run it didn't matter.

I had another interesting coining case when I was in charge of the Hammersmith district many years later. Twickenham–a very charming place in those days–came within the scope of my supervision. Not the sort of place one would connect with serious crime, much less a coiner's den, which only goes to show how easy it is to be deceived by appearances.

575 "In those days there were no such things as finger-prints in England" in *TWN*, 15 August 1936.

576 Dew was recorded as putting in a word to Melville Macnaghten on behalf of P.C.s Frederick Martin and Daniel Gooch for helping him dig up Cora Crippen's remains and placing them in a coffin. They were each given a 10s. reward. (PRO, MEPO 3/198)

For some time, I had been receiving complaints from all parts of the division about the passing of counterfeit florins. These all found their way into the tills of the tradesmen, none of whom could provide a clue as to how the dud coins came into their possession.

The local C.I.D. officers had tried to get a line on the problem without success. Were the complaints genuine? I made personal inquiries into this, and found the characters of the tradesmen concerned above reproach.

Next counterfeit half-sovereigns–this was in the good old days of gold currency–began to appear. This was really serious. Time something was done about it.

In another part of my district I had an excellent sergeant named Taylor.[577] I relieved him of all his other duties, and instructed him to devote all his time to the counterfeit coin's mystery.

"It is a sort of roving commission I'm giving you, Taylor," I told him. "Better make a start by interviewing every shopkeeper who has complained, find out all you can about the people who made the purchases, and to whom the change was given."

And so far, as I was able, I worked on the job myself.

At length we got a clue. One of the tradesmen, who had unwittingly accepted a large number of base florins, remembered, when pressed, that he usually found them in his till after he had had dealings with a traveller in sweet stuff. Armed with this information, we jogged the memories of other shopkeepers, several of whom then agreed that there did seem to be a link between the traveller and the counterfeit coins.

It was easy enough to trace the traveller, who was not, as you may be thinking, the culprit, but another victim. He represented a large firm of confectioners, and it was his custom to deliver goods in a horse-drawn van. He also collected money, and, when necessary, gave change. I saw the man, and it did not take me long to make up my mind that he was perfectly respectable. He was in some way being made the coiner's agent. But how?

Our inquiries were complicated by the fact that certain of the shops visited regularly by this traveller were outside my division. In one of these shops, I felt, the key to the mystery lay. A list was

577   Sergeant Thomas Taylor.

made of all the shops which did business with the firm. Everything were discreetly visited.

One of the shops in the "suspected" list was a rather nice confectioner's situated near Twickenham railway station.[578] It had not been opened very long. Another important discovery we made was that the proprietor of this shop was in the habit of paying for his goods with silver, varied only occasionally by the inclusion of a half-sovereign.

These facts decided me to put the place under observation.

Two discoveries were made by the men I put on the job. One was that two men—[579]so far as could be seen without any business—frequented the shop. The other, that a man named R——,[580] whose wife carried on a laundry business next door but one, was constantly in and out.

R——'s name had a familiar sound about it. Some time before I had come into contact with a man of the same name—a shady customer—over a matter which, however, had nothing to do with counterfeiting. Inquiries I then made established that it was the same man. This gave me much food for thought.

All the information my men got confirmed me in my suspicions that there was something wrong with this nice sweet shop.

Of course, I could have kept the place under observation until something more definite emerged. But there was always the chance that a watcher would be spotted. And if that happened, the crooks, if crooks they were, would make a quick getaway.

If circumstances justified it, I never hesitated to take a risk.[581] I decided to take one here.

I prepared a sworn information, and with Taylor and other officers went to the Brentford Police Court, where I interviewed the genial clerk to the magistrates, who was always willing to help me in a good cause.

The clerk and I discussed the pros and cons, and the clerk, after carefully weighing the evidence I had placed before him, decided to recommend the magistrate to issue search warrants for the sweet

---

578 At 10 Station Road.

579 Charles Jewell, aged forty-two and William Charles Trowbridge, aged twenty-two.

580 William Thomas Russell, aged forty-two.

581 This might explain Dew's willingness to pursue the *Montrose* across the Atlantic in 1910.

shop and the laundry premises.

"If I've made a mistake, then I'm for it," was my thought, as I debated the plan of attack with Taylor and the other officers.

We ascertained from the officer who was keeping observation on the shop that one of the suspected frequenters was inside. The moment had come to make the raid.[582]

A number of officers were deputed quietly to approach both shop and laundry, so guarding the exits that every avenue of escape was cut off. And, having given them time to take up their positions, Taylor and I were to enter the shop.

Alas, through a misunderstanding on the part of one of the sergeants,[583] things did not turn out as they had been planned to do, and, as a consequence, I received a bad mauling.

When Taylor and I boldly entered the shop, there were two men behind the counter.[584] The shopkeeper must have guessed our mission, for the moment he saw us he jumped over the counter and dashed into the street, followed by Taylor. His companion, a burly fellow, rushed into the back parlour, and then through another door into the garden. I gave chase.

Thinking my man was running straight into the trap I had prepared for him, I was quite sure as to the outcome, even though I myself did not catch him. But I did catch him–at the end of the garden, or perhaps it is more correct to say that I caught up with him.

The man turned at bay, and a terrific struggle began. He hammered me, I hammered him. First he was on top, then it would be my turn. So the battle went on between two equally determined men, until at length I got the mastery, and kept him down by sitting on him.[585]

Next day I was black and blue, and the only consolation I had was that my prisoner was equally well marked.

582   This took place on 5 May 1903.

583   The other sergeants involved in the raid were Detective Sergeants William Moore and Charles Crutchett. The misunderstanding was not mentioned at the subsequent trial.

584   According to the trial transcript Trowbridge came out from the parlour, while Jewell was out the back of the shop.

585   Sergeant Taylor said that he saw Dew "in a severe struggle with Jewell in the back yard." Dew told the court he "seized him half-way down the garden... [he] struggled to get away."

I had, of course, never anticipated such a fierce, single-handed struggle. If the plans I had made had been carried out I should have had the immediate assistance of the officers I had sent to watch the rear of the house. But somehow or other they "took the wrong turning", and did not arrive on the scene until it was all over. In the meantime, Taylor had caught his man and brought him back to the shop.

When I had first seen my man he had in his hand a brown paper parcel. This he threw over the garden wall as he ran. It was picked up by a woman.[586] Its contents relieved my mind of all anxiety. Inside the brown paper were twenty counterfeit florins.[587]

Our next step was to take possession of the laundry, and, incidentally, my "friend" Mr. R——. Then, having seen the prisoners were securely guarded, I began my search of the premises.

In the top back room, I found a complete coiners' den. There were moulds for making florins–the same as those distributed all over the district–and, in fact, every implement and tool a counterfeiter requires. A large number of "home-made" florins and half-crowns were found, and a few half-sovereigns as well.[588]

It was one of the most complete coiners' outfits I have ever seen.

In the coiners' room stood half of an oval mahogany table, and upon this rested the moulds and other articles.

Where was the other half? We found it later in R——'s bedroom, and this proved a damning piece of evidence against him.

The three men were charged with making and uttering counterfeit coins, and at the Central Criminal Court, where they were eventually tried, found guilty and sentenced to terms of penal servitude.

Taylor and I received high praise from the judge and jury, from the Brentford Bench of Magistrates, and the Commissioner of Police.

---

586 Actually by Charles Bean who lived at 13 Station Road.

587 Bean handed Crutchett eleven coins. Two were in a purse, three loose and six in paper. He found another four the next day. Dew found five in the house which would make a total of twenty. A witness from the Royal Mint described examining twenty florins.

588 Dew told the court he found two counterfeit sovereigns, a half crown, five counterfeit florins and two half-crowns in a cigarette box.

VIII

HARRY the Valet was a thief with a charming smile and gentlemanly manners.

His theft of £25,000 worth of the jewels of a former Duchess of Sutherland at the Gare du Nord, Paris, is one of the classics of crime.

A great deal has been written about this case during the past thirty years, but I played such a big part in it personally that I feel the new light I can throw on it will justify its retelling.

A tremendous sensation was caused when the news got about that the Duchess, returning from the Riviera, had been robbed of her jewels while the train was standing in the Paris station. She had been travelling with her husband, the late Sir Albert Rollett, M.P., whom she married some time after the death of the Duke, and had been accompanied by her personal maid. That was in 1898.[589]

The French police communicated immediately with Scotland Yard, for it is an offence for anyone to deal in this country with property stolen abroad.

Inspector Walter Dinnie, of Scotland Yard, who later became Chief Commissioner of Police for New Zealand, took charge of the London end, and called me in to assist him. At the time I had just been appointed an inspector, and Dinnie was, therefore, my superior.[590]

The information supplied by the French police showed that the theft was the work of a daring criminal. The jewel case, which contained the collection for which the Duchess of Sutherland was famous, had been placed in charge of the maid who, of course, did not travel in the same compartment as her mistress.

At the Gare du Nord the maid left the compartment for a few moments, and then–according to the theory formed by the French police, it must have been then–the robbery took place.

But it was not until the train had reached Amiens that the theft was discovered, and valuable time was thus lost before the French police could get to work.

---

589   The theft took place on 17 October 1898.

590   "my senior." in *TWN*, 22 August 1936. Dew had been promoted to the rank of inspector (2nd class) on 18 October 1898, the day after the theft. (PRO, MEPO 21/39).

It did not follow from the mere fact that the person robbed was an Englishwoman, that the robbery had been the work of an English crook, or that we should find any line to it in London, but the possibility was too obvious to ignore.

So Dinnie and I set to work. We concentrated on international crooks and others who, from their records, might have pulled off such a coup. Our object was to find out if any such criminal had been out of the country at the time when the robbery took place.

After visiting all the known haunts of such men–night clubs, dives, and dens both east and west–we unearthed a piece of information which gave us something to go upon.

What we learned was that a notorious Continental thief was flush. He had been spending money with a lavishness which had called for comment among his associates and, more important still, his sudden access of wealth seemed to coincide with the Paris station robbery.

This man was known as Harry the Valet.[591] He was as well known to the Continental police as to us, and had several previous convictions against him, including a term of penal servitude abroad.

From that moment Harry the Valet came under suspicion, for, quite apart from the evidence of mysterious affluence, we knew that he was just the type of man for such a job.

Handsome, debonair and plausible, no one lacking a knowledge of his past would have taken him for what he was–a clever and audacious criminal. There was something very disarming about Harry. He might easily have been mistaken for a prosperous gentleman farmer.

In one haunt after another we got news of Harry's free spending. He seemed to have spent a small fortune on champagne. But Harry himself had vanished as completely as the jewels. It looked to us as though he had got wind of the fact that we "were on his tail" and had made a bolt.

---

591   The name originated from the time when Harry learned his trade from a London fence named Abraham Mitchell. Someone jokingly said that he was like Mitchell's valet and the name stuck. (Hamilton, *The Unreliable Life of Harry the Valet*, pp. 8-9). The Valet said this was the case. (*TWN*, 27 March 1926). An alternative suggestion was that the name originated from when he used to masquerade as a gentleman's servant to commit crimes. (Dilnot, *Great Detectives and Their Methods*, p. 98).

I doubt very much if the case would ever have been brought to a successful conclusion had there not about this time been a development of a nature quite unexpected.

We had a visitor at Scotland Yard. This was an actress.[592]

Miss X, who was first seen by Dinnie and then by myself, brought staggering news. She declared that she knew all about the jewel robbery and that the culprit was none other than the man we had suspected–Harry the Valet.

Her story was amazing. She told us that she had been friendly with Harry the Valet in Paris. He frequently visited her apartment there.

"One night," Miss X went on.[593] "Harry arrived with the most marvellous jewels I have seen.[594] I didn't know where he had got them–then–but I suspected that they were stolen.

"Harry allowed me to handle the jewels and try some of them on, and I was so fascinated by them that I pleaded with him to be allowed to keep them just for that night. At first Harry was reluctant to allow the jewels out of his keeping, but in the end he gave way. Some of the most lovely of them I wore all that night.

"I had fully intended to give the jewels back to Harry the following morning, but when the time came I felt I could not part with them, and begged to be allowed to keep them a little longer.

"At this Harry became angry. There was a terrible scene which ended with Harry taking the jewels from me by force and leaving the apartment in a rage. I was angry too–so angry that I went straight out and told the Paris police."

The date coincided with the Gare du Nord theft, and if Miss X's story was true, there could be little doubt that the jewels which had so fascinated her were the property of the Duchess of Sutherland.

But why had the French police failed to act upon Miss X's information? She said she had made her report to them on the morning following the robbery. Surely, then, if they had acted promptly they would have caught Harry before he was able to give them the slip and dodge back to London.

---

592   Maude Richardson, alias Louise Ronald.
593   Full stop here in *ICC*. *TWN* had a comma.
594   "I have ever seen." in *TWN*, 22 August 1936.

The only explanation I could think of at the time–and it turned out to be the true one–was that Miss X had been so hysterical when she told her story to the French police that they did not take it seriously, or did not understand her.

I have always held the view that, without Miss X's evidence, while we might have got Harry for unlawful possession, we should have been hard put to it to convict him of the actual theft.

The hunt for Harry now started in earnest, but while we searched for him in all his known London haunts, we kept in close touch with Miss X in case he went to see her.

But Harry the Valet was too cute for that, and unless the meeting had taken place under the eyes of a police officer I doubt very much whether it would have helped us. Miss X was rapidly repenting the part she had played, and beginning to hate herself for giving away Harry.

In the circumstances if she found him, or he returned to her, she was more likely to give him the tip that we were on his trail than to help us to catch him.

In the meantime a substantial reward had been offered by the Duchess of Sutherland for information leading to the recovery of her stolen property.

But many weeks passed before our diligence was in any way rewarded. Then information was brought to us that a man answering the suspect's description was living in an apartment house in Cathcart Road, South Kensington.

We took counsel together at the Yard and decided to make a raid on the premises at five o'clock the following morning.[595]

Inspector Dinnie and Inspector Froest, who afterwards became superintendent and held this position at the time of the Crippen crime, were in the part,[596] which also included several other plain-clothes officers and a number of uniformed police.

Harry the Valet had the reputation of being a desperate character, capable of violence if driven into a tight corner.[597] Knowing this,

---

595   The following morning was 28 November 1898.

596   "in the party" in *TWN*, 22 August 1936.

597   An example of him being violent was when he beat up Maude Richardson after finding out she had told the police about him. (*Lloyd's Weekly Newspaper*, 8 January 1899).

one of the other inspectors–I think it was Froest–brought along a revolver. We were determined to make no mistake.

In reaching the house in which we hoped and believed our quarry to be living, we carefully disposed our forces so that every exit was guarded.

Then Dinnie, Froest and I crept quietly to the front door. We fully expected the door communicating with the street to be locked and had come well supplied with keys. To our amazement the key had been left in the door on the outside, and all we had to do was turn it and walk in.

Without disturbing anyone in the house, we stealthily climbed the stairs to the first floor, for it was the first floor front room which, according to our information, Harry the Valet occupied.

We had previously decided that if the bedroom door was unlocked we would all three dash straight in. If it were locked we would burst it open without ceremony.

I was the first to reach the door. Gently I turned the handle. Once more our luck was in. The door was neither locked nor bolted. Quite obvious that the occupant, whoever he may be, was not expecting us.

According to plan I threw the door wide open, and all three of us burst into the room.

We flashed our lanterns on to the bed, expecting to see a surprised man lying there. The bed was empty. A second later we had spotted him. Fully dressed, except for his coat,[598] he was standing with his back to the fireplace with a sardonic smile on his lips.

"That's him, all right," said Inspector Dinnie, who had had previous dealings with the famous Harry.

The trouble we had half expected didn't come. Our man did not even move as we seized him, and Dinnie told him he would be arrested on suspicion. Perhaps he realized on this occasion that resistance would be useless and that violence would avail him nothing.

To Dinnie he said: "It's all right, Inspector, I shall give no trouble."

The man's calmness was amazing. He must have known that if

---

598 "with the exception of his collar" in *The Times*, 30 November 1898.

we succeeded in pinning the Paris robbery on to him he would get a long stretch at either Dartmoor or Parkhurst, yet he didn't turn a hair. I admired his bearing as years later I did that of Crippen when I arrested him on the charge of murdering his wife, Belle Elmore.

Harry submitted to my search of the clothes he was wearing. I found nothing worth mentioning until I came to the pockets of his waistcoat. Then, as though to dispel any doubts as to the guilt of the man we were arresting, I brought out, one by one, three magnificent diamonds, which sparkled under the light of the gas lamp, which by this time had been lit.

That these were part of the Paris haul I had no doubts at all. But even the production of the stones left our prisoner unconcerned–at least about himself. His only thought seemed to be of Miss X. He began to ply us with questions about her. Had we seen her recently? Was she all right?

The search of the room brought other jewels to light. These, together with the others we had found in his waistcoat pocket, we took with our prisoner to Scotland Yard.

Later other jewellery was recovered–some from a dealer in Middlesex Street, I remember–but of the £25,000 worth stolen only £5000 worth was traced.

While Harry was awaiting trial Miss X became something of a nuisance to Dinnie and myself.

She was continually sending telegrams to the Yard offering more information. On each of these occasions I went to see her, only to find that she had nothing of value to communicate.

Miss X was, of course, one of the leading witnesses for the prosecution, but it was only with the greatest reluctance that she went into the witness-box at the West London Police Court where the preliminary proceedings were heard.

At each police court hearing Harry would plead with me and with other officers to be allowed to see the woman whose evidence was sending him to penal servitude. She was just as anxious to see him.

The name Harry the Valet had given us was William Johnson, while his age he put down as 46. By occupation he claimed to be a dealer. He was–in stolen property.

Among the aliases by which he was known to the police were,

Harry the Valet, Williams, James, Wilson and Villiers.[599]

When the case came for trial at the County of London Sessions, Clerkenwell, Harry saved a lot of time and trouble by pleading guilty.

The indictment charged him with "having in his possession, without lawful excuse and knowing them to have been stolen, a white enamelled cross set with four large diamonds and small rubies; a dog collar, trellis pattern, of pearls and diamonds; a long silver muff chain set with 205 diamonds; a long rope of fine quality pearls; a chain of small rubies and diamonds; a diamond dragonfly brooch; a butterfly of diamonds, rubies and emeralds; a gold purse set with coloured and precious stones,[600] and a large number or opal, diamond, turquoise and pearl rings, the property of Mary, Duchess of Sutherland, which had been stolen outside the United Kingdom."

Mr. R. D. Muir (later Sir Richard and now deceased)[601] prosecuted. Sentence was postponed in order to give Harry a chance to reveal the whereabouts of the jewellery which had not been recovered.

This he flatly refused to do. "Not if I receive a life sentence," he declared.

I interviewed him at the remand prison, Holloway, to try to get him to change his mind, but he was adamant.

I was standing close to the dock when the prisoner was brought up to receive his sentence. He leaned forward and whispered in my ear:

"Tell the Court I wish the money found on me to be handed over to the Duchess."

The amount was £320, made up of one £200 note, a £100 note a £10 note and £10 in gold.

---

599 In his book, *The Unreliable Life of Harry the Valet*, Duncan Hamilton called *I Caught Crippen* "an instant best-seller" in which Dew "lazily called him either Harry or William Johnson." (p. 271). In fairness to Dew, he didn't give the names of any of the criminals he wrote about in *From Pitch and Toss to Murder*, instead using initials, blanks or aliases. If Dew had known the Valet's real name he would not have put it in his book. According to Hamilton the Valet's real name was Henry Thomas Sands. (*Ibid.*, p. 276).

600 *STWN*, 22 August 1936, included, "a gold purse set with diamonds and pearls; a gold bracelet set with coloured and precious stones and a large number of opal, diamond, turquoise and pearl rings."

601 Dew gave a similar description of Muir in the Crippen part of his book. (*ICC*, p. 63).

The judge passed sentence of seven years' penal servitude, and ordered that the £320 and all the jewellery recovered should be handed over to the Duchess.

Harry the Valet remained undaunted by the sentence.

"I've got a lot of clothes. What about them, my Lord?" he asked the judge. "They will be returned to you," he was told.

"Thank you, my Lord," said Harry with a smile which could not have been broader had five years been taken off his sentence.

But this request was not so idle as it may seem. Harry had a wonderful wardrobe. Good clothes were part of his stock-in-trade. He loved nothing better than to live extravagantly and dress in the height of fashion.

His first meeting with Miss X had been at Brighton. Harry the Valet had been having a lean time, and although perfectly groomed as usual, he was practically penniless.

Miss X helped him. The friendship ripened, and this was strong enough in the case of the woman to survive the knowledge which came to her of the man's real character.

Harry the Valet's most profitable game was the stealing of diamond merchants' pocket-books, or as his own counsel once jokingly remarked: "the picking up of unconsidered trifles at railway termini".

Many years passed before I saw Harry the Valet again. And how different were the circumstances!

The man who had been noted for his spectacular crimes, and who had brought off the great Gare du Nord coup, was standing in the dock at the Old Bailey charged with stealing an empty pocket-book from an overcoat at Holborn Viaduct!

But Harry hadn't intended to steal an empty pocket-book. The place at which the theft took place was used by Hatton Garden diamond merchants. Harry doubtless hoped to find some in the pocket-book he stole. He was unlucky to find it empty, and still more unlucky to get caught.

After he had been found guilty I went into the witness-box and read out his long criminal history.[602] The judge then sent him back

---

602   This included four months' hard labour for stealing a diamond merchant's pocket book at the Holborn Restaurant in 1891. (*The Times*, 5 January 1899). Dew later angrily refuted claims he and Crippen had ever dined together at that establishment. (*ICC*, p. 15).

to penal servitude for five years.[603]

IX[604]

STRANGE coincidences often occur in the life of a detective, which appear almost unbelievable, as for instance the following:

Many years ago you could go into many shops in London and other places, and for a few shillings purchase what can be described as an imitation Victoria Cross; but you can't do that now, and I will tell you why.

Many years ago, when I was a young inspector at the Yard,[605] we were somewhat startled to have reports that a dashing young man was visiting military barracks in and around London, dressed in a private's uniform of a famous Irish cavalry regiment, wearing what appeared to be the Victoria Cross and several war medals.

He entertained the soldiers with a vivid story as to how he had won the "Cross" and the medals. He told the story well, and being a fine figure of a man, he was made heartily welcome and treated to the best by the non-commissioned officers and men, sometimes being invited to stay the night.[606]

But alas, very soon after he had bid his farewells, it was discovered that some valuable articles had mysteriously disappeared from the officers' quarters; a gold watch, sleeve links, a valuable fur coat belonging to the colonel, and so on.

At first the N.C.O.'s and men did not attach any suspicion to their visitor, the smart young cavalryman.

They reported the thefts as they occurred to the police of the district in which the barracks were situated, but no clue was obtained as to the man or the missing property.

603 The Valet stood trial under the name of Thomas Williams. He had stolen the pocket-book and three cheque forms at the Holborn billiard-room from Mr. G.C. Bower, a stockbroker. (*Weekly Dispatch*, 5 April 1908). Like Dew, the Valet sold his life story to *Thomson's Weekly News* who published it as a six-part serial from 27 March-1 May 1926.

604 This chapter did not appear in the newspaper serialisation.

605 Dew was based at Hammersmith at the time of this case, not Scotland Yard. (*Police Review and Parade Gossip*, 30 December 1910).

606 He was Thomas Fowell, alias Frank Butler, aged twenty-eight. Fowell's deception was aided by having previously served in the army and having a bullet scar on his left forearm. He knew barrack routines and when rooms were likely to be unattended and easier to rob. (Hertfordshire Archives and Local Studies, HPF/H/24).

When the colonel had his valuable fur coat stolen from Hounslow Barracks he promptly reported it to Scotland Yard, and I was directed to take up the inquiries.[607]

Being at the Yard, I naturally had a roving commission, which gave me an advantage over the divisional detective, who would naturally restrict his inquiries to the particular thefts in his own district, whereas I could embrace them all.

I soon discovered that no Victoria Cross had ever been bestowed on any man by the name this man gave.

I set to work, and having obtained a full description of our "Admirable Crichton",[608] I circulated it throughout the country, for there was no knowing when this man might transfer his attention to barracks outside London.

I then conferred with the various officers who were engaged in the inquiries before I took charge, and arranged that a special look-out should be kept in every district, for surely a man in this very smart uniform, wearing medals and what appeared to be the Victoria Cross, must soon be spotted.

Nevertheless he was not, and neither could I obtain any clue as to his whereabouts, although I almost haunted the places where the barracks were situated. I had no better luck in tracing any of the loot. The officers of all the barracks were requested to have the man detained should he turn up, all without avail.

At this period I believe there was a barracks situated near Dalston in the North of London, where this man had paid one of his profitable visits,[609] anyhow, I found myself frequently in that neighbourhood, thinking it a likely place for our friend to hang out.

What I could not understand was, how could this man, wearing such a striking uniform, stroll about London, without being spotted?

It might be said, that all soldiers wore a striking uniform in

---

607 The theft of Captain Frederick Lehmann's coat took place on 24 January 1901, just three days after Fowell had been released from prison for housebreaking. Two days later Fowell broke into Shorncliffe Barracks in Kent where he stole a gramophone, after which he went to Canterbury where he committed more thefts from army officers. (*The Times*, 27 March 1901).

608 A reference to the J. M. Barrie play of 1902, in which the eponymous Crichton vaults several social classes by virtue of a shipwreck on an isolated island.

609 He had stolen a ring there from Walter Terry on 5 March. (*The Times*, 27 March 1901).

those days; yes, but not one like this famous regiment.[610]

So days passed, until one morning, somewhere about noon, I was strolling along a road of fair class dwelling-houses, between Dalston and Stoke Newington, when I became almost flabbergasted to see approaching me a smart young man dressed in the identical uniform I have described.

I was alone, and thought, now what's best to be done? is it my man or not?

My doubts were soon set at rest, for as he passed me I saw several medals and a cross on his breast, and his description was that of the wanted man.

Without taking any notice of him, I let him pass, then turned and followed him, thinking it wise to discover where he went. He might lead me to his lodgings. Sure enough he did, for after going a short distance, he entered the gateway of one of the houses, mounted the steps, and inserting a key in the lock was about to enter, when I sprang up the steps, grabbed hold of him and forced him into the passage of the house, at the same time telling him who I was, and should arrest him for stealing valuable from various barracks in London.

To my astonishment he put up no fight or resistance.

The landlady hearing a commotion, came up, and after I had explained my standing, she bustled along and showed me the man's bedroom, upon searching which, I discovered pawntickets for all the missing property, which was ultimately handed over to the rightful owners.

When X got over his surprise, he treated the whole matter as a joke, and told me where he had purchased the bogus cross, which was not a hundred miles from Charing Cross, and offered to do all he could in the way of restitution.[611]

I thought this young man had masqueraded long enough in false colours, so I made him strip and get into mufti, after which, the landlady having procured me a four-wheel cab (no taxis in those days), I took him to Hounslow, where he was charged.

---

610   The 5th Lancers.

611   Dew described the replica medal as "an exact imitation of the real thing." Fowell told him that he had just had his name inscribed on it that day. The usual cost of a bogus Victoria Cross was £2. (*The Canterbury Journal*, 30 March 1901).

The three silver medals he was wearing he admitted buying, and although he had been in the army, the army thought they would prefer his absence to his company, and he was not entitled to any decorations at all. This, of course, all happened before the Great War.

After appearing before the magistrates he was finally sent for trial at the Old Bailey.

In the meantime I was making inquiries as to why it was so easy to purchase an imitation of such a highly honoured decoration, the result of which was communicated to high authorities.

The man was tried before Sir Forrest Fulton, K.C., the Common Serjeant (now deceased), and sentenced to five years' penal servitude.[612]

The judge passed some scathing comments concerning the sale of imitation Victoria Crosses, and directed me to place the full facts before the proper authorities, which had already been done.

I am pleased to relate that in consequence the matter was brought before Parliament and a short act passed making it a penal offence to sell these bogus Victoria Crosses.

This was one of those cases in which perseverance and some luck helped in this capture, which earned for me high commendation.

––––––

I could go on recounting stories of my career in the police service, but space and other reasons will not permit.[613]

The cases of murder I have related are not the only ones I had to deal with. Unfortunately there were many others, brutal ones all of them, and most of the culprits found their way to the gallows.

Whatever district I was in murders cropped up, and even at the Yard I was involved in them. Once I was sent to a distant town to investigate a most fiendish murder, which left a lasting impression on my mind. But I refrain from going into the details of these lest

---

612 Actually seven years, although he was released after five on 14 August 1906. That day he went to Shornecliffe Barracks and was caught robbing an officer's room. Walter Dew attended the East Kent Quarter Sessions to give evidence of Fowell's previous convictions. Fowell was given a seven-year sentence with the remaining year and a quarter from his previous sentence added to it. (*The Whitstable Times*, 20 October 1906).

613 This epilogue did not appear in *TWN*.

it should give pain and annoyance to some of the relatives, or those associated with the cases.

Apart from "Jack the Ripper" case, I was never associated with what is described as "An unsolved murder".[614]

What always impressed me was, the amount of sympathy extended to the "murderer", in comparison to the victim and relations.

There were other matters I had charge of, which at the time created wide interest. One in particular was a *cause célèbre*, which for many months kept the world agape. It was a false claim to great estates, and ended in some of those associated with it finding themselves in prison for long periods.[615]

Again I refrain from going into details for the same reason as expressed above.

Looking back at my nearly 30 years' service in the police,[616] and forgetting the black side of it, I could well describe it as a life of thrills and adventure rarely given to one man to experience.

---

614 Dew's assertion may not be entirely true. In 1900 two new-born male infants were found dead in his division. The first was found on a train at Hammersmith wrapped in a parcel. He had been suffocated by having cotton wool stuffed in his mouth. The second was found in West Kensington, wrapped in an apron. He had been choked to death by a piece of tape that was still wrapped around his neck. The verdict at their inquests was "wilful murder by some person or persons unknown." Additionally the Salisbury murder of Edwin Haskell in 1908 was officially unsolved, although Dew and Froest were satisfied that his mother was guilty.

615 This was the Druce-Portland inheritance case that involved a bogus claim to the deceased 5th Duke of Portland's title and fortune. In a bizarre and long drawn out affair, descendants of a London man named Thomas Charles Druce argued that he had in fact been the Duke of Portland who had led an eccentric double life. Their story of Druce staging a fake funeral at Highgate Cemetery in 1864 was disproved when his corpse was exhumed in December 1907 in Dew's presence. After the case had collapsed, Dew arrested Mary Robinson in January 1908 for committing perjury. Robinson hoped to profit by claiming that she knew Druce and Portland were one and the same. If the Druce family's claim had been successful they would have rewarded Robinson handsomely for helping their cause. In her Clapham flat, Dew found many incriminating papers including a diary purporting to cover the years 1861-1862 and 1868-1870. Dew thought it had been written by Robinson, but in one sitting rather than over a period of years. She pleaded guilty and received a four-year sentence. The 6th Duke of Portland gave Dew a cheque for £100 to thank him for his work on the case. A full account of the case can be found in Piu Marie Eatwell's *The Dead Duke, His Secret Wife and the Missing Corpse* (2015).

616 His exact length of service was twenty-eight years and 176 days. (PRO, MEPO 21/39).

A game of pitch and toss.
(Living London)

Umbrella thief Mary Reynolds.
(Hertfordshire Archives and Local Studies)

Inspector Walter Dew.
(Thomson's Weekly News)

Thief and all-round scoundrel Archibald Johnstone.
(Hertfordshire Archives and Local Studies)

A London pawnbroker's shop.
(Living London)

Army barrack thief Thomas Fowell in 1897 and 1914.
(Hertfordshire Archives and Local Studies)

The murder of Edwin Haskell at Salisbury in 1908.
(The Illustrated Police News)

APPENDICES

APPENDIX 1 –
WALTER DEW'S OTHER WRITINGS

W ALTER DEW was a reader of the *Daily* and *Sunday Express* newspapers. In 1926 the *Daily Express* offered a £100 prize for true-life stories. Dew submitted an account of the Crippen case and won the prize.

The author, to whom a cheque for £100 will be sent to-day, is:

EX-INSPECTOR DEW,

25, Ebury-street, S.W.1.[1]

"My Race with Crippen" is the title of the story, which describes Ex-Inspector Dew's dash across the Atlantic to capture one of the most notorious criminals in modern history.

MY RACE WITH CRIPPEN.

By WALTER DEW

(Ex-Chief Inspector, Criminal Investigation
Department, New Scotland Yard).

In this story from real life ex-Chief Inspector Dew tells of his part in the Crippen murder case. Although the writing is a strange blend of the picturesque with the abrupt style of a police report, it constitutes a grimly fascinating narrative.

THE most extraordinary case in my career, brimful of excitement and thrills, was that of the notorious "Dr." Crippen, in which cold, calculated murder and great love and devotion were mingled.

Much has been written concerning this extraordinary little man, but as one of the chief actors in the drama this is the first time I have written on the subject or disclosed anything concerning him.

No one had more opportunity of studying this mild, benevolent-looking man, yet a fiend incarnate, but, strangely enough, in some respects a likeable

---

1   Dew's business address.

person when occasionally he lifted the veil of inscrutability enveloping him and showed the workings of his mind.

His wife, Cora, a minor music-hall artist, had not been seen for some time, and Crippen explained this by saying she was visiting relatives in America: later he said she was dead, and this apparently satisfied most people, but a great friend of Cora returned from America, was not satisfied, and came to the "Yard."

It is strange that a woman with so many associates should be missing for five months and no trouble taken to find her, but so it was.

The matter being placed in my hands, I eventually interviewed Crippen and Ethel Le Neve, and paid a visit to his house at Holloway, but had no power to make an arrest as no crime was disclosed.

Very soon after this they disappeared, the woman disguised as a boy.

How vividly it comes back to me, my search for them, their descriptions and photographs sent all over the world, my frequent visits to the house at Holloway, my search for Mrs. Crippen, or some trace of her remains.

That house in Holloway had a strange attraction for me: always I had a reluctance to leave it: that sinister cellar seemed to draw me to it. A loose board near the door each time it was stepped upon seemed to creak out, "Stop, stop."

The constant delving in that cellar until one day a brick giving way under my continual search, the digging, and finding the awful thing deep in the ground.

Who can imagine the horror and thrill that went through me? At length I had discovered a clue to the poor creature who had vanished many months before as thought the earth had opened and swallowed her, as, indeed, it had.

It was on a beautiful summer's morning in 1910 that the world was horrified at reading of that terrible discovery.

For me there was no rest, night or day, searching here, there and everywhere, piecing the evidence together to prove the remains were those of Mrs. Crippen, better known as "Belle Elmore." Plenty of so-called clues leading nowhere.

One evening, about seven o'clock, I returned to the "Yard" fagged out and somewhat disheartened, but determined to peg away.

At this moment a telegram is handed to me. It is from the Liverpool police, saying: "Wireless received from steamer Montrose, three days out from Antwerp bound for Montreal, two men aboard, suspected being

Crippen and Le Neve."

Why I don't know, but a wave of optimism swept over me. It seemed it must be them.

It took me a moment to jump into a cab and rush off to see my dear old chief, Sir Melville Macnaghten, whose death some time ago I deeply deplore.[2]

Fortunately he was at home, and on reading the telegram he said, "What's your opinion?" On telling him I thought it was Crippen, he said, "So do I. What's to be done?" I replied some one should go after the Montrose.

Always a man to act promptly and of few words, he said, "You are the man to go. Leave at once. You have a free hand to act as and how you like, only bring him back safely."[3]

He wrote this on a small scrap of paper as my authority, shook hands, and wished me good luck, and I left his house ten minutes after I had entered, thrilled and delighted he had reposed such faith in me on a mere telegram.

A few hours later found me on board the Laurentic, under the nom de plume of Mr. Dewhurst, and Liverpool was soon left behind.

How can I describe my feelings of the next few days? Should I overtake the Montrose? Should I find Crippen on board? Or was I on a wild goose chase?

The excitement of constantly trying to reach the Montrose by wireless, yet never succeeding: the suspense was almost intolerable.

Outwardly I doubtless appeared calm and comfortable, but inwardly I was filled with anxiety.

Although not aware of it, my secret departure had been discovered, and great excitement prevailed all over the world.

This accounted for many wireless messages I received on entering the St. Lawrence River, some amusing, some otherwise, but that belongs to another story.

This increased my anxiety, for if people were sending messages to me, might they not be sending them to the Montrose?

I decided to land at Father Point, a tiny hamlet on the St. Lawrence, where the pilots come aboard.

Arriving there on a Friday afternoon I was disconcerted to see the pilot's launch crowded with journalists and camera men.

---

2   Macnaghten had died in 1921.
3   Why only bring "him" back? Ethel Le Neve was wanted too.

I knew secrecy was no longer possible when, on seeing me, they gave a mighty cheer and shouted my name and levelled a whole battery of cameras at me. However, we got on well together.[4]

I was relieved to hear from the genial French-Canadian pilot that the Montrose had not passed nor been heard of.

I rushed to the wireless station, where the operator became quite enthusiastic in his efforts to help me get in touch with the Montrose.

At last, what joy, he had got the Montrose: then messages to and fro to the captain. I knew then I must possess my soul in patience until Sunday, before which time the ship could not reach Father Point.

During this period, owing to the courtesy of the representative of a great London newspaper, I heard of a scheme of some of the very enterprising journalists to construct a raft, find their way down the St. Lawrence, and be taken on the Montrose as shipwrecked mariners, and endeavour to interview the suspects.

This expedition had to be frustrated, because if Crippen was on board and became suspicious, he would commit suicide. Therefore I must board the Montrose before any one else.

In the end I succeeded by a little diplomacy in making such arrangements as would satisfy every one.

It was a delightful Sunday morning, in the distance a church bell ringing, all apparent peace. At this moment I was not so much the Scotland-yard officer as the small boy who went to Sunday school in response to a similar bell.

A great pity overwhelmed me at the thought that in a few minutes I should perhaps confront a man who would never more know the delights of freedom.

The Montrose is seen approaching: the gentlemen of the Press on the pilot launch. I have donned the pilot's uniform lent me by the genial pilot.

This disguise is necessary because Crippen may recognise me. At last we are being rowed towards that towering ship which even in this contingency must keep on its way: I must board her as she glides along, and I wondered how, as I am no sailorman.

I am alongside. I see a rope ladder dangling from what appeared to me the top of St. Paul's. I gave a gasp, the pilot shouted: "Jump for it." I did, and by the help of Providence caught it, and found myself twisting and twirling with one foot in the water and my back knocking the ship's side.

---

4   They did not and Dew would later admit this.

Somehow I climbed it and was never more relieved when two pairs of hairy arms hauled me on deck.

After paying my compliments to the captain on the bridge, I turned and saw a little man on the deck below. A sigh of relief escaped me. It was Crippen.

Approaching and holding out my hand I said: "Good morning, Dr. Crippen." He looked up wonderingly as much as to say, "Why does the pilot address me?" I said: "I'm Inspector Dew." He gave a start, turned a greenish hue, the apple of his throat throbbed up and down, then calmly clutching my hand, he said, "Good morning, Mr. Dew."

I found the whole of the murdered woman's jewellery pinned on the undervest he was wearing.

Proceeding to his cabin, I found his companion dressed as a boy. She turned, recognised me and gave a terrific shriek and fainted.

Thus ended my 3,000 miles chase and capture of a monster in human form, yet who proved there is good in the worst of us.[5]

In December 1926 Agatha Christie, the well-known author of detective stories, mysteriously disappeared. Her car was found abandoned halfway down a grassy slope at eleven o'clock one morning with its headlights still on. The newspapers made much of the disappearance of the writer whose work was so closely associated with crime and mystery. The *Sunday Express* asked Dew for his opinion and he was forthcoming:

VANISHED WOMAN WRITER NOT DEAD.

CHIEF INSPECTOR DEW'S THEORY.

WANDERING.

MIND AFFECTED BY HER NOVELS?

By Ex-Chief Inspector WALTER DEW

(The man who caught Crippen).

IT is natural with many of us to fear the worst in a case that excites public attention. Foul play is one of the many theories that are being advanced privately and publicly to account for the disappearance of Agatha Christie.

Foul play is possible, but I do not think there has been foul play. It is just conceivable that she has been murdered, and that her body will soon be

5   *Daily Express*, 23 November 1926.

discovered, hidden, say, in some spot near the house, or perhaps where her car was found.

Those who support this theory say that it must be the secret belief of the police, or they would not have carried out such a thorough search in the case of a missing woman. They point out that this is not usual in all cases of disappearance.

NO FOUL PLAY.

Even if the missing woman is safe and well, and, as some think, laughing in hiding at the hullabaloo she has caused, I think the police are justified in the course they are taking. They would look ridiculous if they had given up on the search and the body of the woman–possibly murdered–were found subsequently.

I cannot subscribe to the theory of foul play, however. I have had experience of one famous case of a woman's disappearance–that of Belle Elmore–and of her murderer, Crippen. This case is altogether different.

Agatha Christie has been writing detective stories, and one suggestion is that the publicity of a disappearance would be good for the sales of her books. That might be the view of an unknown actress out for publicity, but no clever woman novelist of her standing would believe that to disappear for publicity's sake would be of service to her in her work.

I reject the theory of voluntary disappearance for pecuniary advantage, as I do the murder theory.

She may have had other motives for disappearing besides publicity, such as that of causing annoyance to some one else. That time may prove or disprove.

I am content to accept loss of memory or hysteria as the likeliest reason for her absence.

Against that one has to set the fact that the district is being combed thoroughly, so far without success. Surrey is a large place, however. There are thousands of acres that might conceal an exhausted or dead body.

HYSTERIA?

I remember that in Richmond Park, only ten miles from London, a dead body escaped discovery for a long time.[6] There are numerous other places in Surrey that have not been searched.

---

6   This might refer to the discovery of the remains of William Ellacott. He had been missing since 16 July 1920 and "little more than a skeleton" was all that was left of him when he was found in Richmond Park in October 1920. At the same time the skeleton of an unknown man with a bullet wound to the head was found in the park. (*The Times*, 16 October 1920).

Agatha Christie is a woman whose work focussed her attention on crime and things sinister. She wrote detective stories, thought about crooks and murder all day, and possibly her subconscious brain was at work on these subjects all night.

These reflections might affect the minds of strong men; even public executioners have gone crazy. Agatha Christie may have had other, possibly smaller, things than plotting novels to worry her. These together may have brought on a condition of hysteria.

All women are subject to hysteria at times. If Mrs. Christie's mind became hysterical she may have gone wandering over the country, on and on, with the false strength of the half-demented, until she dropped in some spot miles away from where she is being sought now.

She even may have found her way to London, or some other town.

It is said there has been so much publicity that it would be impossible for her to hide in London. I do not believe it. London is still one of the easiest places in which to hide.[7]

Dew had certainly hedged his bets over what had happened to Christie. The writer did have other matters on her mind. Her mother had recently died and she had discovered that her husband Archibald had fallen in love with a friend's secretary named Nancy Neele. Agatha had booked into a hotel in Harrogate under the name of Neele and was found there on 14 December. Dew commented again on the case:

MRS. CHRISTIE'S SECRET.

By EX-CHIEF INSPECTOR DEW

(late of Scotland-yard).

The explanation offered to account for the disappearance of Mrs. Christie is that she has been suffering from loss of memory.

If this is so hers is indeed a remarkable case. In my long experience I have known of many authenticated cases of disappearance caused by loss of memory, but in every one of these cases there has been evidence of some mental aberration on the part of the person who has been missing.

I have known of a number of cases in which the missing man or woman has wandered about aimlessly for some considerable time, and has been found eventually in an exhausted condition or in an institution, but I have

7   *Sunday Express*, 12 December 1926.

never known of a person suffering from loss of memory found in such circumstances as Mrs. Christie.

Mrs. Christie was able, after her motor-car was abandoned, to make her way to London, where a letter was posted to Colonel Christie's brother, and from London she was able to proceed to Harrogate. It appears that Mrs. Christie has been living a normal life at the hydro where she was found. If the explanation of loss of memory is to be put forward, it must be considered in the light of all the surrounding circumstances.

The acumen displayed by Mrs. Christie makes the explanation all the more remarkable.

The climax of the mystery will come as no surprise to those who have studied human nature and have had long experience of the investigation of mystery cases.

No trained investigator could have failed to notice that the most significant feature of Mrs. Christie's disappearance was that there was so much mystery about it, and those of us who have had to deal with human conduct in many strange phases have found time and time again that there are persons, chiefly women, of such curious mentality that their actions cannot be accounted for according to normal standards.

The psychology of Mrs. Christie is difficult to understand. Here we have a woman of ability and position, and with a considerable experience of the world, who takes it into her head to vanish in mysterious circumstances which must have caused her family and friends great anxiety and distress.

Why should she have chosen to disappear? Was she suffering from what psychologists might describe as a publicity complex, or was it just sheer curiosity to test whether a person could disappear and remain hidden for a considerable period in spite of a hue and cry?

We know Mrs. Christie was a writer of detective fiction, and that she was continually busying her mind evolving sensational plans for her stories of crime and adventure. Mystery seems to have had a fascination for Mrs. Christie all her life, and I am inclined to think that she had allowed this fascination to become almost an obsession.

Morbid curiosity is sometimes the cause of irrational conduct. I can only imagine that Mrs. Christie had an insatiable desire to figure as the central character in a great disappearance mystery which would prove or disprove the theories she held.

The police had no alternative but to assume that a tragedy might well have occurred. They have had to assume that a woman of Mrs. Christie's education and position would have relieved the anxiety that was felt for her had she been able to do so.

It may be that when Mrs. Christie vanished the tremendous publicity given to her case was rather more than she had bargained for. If this was so we can understand a little better why she remained silent so long.[8]

The Christies divorced in 1928.

The year after Agatha Christie's disappearance Dew was once against asked by the *Sunday Express* to comment on a headline-grabbing story. This time it was the murder of P.C. George Gutteridge on the Romford to Ongar road in Essex on 27 September 1927. The murder was particularly shocking as the killer had shot Gutteridge in the head several times including in both eyes. This may have been in the belief that, as in the case of Mary Kelly in 1888, the murder victim's eyes retained an image of the last thing they saw. James Berrett, with whom Dew had worked with on the case of Conrad Harms in 1909, led the investigation:

PANIC THEORY OF THE ESSEX MURDER.

FAMOUS DETECTIVE RECONSTRUCTS THE CRIME.

BLIND FEAR.

PART PLAYED BY THE STOLEN CAR.

By Ex-CHIEF DETECTIVE INSPECTOR WALTER DEW.

(The man who caught Crippen.)

WERE the murderers of Police Constable Gutteridge, the Essex rural policeman who was shot dead in the lonely lane between Stapleford Abbots and Romford, desperate and experienced criminals, or were they comparatively inexperienced men, one of whom shot the constable under the nervous tension of fear and apprehension caused by his unexpected appearance and probable questions?

Why were these men in the neighbourhood, and why did they stop their car in that lonely road just before dawn?

These are the questions which present themselves to my mind in connection with this, the latest murder mystery, which the police have to unravel.

THE MOTIVE.

I have no actual experience of this crime or of the clues which are being

8   *Daily Express*, 15 December 1926. See also PRO, HO 45/25904.

followed, but as an interested member of the public, and as one who has assisted to unravel many murder mysteries–from that of the notorious Dr. Crippen to many lesser-known "lights" of crime–I feel inclined to put forward my own hypothesis of the probable cause of the crime.

But, it must be remembered, it is only an hypothesis. I do not pose as an authority on this latest mystery, or even as one possessing any inside information.

My theory, then, for what it is worth is this. We may assume that the murderers were out for robbery on a far more important scale than the mere theft of the car itself. Strangers would not travel to an obscure country town merely to steal a small car.

Many large houses in the neighbourhood contain objects of considerable value, and one or more of these houses may have been the object of the projected raid. We will assume, for the sake of argument, that it was either Lord Lambourne's house, Bishop's Hall, or that of a woman who is known to posses a valuable object of art.

MIDNIGHT WATCH.

The men decided then on their plan of campaign, the first step in which was to steal the doctor's car, for presumably they had found out that it was always kept ready for the road.

Previously they, or men who are supposed to be them, met at an inn in Billericay, where their earnest and secretive conversation and nervous manner are said to have attracted some attention.

The next we hear is that a man and woman who left Dr. Lovell's house well after midnight noticed two men in the road near the doctor's house, and commented on the fact. It was late for people to be abroad in such a quiet district.

Probably those two men were keeping a watch on the doctor's house to see when his guests departed and his household went to bed.

The doctor may not have retired immediately, or, if he did, there may have been sounds about his house which convinced the would-be car thieves that all was not yet quiet enough for them to rob the garage. That would account for the lateness of the hour at which the car was stolen.

Personally I believe that had Dr. Lovell not had guests that night his car would have been stolen some hours earlier.

WHY THEY STOPPED.

However, it was stolen, and the thieves drove off at high speed. At the fatal spot they stopped. Why?

I do not believe that they stopped because the murdered constable called on them to do so. No desperate man in a car at night would be likely to stop for a pedestrian.

My view is either that in the fog they missed a side turning–there is such a lane leading to Lord Lambourne's house, I believe–or that they halted for some adjustment to the car.

Then the constable came on the scene. He saw the stationary car and stopped to examine it. Possibly he recognised it.

Again, his suspicions may have been aroused by the mere appearance or demeanour of the men in it.

Whatever the reason he apparently thought that the circumstances warranted his taking a note of the car and the passengers.

He stood well in the light of the lamps and pulled out his notebook and pencil to do so. Then some one shot him.

He staggered, clutched at the car for support, and fell forward. The murderer or murderers, realising that desperate circumstances needed desperate measures, turned him over on his back and shot him again, twice, through the head. They wanted to make sure that he was dead. Then they fled.

Why was the constable shot?

"SHOT IN FEAR."

Every sort of theory has been advanced, but mine is simply that he was shot by a man in a bad state of nerves, whose fears and apprehensions were doubled by the sudden appearance of a policeman and the production of a notebook.

The murderer, I believe, was a young and possibly inexperienced man, jumpy and nervous, and so obsessed with the further crime which he and his companions had in view that the appearance of Police Constable Gutteridge acted on him like a shock.

He shot the policeman in blind fear.

This theory, is, I think, born out by the fact that many criminals, particularly burglars, are in a highly nervous condition while they are committing their crimes.

The public conception of the criminal as a man of callous, cold-steel nerves and unshakeable calm is by no means correct.

He is often in a state of bine [sic] funk the whole time. I have known case after case of this description. I have even known men who had committed a burglary almost faint with fright when the policeman's hand fell on their shoulders to arrest them.

Crippen was one of the rare exceptions, but he was a man of great intellectual qualities and iron self-control.

When I stepped aboard the ship to arrest him on his arrival in America [sic–Canada], six months after he had committed his crime, I said, "Good morning, Dr. Crippen."

He replied, "Good morning, inspector," but, although he must have known that I had come for him, he never flickered an eyelid. The only sign of emotion was that his Adam's apple moved convulsively up and down, as though he was gulping.

But I do not assume that the man or men in this case are criminals of the calibre of Dr. Crippen.

Finally, let me say that I am quite convinced that the murderer or murderers will be arrested within a short time. I know Chief Detective Inspector Berrett well. He is one of the most capable men at the "Yard," and any case which is entrusted to him is not long in being solved.[9]

Two car thieves, Frederick Browne and William Kennedy, were arrested in January 1928, found guilty of the murder and executed on 31 May 1928.

In 1929 Dew was interviewed by the *Sunday Express* and asked to give his views on the Croydon poisoning mystery which was making the headlines. Three members of the same family living in Birdhurst Rise had died from poisoning within an eleven-month period. The retired detective had a great deal of sympathy for the Scotland Yard officers investigating the case. Having been involved in perhaps the most famous poisoning case of all, Dew, who had lived in Croydon just a few years earlier, knew just what they had to contend with. His comments on the case echoed some of his feelings about the Whitechapel murders and the Crippen case.

NEW EXAMINATION OF THE DUFF CASE DOCUMENTS.
WHOSE POISON?

Ex-Inspector Dew, the man who caught Crippen, discusses the many obstacles which face the police in this baffling mystery.

By EX-INSPECTOR WALTER DEW.

---

9   *Sunday Express*, 2 October 1927. See also PRO, MEPO 3/1631.

SCOTLAND-YARD–in the Croydon poison mystery–is faced with a problem which might have been staged by the creator of Sherlock Holmes, and it is a problem which will require the assistance of a good many Dr. Watsons if it is to be solved.

Poison is elusive–particularly so far as a criminal investigation is concerned. The bullet or the knife finds its mark, but must leave behind the source of its origin, and therefore provide a clue to the murderer–a clue which incidentally seldom fails to reveal the culprit.

So far as the bullet is concerned, the Brown and Kennedy case proved to us that scientists–or even gunsmiths–can tell us by microscopical investigation the actual weapon by which a bullet is fired.

The poisoner, however, is the most difficult murderer with whom the police have to contend. He is subtle and cunning, and he is aided by the fact that his crime is rendered comparatively easy.

The victim may be attacked in a thousand different ways. I believe, in fact, it is on record that a subtle poison has even been impregnated into a glove, by which means the person who wore it met with an untimely death.

THE ACCUSING FINGER.

In the Duff case my whole sympathy goes out to the officers engaged in solving this mystery which has intrigued the world.

We have three persons dead–all of whom, after exhumation, were discovered to have died from arsenical poisoning.

First, we have Mr. Creighton Duff, who died on April 27, 1928. The coroner's jury brought in a verdict that he had been murdered by some person or persons unknown.

Secondly, there is Miss Vera Sidney, his sister-in-law, who drank arsenic in soup on February 14 this year, and died a few hours later. A similar verdict was returned in her case.

Then there is Mrs. Violet Sidney, the mother of Vera and mother-in-law of Mr. Duff. She died from arsenical poisoning nineteen days after her daughter, and in this case, the jury returned an open verdict, deciding, on the advice of the coroner, not to eliminate the possibility of suicide.

Now, what is the problem which presents itself to Scotland-yard? The accusing finger has failed to point itself to any particular individual.

The coroner, in his particularly careful analysis of the cases to the juries, bore on the point that it might be "this, that, or the other person" who had committed the crimes.

And as there was not a scrap of evidence to point to a murderer or a suggestion of motive the verdicts do not help the police in the slightest.

One is tempted to the conclusion, however, that one hand must have been responsible for the deaths of all three members of the family.

Whose hand, then? Assuming that since at the inquests no new facts have come into the possession of the detectives in charge of the case, then, indeed, it looks as if the police are faced with such an unfathomable mystery that no blame could possibly be attached to them if it passed into the lists of unsolved crimes.

The public little dream of the enormous amount of work entailed in endeavouring to solve such a mystery as this–of the heartbreaking disappointments in following clues which breathe success, and which are shattered after sleepless nights of investigation.

Arsenic can be obtained in many other forms, and here it must be apparent how difficult and prolonged were the inquiries of the police in endeavouring to trace the purchase of such a poison.

Chemists, probably throughout the country, would have to be interrogated on this point alone–obviously involving many officers and hundreds of hours of inquiry.

In all cases of poisoning, however, the chief difficulty is to prove, not that the person was poisoned, but that the accused person possessed the poison, had the opportunity and actually administered it.

It is certain, however, that so far from the negative results of the inquests deterring the police from following up the matter, I am convinced that it will only encourage them to renewed efforts, and although at the moment these mysteries seem to be insoluble, I still have hopes that Scotland-yard will eventually succeed in bringing to justice the murderer or murderers.

They accomplished this in the case of the murder of P.C. Gutteridge at a time when probably the public had come to the conclusion that there were no hopes of the murderer being traced–and they can do it again.

The apparent absence of motive in the Croydon case might lead to the supposition that the crimes have been the work of some person with the poison mind–that mysterious individual who kills without motive or idea of gain.

We shall see.[10]

---

10   *Sunday Express*, 1 September 1929. See also PRO, MEPO 3/861. The murders remained unsolved. The best account of this case is Richard Whittington-Egan's *The Riddle of Birdhurst Rise* (1975).

In 1934 Dew was upset to read an article that mentioned the Crippen case. The offending text appeared in the *Daily Mail* and was titled "WHAT A BIG CRIME COSTS THE NATION". It read:

Dr. Crippen, the murderer of Belle Elmore, his actress wife, made a dash for Canada with a woman companion. Before the first wireless message used in crime reached England–it revealed the whereabouts of Crippen– something like £10,000 had been spent in the search for him.

The trial that led to the conviction and execution added thousands more to the bill of costs against the public. It was, the authorities considered, money well spent, for the case showed how really strong the law is when a murderer's identity is known.[11]

Dew immediately wrote an angry response to the article to the editor of the *Daily Mail*, but it was not published:

"The Wee Hoose,"
10 Beaumont Road,
Worthing.

10th July, 1934.

To
The Editor
"The Daily Mail",
Northcliffe House,
London, E.C.

Dear Sir,

Re "What a Big Crime Costs the Nation".

I was interested to read the above mentioned article in to-days "Daily Mail".

I was more than interested, and indeed staggered, at the statement therein as follows:-

"Dr Crippen, the murderer of Belle Elmore, his actress wife made a dash for Canada with a woman companion. Before the first wireless used in crime, reached England – it revealed the whereabouts of Crippen – something like £10,000 had been spent in the search for him."

As the officer in charge of the inquiries, and the one who chased and

---

11   *Daily Mail*, 10 July 1934.

captured him in Canada, I should know something about the expenses incurred up to the time stated. I am puzzled indeed to know how £10,000 was spent?

Not one extra police officer was recruited and the pay of those engaged would still have gone on, whether Crippen had committed a crime or not, so it cannot be said that that was an extra charge on the Nation, and I doubt if my own expenses for cab fares up to the time the wireless was received, exceeded £2, and the extra costs, whilst I was making enquiries, as a Chief Inspector, for food allowance, would be 3/- per day, always supposing I could not reach home for a meal for a continuous period of nine hours, other officers of less rank would be paid in proportion.

Of course there was the printing of the Reward bills and other expenses, such as medical men, etc., and I should have thought I was exaggerating if I had suggested that up to the time of the wireless being received the cost would have exceeded £500.[12]

Maybe, Mr Hugh Brady [the author of the article] has some information as to the expenses incurred which I am ignorant of, but oh! £10,000 extra cost to the Nation before that famous wireless was received and that in 1910, too!

I really should be glad to be enlightened, and doubtless so would the taxpayers.

I am, Sir,

Your obedient Servant,

Walter Dew
Ex Chief Inspector,
C.I. Dept.,
New Scotland Yard.[13]

Nine days before the execution of Dr. Buck Ruxton for the murder of his common-law wife Isabella Van Ess and their nurse-maid Mary Rogerson at Lancaster on 14 September 1935, Walter

---

12   This was reduced to £300 when he wrote about it in *TWN*, 27 October 1934.

13   The letter is reproduced in Goodman, *The Crippen File*, p. 90. Dew also refuted the £10,000 claim in *TWN*, 27 October 1934, (see footnote 251), but this was left out of *I Caught Crippen*. Coincidentally the *Mail* had previously questioned the cost of the Crippen investigation, suggesting that it could amount to £5,000. They estimated that sending telegrams with descriptions of Crippen and Le Neve all over the world would cost £400. There were also 5,000 wanted posters, 2,000 extra copies of the posters in various languages and the employment of clerks to wrap and distribute the posters. (*Daily Mail* (overseas edition), 6 August 1910).

Dew gave his thoughts on the case. Ruxton had probably strangled his victims before dismembering their bodies. These he wrapped in newspaper and threw into a stream in Moffat, Dumfriesshire. Ruxton left behind a wealth of circumstantial evidence that led to his conviction for double murder and execution at Strangeways Prison in Manchester on 12 May 1935:

It Might Have Been the Perfect Murder

EX-CHIEF INSPECTOR DEW, the man who caught
Crippen, analyses the mistakes that condemned Dr Ruxton.

DR BUCK RUXTON is now lying in a condemned cell because, like many others, he attempted the perfect murder–and bungled it.

Yet all the circumstances may be said to have favoured him.

He was a doctor enjoying a wide practice. He was respected in the community.

His wife, we have been told, had often been away from home.

At the time of the murder he was the only man in the house. He could have carried out his crime, and, with his professional knowledge, defied all suspicion–but for his own mistakes.

Vanity contributed as much as anything to his undoing. He over-estimated his own cunning. He under-estimated the searching skill which, in these days, science brings to the aid of the police.

Dr Ruxton staked his life on the success or failure of his efforts to destroy every mark of identification on the bodies of his victims.

He might have succeeded, and become the perfect murderer, had he exhibited in other matters the same attention to detail which he mistakenly displayed in his cold-blooded surgical work.

RUXTON here made the same mistake as his fellow-doctor and fellow-murderer, Hawley Crippen, whom it was my good fortune when in harness at the Yard to catch and bring to justice.

When Crippen consigned the mutilated remains of Belle Elmore, his ill-fated wife, to their temporary grave underneath the coal cellar of their home in Hilldrop Crescent, Camden Town, he was so confident they would never be traced, he wrapped certain portions of the remains in his own pyjama suit.

This proved one of the most damning pieces of evidence against him.

Ruxton, though perhaps not from the same cause, fell into precisely the same error. With the remains at Moffat was found a blouse, which was recognised as the property of Mary Rogerson, the nurse-maid.

THE identity angle, to my mind, was the crux of the whole case.

Had the police failed to prove beyond all reasonable doubt the bodies were those of Mrs Ruxton and Mary Rogerson, it is quite possible, instead of now lying in a condemned cell, Ruxton would still be carrying on his practice at Lancaster.

The fact that he was a doctor aided the murder in eradication of all marks of identity on his victims.

But in another way his skill with the knife undoubtedly reacted against him.

One of the first conclusions reached by the doctors who examined the remains was that the bodies had been dismembered by a person with a thorough knowledge of anatomy.

Would he not have been wiser to have displayed less deftness in the use of that knife?

RUXTON'S first mistake was to murder TWO women.

My theory, and I believe it was the theory put forward by the prosecution at the trial, is that this was not a premeditated crime at all.

The doctor is clearly a man of violent passions, and I believe it was in a fit of frenzy he murdered his wife, probably by strangulation.

Poor Mary Rogerson was either an eye-witness of the crime or became cognisant of it soon afterwards, and she was killed for the simple reason she possessed the knowledge which would have sent Ruxton to the gallows.

Ruxton found himself with two bodies on his hands. Can you imagine the feelings of this highly-strung man?

That he was able in the circumstances to accomplish what he did— disfigure the bodies, mutilate them, and get them to that lonely spot in Scotland without serious suspicion falling upon him was little short of a miracle.

WHILE awaiting Nemesis to overtake him, Dr Ruxton made many mistakes, but these were the errors of a man driven to distraction by the thing he had done.

He lied. He had to do so. The sudden disappearance of his wife and the nurse had to be accounted for.

For an innocent man he was too talkative. He protested too much.

His requests to various potential witnesses to say things which were not true in order that he might account for his movements at vital periods also told heavily against him.

The plain fact was that Dr Ruxton had not the temperament to play his part and hide his guilt from the world.[14]

In May 1936 Dew wrote an article for *Thomson's Weekly News* after the murder by strangulation of two young women in the Soho district of London. Dew dismissed the suggestion that the murders were part of a series like the Jack the Ripper murders. Ultimately three women were murdered; two prostitutes, Josephine Martin (alias French Fifi, strangled with a silk stocking), Constance May Hind (strangled with an electric-light cord and beaten around the head with a blunt instrument), and a charlady called Jeanette Cotton (strangled with a silk scarf).

THESE SOHO CRIMES
By Ex-Chief Inspector Dew, of Scotland Yard.

I AM reluctant to believe that these Soho crimes can be attributed to what is thought to be a criminal of the type of Jack the Ripper, who caused such consternation in 1888.

In fact, I would go so far as to say there is nothing to cause alarm in the minds of women.

This class of murder, if it is murder, occurs periodically or in cycles. The victims in each case are women who live alone, as a rule. They are of a Bohemian character and invite strange men sometimes to their rooms or flats.[15]

In so doing they thus render themselves liable to attack by their visitor, who may or may not become enraged at some act or some conduct of their hostess–either fancied or real.

This class of woman is frequently attacked by men, and these attacks do not always come under the notice of the police.

They Won't Tell.

These women are never by any means anxious to expose their mode of

14   *The Sunday Post*, 3 May 1936. See also PRO, MEPO 3/793.
15   Dew was being very chivalrous with this description. He was hardly a stranger to investigating crimes involving prostitutes.

life, either to the police or the neighbours. I have known many instances, where an ill-tempered brute has wantonly attacked women without any or little provocation, but no prosecution has followed owing to the woman's reluctance to open her mouth.

It may be that some of the women of Soho are disinclined to talk about the present crimes, but I should doubt if this extends to many who could give the police any reliable information.

It is always found in any sort of crime that many are diffident about giving evidence owing to the fact that they have a very strong antipathy to attending to give evidence in a public court.

On the other hand the police are frequently overwhelmed by people who, in the main, wish to help them, but whose statements when inquired into are found to be quite valueless.

For my part, I have not the slightest doubt that in the end the police engaged on these particular crimes will run the culprit to earth.

It is only a matter of time and patience.

It does not follow that because no arrests up to the moment have been effected that the police are not in possession of evidence, although not of a sufficiently strong character to satisfy a jury.

What Police Must Consider

We have seen innumerable instances of this sort of thing. The public have become impatient at an immediate arrest not being made, when suddenly they are confronted with the fact that the police have got the "suspect" in their hands.

But the points I have to consider are these:

Within a very short space of time three women have been found strangled.

The first was a woman known as French Fifi who was found in her flat in Archer Street, Soho, with a silk stocking round her neck.

The second was Jeanette Cotton, another Frenchwoman, who was discovered in Lexington Street. A silk handkerchief was round her neck.

The last, and most recent case was that of Constance May Hind. Round her neck was a piece of copper wire.

All three women lived within a reasonable distance of each other.

Because of these facts, are we justified in assuming that each death had been brought about by the same hand?

I am inclined to believe that it is not so.

For the sake of argument, let us assume that these are the work of one person.

The natural inference then, is that either this person is carrying out a scheme of punishment or revenge, or, on the other hand, that he is a person of weak intellect.

First of all let us take the theory of revenge. I do not believe or support this theory. My reason is that there is nothing to indicate, so far, that there is any connection between the cases.

It is not even suggested that the women knew one another. Another thing I would like to emphasise is this–Great Britain is not a country in which this class of crime is perpetrated. However much foreigners may nurture a desire for revenge they are not inclined to follow their inclinations for two reasons. First of all, they know justice is swift over here, and, secondly, they do not want to do anything to destroy their residence in this hospitable country.

This leaves us with the other consideration.

Is it the work of a person of weak intellect?

Personally, I have never come in contact with a person of weak intellect who committed murders on a wholesale scale.

There have been a series of murders committed by one individual in the past.

I recollect, and the public will remember, the notorious Neil Cream. This man was convicted and executed for a series of murders of women of loose character in South London, to whom he gave pills containing poison.

Another well known case is Smith, of the Brides in the Bath murders. These two will suffice for the point I wish to make.

The point is this. Could either of these two men be looked upon as maniacal or insane? On the contrary. Neil Cream was a person of intelligence and cunning.

He certainly had a vein of cruelty in him, but I think notoriety more than anything else moved him to carry out his designs. I saw this man several times.[16] From my study of him, I wish to emphasise that there was nothing whatever of the madman about him.

And so far as Smith is concerned, his murders were committed for the purpose of becoming possessed of his poor victims' property. He married them, got their money and drowned them.[17]

---

16   Where had Dew seen Cream?
17   George Joseph Smith (1872-1915). Smith bigamously married a number of women and murdered three of them for their life insurance by drowning them in baths. Their deaths were initially recorded as accidental, but he was eventually arrested, tried and executed.

A Man Who Could Think.

It was systematic but, above all, the act of a man who could think out his schemes very cleverly.

There is nothing in the Soho crimes to indicate any of the traits shown by these two murderers.

It would appear that French Fifi was living in quite a different sphere of life to that of either of the other two women. It is doubtful if the same person who would be received at a comfortable flat would be in contact with the latest victim who lived in, shall we say, a less comfortable apartment in Old Compton Street.

Soho has recently come into notoriety by the fact of the murder of the man known as Red Max. Under no consideration could this have had anything to do with the other deaths in Soho and neighbourhood.[18]

Doubtless this has caused many of the public to believe that Soho is a hot-bed of crime and bad characters. It is nothing of the kind. It is the home of many hard-working and highly-respectable English and foreign shopkeepers and others.

These are just as law-abiding people as you will find in any other district or great city. True, it has its bad characters. But what district has not?

My advice is, don't be too ready to dwell on certain points as being too coincident, and jump to conclusions–particularly melodramatic conclusions.

My suggestion is to rely upon the great efficiency of the police officers who have charge of these cases and who, in my opinion, will eventually bring the culprit or culprits to justice.[19]

An unusual story appeared in the *Bromley & Kentish Times* in 1938. Written by Clayton Kent, it was titled "DREAM-SOLVED MYSTERIES" and concerned the police solving crimes from information received from people who had dreamt the solutions.[20] Dew's response to the article included a description of Crippen as "this unfortunate man", probably indicating that Dew thought Crippen was unfortunate to have been caught so close to escape.

---

18   Red Max was a pimp named Max Kassel who was shot in his Soho flat by George Lacroix, another pimp. His body was put in a car and dumped at St. Albans. Lacroix was later arrested in Paris and imprisoned for the murder. (PRO, MEPO 3/795).

19   *TWN*, 16 May 1936. See also PRO, MEPO 3/1702; 1706 & 1707. The crimes remained unsolved and Scotland Yard believed they were unconnected.

20   *Bromley & Kentish Times*, 24 June 1938.

"DREAM-SOLVED MYSTERIES."

To the Editor.

DEAR SIR,–My attention has been called to an article in your issue of the 24th ult., under the heading, "Dream-Solved Mysteries." Under the caption, "Doom of Crippen," your contributor says : –

"Had a friend of the unfortunate Belle Elmore not dreamed grimly of her one night and insisted on a search that led the detectives eventually to dig beneath the hearthstone of the infamous Dr. Crippen's house in North London, it is possible the crime might not have come to light."

As the officer who had charge of the Crippen case from the commencement of the inquiries to the end, who discovered the remains, and who chased and captured this unfortunate man on board the s.s. Montrose in Canada and brought him back to England, I hasten to say that the remains were not buried under the hearthstone, but under the bricks in the coal cellar.

The search was not instituted and insisted upon by a person who had had a grim dream concerning Belle Elmore.

The matter was taken up by me in consequence of a famous music-hall artist of that period calling at the Yard on her return from the U.S.A. and saying she was not satisfied with Crippen's story concerning his wife's death in America. After hearing her story I took the case up and made personal inquiries. She certainly did not insist that inquiries be made, but left it to the good sense of the police, and she certainly never mentioned anything about dreams.

It was my own perseverance which led to the discovery of the remains and capture of Crippen.

I feel sure your contributor wrote, and you published this in good faith, and under ordinary circumstances I should have taken no notice of the matter, but on May 19 last Messrs. Blackie and Son, publishers, London and Glasgow, published a book written by me under the title of "I Caught Crippen," Memoirs of ex-Chief Inspector Walter Dew, and this has aroused great interest throughout the country.

It may well be that many persons who read your paper will also read my book, which has already had a wide circulation, and wonder why I make no mention of this alleged incident.

Trusting you will give this the same publicity as the article.–Yours faithfully,

WALTER DEW,
Ex-Chief Inspector, C.I.D.,

New Scotland Yard.
The Wee Hoose, 10, Beaumont-road,
Worthing.[21]

Dearly Beloved Wife was a play based on the Crippen case that
was reviewed in *The Times* in 1938. The review commented on how
"the murderer's successful disarming of police suspicion" reflected
the real events of 1910.[22] Dew responded in a letter to the editor:

THE CRIPPEN CASE

TO THE EDITOR OF THE TIMES

Sir,–In your issue of October 31, under the heading of "London
Playgoers' Club" and *Dearly Beloved Wife*, your critic says: "The play is
readily recognized as a dramatization of the Crippen case." Further on it
says: "The story of a quarter-century ago is followed to the end, including
the murderer's successful disarming of police suspicion, the panic," &c.

I am the officer who had sole charge of the case from the moment it was
reported to police that Mrs. Crippen was missing. It was I who discovered
the remains and later chased and captured Crippen in Canada. Therefore
it must refer to me when it said: "Crippen successfully disarmed police
suspicion."

Will you permit me to say that from the moment I took up the inquiries
concerning the missing Mrs. Crippen I never for one minute (except for
a few hours' sleep) relaxed my efforts to clear this matter up, until on the
Wednesday I dug up the remains of this unfortunate woman in the cellar
at Hilldrop Crescent. This was all within a few days of my undertaking
the inquiry, and the very day after I interviewed Crippen I circulated the
description of Mrs. Crippen far and wide.

It is strange that if police suspicion was disarmed that I should have
done this and persisted in my efforts until I succeeded in discovering the
gruesome remains in the cellar, and all within such a short time, and it must
be remembered that until those remains were found there was no suggestion
of Crippen having committed any crime whatever.

I do not for a moment suggest that your critic intends to cast any reflection
on me–in all probability he does not know me–but some who read it might
take it in a different light.

I am, Sir, yours faithfully,

21   *Bromley & Kentish Times*, 8 July 1938.
22   *The Times*, 31 October 1938.

WALTER DEW (ex-Chief Inspector, C.I. Department, New Scotland
Yard, S.W.)
The Wee Hoose, 10, Beaumont Road, Worthing, Sussex.[23]

Dew attended a lunch at the Worthing branch of the Overseas
League in January 1939 and gave a talk to them at The Burlington
Hotel on 12 April that year. It was called "Leaves from my Notebook"
and touched upon the Crippen and Jack the Ripper cases, as well as
police conditions when he joined the Metropolitan Police:

Some people have the idea that the police have no feelings except the
desire to get convictions. It's queer, but people always seem to think of
a detective as a great, massive, brutal fellow, whereas in reality most
detectives are among the kindest-hearted men you can know.

So far as I can remember, I've never had a prisoner through my hands
without finding a little bit of good in him somewhere—although I must say
that sometimes it was very difficult to detect.

I've known very kindly things done by most criminals, and although
sometimes they might make the detective's blood run cold by telling him
on their way from the dock what they're going to do to him when they are
free, very often he will have a letter instead thanking him for various things
he may have been able to do.

He had this to say about the Whitechapel murders:

In 1887 I was appointed a detective. I was transferred to Whitechapel,
which was in those days was a den of thieves, ill-lighted and where it was
regarded as really dangerous to walk alone. The haunts and alleys were
infested with the worst gangs, and in some parts it was necessary for two
policemen to patrol together.

How the murderer, finally known as 'Jack the Ripper' time after time
could have got away after the crimes, is a mystery to this day. One would
have thought he could not have got ten yards for, apart from anything else,
he must have been covered with blood, yet he would manage a mile, and no
one would set eyes on him.

The police never, so far as I know, had the slightest inkling of who the
criminal was. In a library copy of my book of reminiscences, where I have
mentioned this fact, a reader has written against the text: Perhaps Inspector

23   *The Times*, 21 November 1938.

Dew did it.[24]

In 1943 the *Sunday Express* ran a story "that has nothing to do with war". It was a feature on the Whitechapel murders, extracted from the book *Sober Truth* by Margaret Barton and Osbert Sitwell.[25] Dew read the article and a fortnight later the newspaper published his response:

Jack the Ripper detective

AS perhaps the only police officer alive who assisted in inquiries throughout the series of "Jack the Ripper murders,"[26] I still retain the awful memory of seeing each of the victims.[27]

I was the first officer on the scene at Millers-court. What a fearful shock when I peeped through a window in that small back room!

It was suggested that the mutilations showed evidence of medical skill. I have always maintained that this was not so.

The poor girl Kelly was cut to ribbons as if a raging lunatic had been let loose with a knife. I have always considered that was the last murder committed by Jack the Ripper.

With regard to photographing the retina of the eye to see if it retained the picture of the murderer, Sir Charles Warren, the then Commissioner, visited Millers-court soon after we had the door opened, and at once had the girl's eyes photographed, in my presence, but, of course, without result.

Walter Dew,
Ex-Chief Inspector,
New Scotland Yard
10, Beaumont-road, Worthing.

[Chief Inspector Dew is famous as the man who caught Crippen.][28]

---

24   *The Worthing Herald*, 14 April 1939; *Worthing Gazette*, 19 April 1939. Dew gave a further talk to the League on 7 November 1939 entitled "More Leaves from My Note Book." It included the Crippen case. (Mentioned in *The Worthing Herald*, 10 November 1939, but no transcript of the talk was given).

25   *Sunday Express*, 3 October 1943.

26   There was at least one other retired police officer alive at that time who had worked on the investigation. James Stockley (1863-1954), joined the Metropolitan Police in 1885 and retired in 1911 with the rank of chief inspector. (PRO, MEPO 21/39).

27   In *I Caught Crippen* Dew wrote: "I did not see all the murdered women, but I saw most of them". (*ICC*, p. 127).

28   *Sunday Express*, 17 October 1943.

Colin Bennett from Devon read Dew's letter in the *Sunday Express* and wrote to him about the Crippen case. Bennett's theory was that "while Crippen did unquestionably cut up and bury his wife's body he did not kill her." He suggested that an unnamed assistant may have been responsible for the murder. "Are you still as sure as ever that in Crippen you hanged a murderer?" Bennett asked. Dew bluntly replied:

10 Beaumont Rd
Worthing
20.10.43

Dear Sir

Re "Crippen."

I beg to acknowledge yours of the 18th, and to inform you that I am not prepared to enter into any discussion on this subject, other than to say my conscience is quite at rest as the result of the case.

Yours faithfully
WD[29]

---

29 Reproduced in the *Western Daily Press*, 10 August 2007. There have been believers in Crippen's innocence since 1910. Some have even gone so far to suggest that Dew planted the remains in the cellar at 39 Hilldrop Crescent. For a discussion of the various claims about Crippen being innocent see Connell, *Doctor Crippen* (2006), pp. 168-191.

APPENDIX 2 –
CONTEMPORARY WRITINGS
ABOUT WALTER DEW

RETIREMENT OF INSPECTOR DEW.
Detective Who Tracked Crippen Takes His Pension.
IN MANY FAMOUS TRIALS.
Investigated Druce, Big Jewel, and Ripper Mysteries.

Last evening "Lloyd's Weekly News" was authoritatively informed that Chief Inspector Dew, of Scotland Yard, had tendered his resignation to the Chief Commissioner of Police.

It is a coincidence that the day is that of the final scenes in the High Courts of a case which has made the retiring officer's name famous. Although coinciding with the dismissal of the Crippen appeal, it is stated that Mr. Dew's decision has not been in any way affected by this case. He had already seriously considered his resignation before he was concerned in it, but consented to remain in office until its completion.

Chief Inspector Dew will not actually leave Scotland Yard for several weeks yet.[30] When he does, it is stated, he will set up in business as a confidential inquiry agent.

Joining the Metropolitan Police Force nearly twenty-nine years ago, Mr. Dew has been associated with the leading criminal cases of the past quarter of a century. He first came into prominence at the time of the "Jack the Ripper" crimes. For his services in relation to those cases he was promoted to the rank of detective-sergeant.

Since that time rapid progress has marked his career, until he came to one of the foremost positions in the service. After some years as inspector at Bow-street he attained the aim of every detective of the C.I.D.–he was four years ago appointed a chief inspector in succession to Mr. Frank Froest.

Chief Inspector Dew has produced proofs in hundreds of forgery charges.

---

30   His leaving date was 5 December 1910. (PRO, MEPO 21/39).

Several difficult murder cases were cleared up by him, and many huge frauds were exposed. Mr. Dew, after months of inquiries, had the satisfaction of securing the conviction of a clever swindler named Nicholson, who as an "orthnologist" [sic-ornithologist] specialist, obtained thousands of pounds by a clever advertising method in connection with the solving of easy rebuses.

In was in 1907 and 1908, when the Druce case was in full swing, that Mr. Dew was given a watching brief by the Commissioner, as the result of which one Saturday night in January, 1908, he arrested at Sisters-avenue, Lavender Hill, Miss Robinson, the Australian witness, on a charge of perjury. It will be remembered that Miss Robinson, the daughter of an ex-policeman, swore that she was an Australian, and that she was formerly a maid in the service of the fifth Duke of Portland at Welbeck, and that she knew, both from the duke and the late Charles Dickens, that Druce was an assumed name of the duke.

Prior to her arrest Miss Robinson had created some sensation by offering a hundred pounds reward for the recovery of a mythical diary which she said had been stolen from her to prevent her giving evidence in the case. Inspector Dew arrested her on the collapse of the Druce prosecution, and secured her conviction on the perjury charge at the Old Bailey.

This Year's Sensation.

It was whilst at Hammersmith that Mr. Dew broke into a flat in the Fulham-road and arrested "Harry the Valet," one of the most expert jewel thieves in the country, and the man who stole the Duchess of Sutherland's £20,000 jewels from the saloon carriage at the Gare du Nord.[31] "Harry the Valet" was a very tough criminal, but he was taken by surprise, and gave no trouble.

In June of last year Mr. Dew obtained a long term of penal servitude for Conrad Harms, alias Henry Clifford, the clever swindler, who drew £1,700 from Parrs Bank at Notting Hill after a forged note of credit had been sent there from one of the London branches of a well-known foreign bank.

This Harms had cleverly forged in America and sent on in advance. When he came over his arrest was brought about in a curious way. With one of the £100 notes, the proceeds of the fraud, he purchased a watch in the Strand, and, later, as the watch did not keep proper time, he took it back to the tradesman to have it adjusted. In the meantime the note had found its way to the Bank of England, and the inquiries which followed led to the

---

31   Dew was at Scotland Yard then, not Hammersmith.

watchmaker communicating with the police.

Eighteen months ago Mr. Dew was sent to Salisbury to take up the case in which Mrs. Haskell was accused of the murder of her cripple son. It was only after a second trial that she was acquitted.

During the whole of the "Jack the Ripper" outrages Inspector Dew was stationed in Whitechapel, and took part in all the exciting searches, incidents, and inquiries which these crimes entailed.

He was entrusted with the difficult task of unravelling the mysterious disappearance of Belle Elmore, and after the flight of Dr. Crippen he directed the excavations at Hilldrop-crescent which resulted in the discovery of the remains of the missing woman.

When news came by the "wireless" of Dr. Crippen's presence on the Montrose, Chief Inspector Dew was able to take a faster boat to Canada and await the vessel at Father Point.

Chief Inspector Dew has served twenty-nine years in the Metropolitan Police Force, and was, therefore, entitled to a pension three years ago. On the Continent, as in this country, his astuteness and tact have won him fame. Many times he undertook long journeys across the Continent in pursuit of notorious criminals.

During the time he has been at Scotland Yard Mr. Dew has been in charge of the leading investigations. His quiet, unassuming disposition secured him considerable popularity among his colleagues, and the intimation of his ensuing resignation had been received with universal regret.[32]

MR. WALTER DEW,
Ex-CHIEF INSPECTOR, METRO.

MR. WALTER DEW has just retired from the Criminal Investigation Department, New Scotland Yard, after nearly 29 years' strenuous and exciting service. He was born 47 years ago within a mile of the busy town of Northampton. When he was ten years old he came to London with his parents, and has practically lived in the Metropolis ever since. Being of a somewhat hestless [sic–restless] disposition, school became irksome to him, and at the early age of 13 he left and obtained a situation in a solicitor's office in the neighbourhood of Chancery Lane. Whilst so employed, Mr. Dew's duties frequently took him to the old Law Courts, at Westminster, where he was never tired of listening to the cases, and the experience thus gained was very useful to him in after years. Subsequently he came to take

32   *Lloyd's Weekly News*, 6 November 1910.

charge of this district as Detective Inspector at Bow Street.

Tiring of this somewhat monotonous work, after a year or so he obtained a situation as junior clerk at a famous seedsman's, but being fond of outdoor life, this soon palled upon him, and his next step was to obtain a situation on the L. and N.W. Rly., his father being one of the oldest and best known guards on that system. During the next four or five years he went through various grades, his great ambition being to become a "guard," but this was destined not to be, for just before he attained the age of 19 years he was advised to enter the Police Service.

For some reason or other, he had always stood in mortal dread of Policemen, and so it was with mixed feelings that he decided to make the attempt, never believing that he would succeed, because he was very slim and boyish-looking. To his surprise he passed the medical test, and after spending ten days at drill at Wellington Barracks, he was duly posted to Paddington Green Police Station, then in the X Division, on the 12th June, 1882. He was agreeably impressed with the reception he had from the then Chief, the late Supt. Foinett, of whom he speaks in high praise.[33]

He had not been many months at Paddington before he brought himself under notice by the various good captures he made, for which he was rewarded and commended by Judges and Magistrates. This apparently attracted the attention of the Detective Chief, the late Mr. Daniel Morgan, of whom Mr. Dew cannot speak highly enough, considering him the finest Detective he had ever known, and brimful of confidence. Soon after this Mr. Dew was chosen for plain clothes duty.

Many and varied were his duties after this, the young Officer being entrusted with important and intricate inquiries. In June, 1887, he was appointed a Detective and transferred to H, or Whitechapel Division, being stationed at Commercial Street. Here he spent a very exciting period of nearly two years, for besides effecting the arrest of many desperate criminals for highway robbery, coining, van robberies, burglaries, etc., and being many times assaulted, he was engaged throughout the whole of the "Jack-the-Ripper Murder" inquiries, and from his superiors he received high praise for his conduct of these cases.

Whitechapel and Spitalfields, however, were not at all to his liking, and so in December, 1888, he obtained a transfer to his old Division, then called F, and was for several years stationed at Kensington and Notting Hill. The cases he had in this district are far too numerous to deal with here, but

---

33   Superintendent Thomas Foinett (1835-1908). He joined the Metropolitan Police in 1856 and retired in 1887. (PRO, MEPO 21/18).

he effected many good captures. In the course of his duty, especially at Notting Dale, which was then known as "The Avernus of London," he was frequently assaulted, but being of a wiry nature, he never felt any serious effects from these attacks. Indeed, during the whole of his life in the Police, he has only been on the sick list for two or three weeks, from influenza, and similar minor complaints.

In December, 1889, he was promoted Sergeant. His good work brought him frequently under the notice of the Authorities, so that he was, in May, 1894, advanced to second class and transferred to Headquarters. Two years later he was advanced to first class, and in a little more than two years after this he was promoted to Detective Inspector and retained at "The Yard."

During this period he never had an idle moment, and one of his best captures was that of "Harry the Valet" for stealing the Dowager Duchess of Sutherland's jewels at the Gare du Nord, Paris. The thief got away with about £20,000 worth of property, and was subsequently arrested in a house within a short distance of her Grace's London residence, under most exciting circumstances.

In February, 1900, Mr. Dew was deputed to take charge of the T, Hammersmith, Division, which covers a huge area, extending to Staines. Space will not permit us to recount all his doings there, but he brought many clever swindlers and others to justice, including a notorious gang of coiners whom he and others arrested at Twickenham after a most desperate resistance. As a reward he was advanced to first class Inspector in July, 1903, and in October of the same year he was given charge of the E or Bow Street Division. Here he had many exciting experiences in arresting criminals of every type, and practically cleared the whole district of gaming houses, etc. He also brought to justice several "Theatrical Agency" swindlers and others, and earned the thanks of many deluded stage struck girls, as well as the thanks of the genuine theatrical agents.[34]

On November 1st, 1906, Mr. Dew was advanced to Chief Inspector, and again found himself at "The Yard," and at the outset was engaged in

---

34 One of the fraudulent theatrical agents arrested by Dew was William Cecil Watson, an elocutionist, who advertised stage work for people with no experience. He took their money but never found them any work. Watson was tried at the Old Bailey in 1906 and sentenced to eighteen months' hard labour. The same year Dew arrested Charles Henry Houghton and Hedley Howard for similar offences for which they were both sentenced to twelve months' hard labour. At the committal hearings their lawyer asked Dew, "Have you had much experience as to the way in which theatrical agencies are run?" Dew replied "No, but I have had a great deal of experience as to the way in which swindles are run." (*The Era*, 28 April 1906).

connection with the Royal Commission on the Metropolitan Police.[35] After this he was busily engaged in various parts of the country in connection with the larcenies of Government stores and many other cases too numerous to relate. He had a very trying time in investigating what was known as the "Salisbury Murder," which created a great sensation. He was also in charge of the "Druce" case, and arrested two of the female witnesses for perjury, etc. He also had many heavy cases of forgery to deal with, and at the beginning of this year he was engaged in the North of England in investigating the larcenies of Government cartridges.[36] He obtained convictions against various men for stealing these, and by his successful efforts has, it is said, put a stop to a pernicious system, which will save the country a great deal of money annually. For his action in this case he received high commendation from H.M. Army Council, and a very substantial reward. After this came the recent "Crippen" case, which put the coping stone to a brilliant Police career.

Mr. Dew has served under no less than five Chief Commissioners,[37] and has been commended and rewarded by the Commissioner, Judges, Magistrates and other high Authorities about 130 times, and in leaving the Service on pension received an "Exemplary" certificate, the highest certificate of conduct that any officer can obtain.

Mr. Dew is the first of his family to serve in the Police. He did not know a soul in it when he joined, and he thinks that this speaks well for the fact that any young officer of ability can, by perseverance, etc., succeed in the Metropolitan Police of which he speaks in the highest terms. He leaves his eldest son in the Force.

Mr. Dew has started in business as a "Confidential Enquiries" Agent, his offices being at his private house, 16, Allfarthing Lane, Wandsworth, S.W.[38]

THE TWELVE GREATEST DETECTIVES OF THE WORLD
THE TRUE STORY OF THEIR MOST FAMOUS CASES.

THIS WEEK–INSPECTOR DEW,
THE MAN WHO CAUGHT CRIPPEN.

---

35   Dew's name was not on the list of witnesses examined by the commission, but he was
      mentioned as having been present. (*The Royal Commission on the Duties of the Metropolitan
      Police*, vol. 2, p. 512).

36   There was a spate of such cases heard at the magistrates' courts and assizes at Newcastle and
      County Durham in January and February 1910. Dew and Sergeant Berrett worked together
      on the investigations.

37   Edmund Henderson, Charles Warren, James Monro, Edward Bradford and Edward Henry.

38   *Police Review and Parade Gossip*, 30 December 1910.

"IT is the finest profession in the world, and if I could start life all over again I would rather be a detective than anything else. My elder boy is a detective-sergeant at Scotland Yard now. That proves what I think of the profession."

Ex-Chief-Inspector Dew summed up his twenty-eight years' experience of Scotland Yard in those words, and no one listening to him could doubt for a moment his sincerity.

To-day he is one of the best known private enquiry agents in London, possessing a large clientele, and proving that even without the help of the official forces he is as good a detective as ever.

In appearance Mr Dew suggests the retired army officer rather than the detective. Imagine a man just above medium height, with a dark moustache, hair turning grey, a strong face tempered by a pair of kindly eyes, a clear-cut figure reminiscent of the barracks, and you have Mr Dew as he is to-day at the age of fifty-three. A major in mufti is as good a description as any. You will find many like him in the famous military clubs in West End London.

Began Life in a Solicitor's Office.

In his early days Mr Dew had visions of legal glory, and entered the office of a solicitor, where he picked up much valuable information that helped him greatly later on when he was placed in charge of important criminal cases. But eventually the "Force" had an attraction for him, because he resisted the blandishments of the solicitor's office and enlisted as an ordinary police constable at the age of nineteen.

It is the ambition of every young constable to exchange his uniform for plain clothes–in other words, to be promoted into the ranks of the detectives. Mr Dew achieved this in a few months. That showed the quality of the new recruit.

They were on the lookout in the early eighties for clever, shrewd, resourceful, and fearless young men who possessed the necessary initiative that makes the successful detective. Walter Dew was very soon in the "good books" of his superiors, and by his handling of several larceny cases he attracted flattering attention to himself. After that it was only a matter of time for the highest honours of his profession to come his way.

Hunting For "Jack the Ripper."

But the training he underwent was severe, for he was one of the small army of detectives which hunted in vain for the infamous "Jack the Ripper."

When that series of fiendish murders began Dew was stationed at Whitechapel. He was, of course, only an ordinary detective at the beck and call of his superiors, and it was as one of the rank and file that he joined in the chase. The police have their own theories as to the identity of "Jack the Ripper," but the fact remains that the murderer was never arrested, and to the general public it must remain a mystery for all time.

To Walter Dew, however, the Whitechapel murders brought promotion. He did all that was humanly possible, and as a special reward for his untiring services he was given the rank of detective-sergeant. Few men earned such a reward during a period when the whole of Great Britain was criticising the police for their failure. More than one reputation was sadly tarnished thereby, but Walter Dew's was enhanced.

When a detective reaches the rank of sergeant he knows that he is going to get a good chance to distinguish himself. He takes charge of certain cases, and even when only second in command has every opportunity for displaying his capabilities. If his responsibilities increase with promotion so do his privileges, and to the man who can think for himself the latter make all the difference in the world.

"Doesn't Look Like a Policeman."

During a period of nearly thirty years in the public service Dew handled hundreds of cases, from commonplace forgeries to sensational murders. He was never idle.

If a swell "mobsman" had to be shadowed the usual order was "Send Dew. He doesn't look like a policeman," and Dew went into fashionable houses, restaurants, and theatres. He mixed in society without the slightest difficulty for no one could suspect the faultlessly-dressed, military-looking man of being an emissary from Scotland Yard.[39] Certainly his appearance has helped him considerably.[40]

The case of Nicholson, the self-styled "Ornithologist Specialist," is practically forgotten, but it deserves to be remembered for more than one reason. It had its humorous side, too. Nicholson was finally outwitted by Dew, and the story is worth telling.

The swindler managed to extract thousands of pounds from the gullible public by means of "puzzles" which he advertised extensively. They took the shape of a certain number of letters out of which the guileless were to

39   When taking part in a raid on an illegal betting shop in Holborn in 1904 Dew was mistaken for a bookmaker and handed some betting slips and money by a man who entered the shop. (*The Globe*, 15 October 1904).

40   A more irreverent description of Dew appeared in the literary periodical *The Academy*. He visited their office in 1908 to say that Scotland Yard would not be taking any action against a publisher who had recently published a book that *The Academy* considered indecent. Dew, they reported, "dropped in on us like the gentle rain from heaven... He came like water and like wind he went." (*The Academy*, 10 October 1908).

evolve the names of birds. Alluring and valuable prizes were offered to the successful. Dew saw the advertisement and decided to enter, because it was on the face of it a swindle. Thus the jumble of letters "NVARE" obviously meant "raven," and the others were equally simple. The detective, however, instead of inserting the names of birds, took the liberty of filling in the names of animals, chiefly quadrupeds.

A few weeks later he received a letter from Nicholson which said– "The arbitrators have carefully considered your list, and have come to the conclusion that it is the best list of birds' names sent in!" Then followed a demand for a subscription to a bogus paper–the sole condition before "the valuable first prize" was awarded. Of course, the same letter had been sent to every competitor, and it equally followed that not a single list had been examined except for the purpose of copying the address. That was the end of the "Ornithologist Specialist," for he was convicted and sentenced.

The Duchess of Sutherland's Jewels.

The theft of the late Duchess of Sutherland's jewels–valued at £20,000– was a sensational affair. It took place at the Gare du Nord, the great Paris railway station. Scotland Yard was notified at once, and there it was agreed that one of the most expert jewel thieves had carried out the job. Dew was of opinion that "Harry the Valet" was the guilty person, for Harry was renowned for his neat work, and was a veritable king in his own particular line of crime.

In due course he came to London in order to lie low for a time, but Dew seldom lost sight of him, and "Harry the Valet," who was always on the lookout for detectives, did not suspect the quiet, gentlemanly individual, whom he must have seen at least once, of being on his track.

The thief was a dangerous person to tackle, but desperate criminals require desperate measures, and when Walter Dew decided to arrest his man he did not put kid gloves on. He simply went to the small flat in the Fulham Road, where the fellow lived, and without troubling about formalities, he burst open the door of the room where the wanted man was hiding, and without hesitating flung himself on his "quarry." The thief, however, was so astounded that he scarcely offered any resistance, and a life and death struggle was avoided. Dew had summed up his man, and his knowledge of human nature saved him much trouble.

Another criminal with whom Mr Dew had more than a passing acquaintance was Conrad Harms, a German-American forger of more than average ability. Harms forged a letter of credit in America, which he forwarded to Parr's Bank in Notting Hill via the London office of a well-known foreign bank. Here the letter of credit awaited Harms' arrival, and when he presented himself at

Parr's Bank the money–£1700–was paid without the slightest suspicion.

When the inevitable discovery of the fraud came Dew was sent for, and the only clue he was given was a Bank of England note for a hundred pounds. This had been paid to a Strand jeweller, who in an interview with the detective explained that it had been received by him in payment for a gold watch.

Luck on Dew's Side.

That was all, for the jeweller could only give a vague description of his customer. Meanwhile Conrad Harms had disappeared completely, and it must have struck Dew at the time that his chances of capturing him were remote.

But the luck was on the side of the detective. Conrad Harms, having paid a hundred pounds for a watch, expected it to keep good time, and when it refused to work he took it back to the jeweller in a passion, loudly complaining that he had been swindled.

"It will be ready to-morrow morning, sir," said the jeweller, politely. "If you will call then I will convince you that you will have no more trouble with the watch."

Harms gruffly promised to keep the appointment, unable to fathom the real meaning of the jeweller's words, and when he did return there was one other "customer" in the shop. A gentleman was examining a showcase, and for a few minutes he ignored the presence of the American, but once the gold watch was in the forger's pocket Dew acted, and another swindler eventually saw the inside of a prison.

Criminals Bear Witness to His Fairness.

One of Mr Dew's most charming characteristics is his fairness. Many criminals have borne witness to this. Whenever engaged upon a case he has never permitted his zeal to secure a conviction to tempt him into acting unfairly towards the accused, and one remarkable result is that he has never been threatened with "reprisals" by convicts or their friends. It has happened now and then that the famous detective has failed to convince a jury of the guilt of his prisoner, and even in cases such as this detective and accused have parted good friends.

The double trial of Mrs Haskell, of Salisbury, may be recalled in this connection. She was accused of the murder of her cripple son, and for many reasons the case excited tremendous interest throughout the country.

Inspector Dew was sent down specially to take charge of the police inquiry. He had a hard task, although there were plenty of persons to volunteer evidence. The prejudice against the accused woman was strong in numerous quarters, for the tragic death of the poor cripple had excited the public imagination. But Inspector Dew kept his head. He had his duty to do, which was to place on record all the evidence that the police could procure. It was no business of his to take sides, and, with his usual fairness, he did not. Mrs Haskell was tried twice, and the second trial ended in a verdict in her favour.

With her vindication came the parting between her and the detective, who had, as a duty, done his best and fairest to secure her conviction, but there was no ill-will on either side; indeed, the officer could sympathise with one who had undergone such a terrible ordeal as a trial for murder.

The Druce Case.

During the past nine years there have been two exhumations which have become historic, and it is something of a coincidence that Inspector Dew was present at both as the representative of the police. The first took place at Highgate Cemetery; the second in a house in Camden Town. One settled finally the question as to the ownership of vast estates and a ducal title; the other started a chase across the world that led to the capture of the author of one of the most cold-blooded murders in the long and terrible records of crime.

The Druce case raged furiously in the years 1907-8. A dukedom was claimed – that of Portland–by the son of a Baker Street tradesman, who declared that his father was the fifth Duke of Portland, who had assumed the name of Druce and turned tradesman because he wished to have two personalities–at Welbeck Abbey he was his Grace the Duke of Portland; at Baker Street he was Mr Druce, the owner of a furniture depository. This was what the claimant based his case on, and if he proved it he would gain the dukedom, because the fifth duke officially left no children, though "Thomas Druce" had a son. If Thomas Druce was the fifth duke his son was obviously entitled to inherit his eccentric father's title and property.

Claiming a title and estate is not a criminal offence, and the Druce case did not affect Scotland Yard, but the authorities there realised that a claimant, however honest he may be, is nearly always a magnet that attracts swindlers prepared to swear to anything if there is a chance of making money. For that and other reasons the head of the Criminal Investigation Department sent for Chief-Inspector Dew, and instructed him to keep an eye on the Druce case. In other words, he was given a watching brief.

The Missing Diary.

It was a period crammed with sensations. The claimant's witnesses backed him up loyally. One of them, Miss Robinson, the daughter of an ex-policeman, told the story of her early life, which had been passed in the service of the fifth Duke of Portland at Welbeck Abbey. She remembered incidents at the ducal residence, when the great ones of England visited the famous mansion.

The name of Charles Dickens was dragged in, and Miss Robinson swore that she had heard both the Duke and the novelist discuss the personality of "Thomas Druce," and that both admitted in her hearing that the Baker Street trader was the Duke himself. "Here was richness!" The mention of Charles Dickens recalled the spacious days of English literature, and at once it lifted the Druce case appreciably higher.

To crown all, Miss Robinson inserted an advertisement in several papers offering a reward of one hundred pounds for the recovery of her private diary which had been stolen, she said, to prevent her giving evidence in favour of the claimant. This supplied another melodramatic touch to the whole case. Amongst those who searched for the missing diary was Chief-Inspector Dew of Scotland Yard.

Meanwhile the affair began to be taken more seriously by the public, and when the claimant asked that his father's alleged grave at Highgate should be opened to see if the coffin actually contained a body the request was generally deemed to be a reasonable one.

The claimant declared that the funeral of "Thomas Druce" had been a bogus one, for his father, anxious to end his "Druce personality," had only pretended to die, and had in reality only retired to Welbeck Abbey after having had a coffin filled with lead and buried in Highgate Cemetery in the name of Thomas Druce. Thenceforward the Duke had ceased to use any other name, and when he did actually die, was buried at Welbeck as the fifth of his title.

"The coffin at Highgate does not contain a body," said the claimant in effect. "It is merely filled with lead. Open the coffin and you will prove my case. My father lies buried at Wellbeck, and on his coffin plate you will read his real name."

At first difficulties were created to prevent the exhumation. Naturally the claimant made the most of them, and the public which likes to give both sides fair play, began to suspect that the defendants were afraid to put the matter to the final test.

Public opinion veered round to Mr Druce, and as the proposed test was simple enough the newspapers advised the authorities to grant permission for the coffin to be opened. The Druce party gained their point, and the grave was ordered to be examined by the Home Secretary.

When the Coffin was Opened.

Mr Dew was there on behalf of the police, and, in all probability, he was the least excited of the numerous witnesses who attended. It was certainly an exciting moment when the coffin was hauled up and the lid was being prised open. What would it reveal? A Dukedom might change hands as a result of this exhumation. Did the coffin contain lead, or did it hold the body of a man who had attained a good age? The lid was lifted; all eyes were fixed on the coffin, and everyone gazed at the white, bearded face of Thomas Druce, the Baker Street tradesman. The Druce case was over!

It was over in the sense that the present holder of the Dukedom was left in undisturbed possession, but there was a sensational sequel that kept the Druce case in the papers for months afterwards.

Mr Dew arrested Miss Robinson on a charge of perjury, and she was committed for trial. Then the detective went after Robert Caldwell, another witness, who had sworn an affidavit, but he was an old man and he escaped prosecution when he was certified to be insane.

The principal charges against Miss Robinson turned on the diary which she declared she had lost. Mr Dew said that the diary had never existed, and that her offer of a hundred pounds reward for its recovery was a piece of sheer bluff. At the Old Bailey the prosecution proved their case, and Miss Robinson was convicted and sentenced.

One of these days the inner history of the Druce case will be written, and it should prove a fascinating romance. The claimant had several wealthy supporters, who subscribed lavishly in the hopes of sharing the spoils when he gained the rich dukedom. It is said that a certain insurance magnate invested twenty thousand pounds in the claim, and had the plaintiff won he would have made a profit of over two hundred thousand pounds!

The Arrest of Crippen.

Ask the average person who Walter Dew is, and he will answer, "The man who arrested Crippen." Some will cut down the answer to "Crippen Dew." Such is fame.

Until the early part of 1910 Chief-Inspector Dew's reputation was practically confined to police and criminal circles. The Druce case had brought him into prominence so far as the public were concerned, but they were not unduly excited, and continued to confound him with Inspector Drew, because of the similarity of their names.[41] But the Crippen affair altered all that, and at one bound Chief Inspector Dew, of Scotland Yard, became famous the world over.

With the possible exception of the recent "Brides in the Bath" case no murder has excited more interest than that of Belle Elmore, the music hall artiste, by Crippen, the self-styled doctor from America. There was

---

41   Detective Inspector Edward Drew (b. 1859) joined the Metropolitan Police in 1881 and retired in 1908. Like Dew, he was promoted to the rank of chief inspector in 1906. At some time during his service he had been stabbed in his right hand. (PRO, MEPO 21/37).

something hauntingly sinister in the crime, which had taken place in the midst of a densely-populated London suburb, and the manner of its discovery intensified the over-wrought feelings of the public.

The personality of the victim was another important factor. Belle Elmore was the sort of girl who is always smiling, in good luck or in bad. She was happy-go-lucky, careless, generous to a fault, quick-tempered, but always ready to forgive and forget. All who knew her liked her. Had it been otherwise it is safe to say that her fate would never have become known.

It is nearly six years now since a small party of well-known music hall artistes called at Scotland Yard, and asked to see someone in authority. They were taken to Mr Frank Froest, the chief of the C.I.D., and he passed them on to Chief-Inspector Dew. The deputation asked Mr Dew to have inquiries made in America concerning the death of their friend Belle Elmore. They produced a copy of a theatrical newspaper containing a brief notice of her death.

"We have written asking for particulars," said a lady in the party, "but we can get no answer. Perhaps they will take Scotland Yard more seriously."

Mr Dew asked several questions, and was given a brief account of the dead woman's career. He promised to do what he could, and the deputation left him.

There was nothing about the inquiry at this period to warrant the assumption that it was destined to hold the attention of two continents. Mr Dew cabled several questions to the police of the American town where Belle Elmore was supposed to have died. When he was informed that no such person had died or had been buried there he realised that things were beginning to look serious.

"Dr" Crippen, the husband of the unfortunate woman, was living in London, and besides the house in Hilldrop Crescent, Camden Town, he had offices in a more central position in London. Here Mr Dew paid him a visit, and the bereaved widower answered all questions with apparent frankness. He had a reply for every question, and as there was as yet only suspicion against Crippen he could not be arrested.

In English law no man can be convicted of murder unless the body of his victim is found. In the old days innocent men have been hanged for murder, and afterwards their supposed victims have turned up alive and well. Nowadays such a tragic mistake is impossible.

The House in Hilldrop Crescent.

The police, under Chief-Inspector Dew, worked assiduously, and the papers helped considerably. Suddenly Crippen bolted. From the first he had feared the quiet-mannered detective who was unobtrusively yet relentlessly getting nearer and nearer the solution of the terrible problem. When Crippen disappeared Dew was convinced that Belle Elmore had been murdered in London and that her body was hidden.

A thorough investigation of the house in Hilldrop Crescent followed as a matter of course. Mr Dew was in charge of the search party, and he went over the ground with a view to selecting a spot where the body was likely to be concealed and ordering it to be excavated. Eventually he settled upon a gloomy room in the basement, half-kitchen, half-cellar, and here the police dug until they came upon the remains of Crippen's wife.

The moment the result of the excavation was announced a howl of indignation went up that Crippen had been allowed to escape. The police were severely blamed for not having arrested the murderer when suspicion was first directed against him, but quite apart from this suggestion that the liberty of the person should be subject to the whim of any police officer, the critics were wrong in supposing that Crippen had escaped. He had merely taken steps to delay his arrest, for in modern times it is practically impossible for a "wanted" man to disappear. His only way of escape is by the gate of suicide, but the most callous of murderers is always terribly afraid of death, and Crippen was no exception to the rule.

The Chase Across the Atlantic.

The chase was not so long as many imagined, though it was a severe strain on one's patience to open the paper morning after morning and fail to read of the miscreant's capture. Everyone was hot with anger against the criminal, and it was this indignation and fierce desire for revenge that made the waiting seem so long to a public in a state of nerves.

But the great invention of wireless telegraphy came to the rescue, and for the first time Signor Marconi's genius aided in the capture of a notorious criminal.

Crippen, after a brief Continental trip, left England on the s.s. Montrose, bound for Canada. He was disguised as a clergyman,[42] the sort of disguise that invariably attracts attention, and is, therefore, a bad one. But Crippen moved about the ship freely enough, and he was a regular attendant at the concerts which passengers find a welcome antidote to the monotony of a long sea voyage. It was remarked by more than one passenger that the "clergyman" had been particularly amused by one song, the first verse of

---

42   He wasn't, but on 13 July in London Detective Sergeant Francis Barclay of the Thames Division told an officer on the *Montrose* that Crippen might be disguised as a clergyman. (PRO, MEPO 3/198).

which was–

"Then we all walked into the shop
To shelter from the rain.
We looked at a plate of cakes;
Then we all walked out again."[43]

Of course, everyone on board the ship had heard of the Belle Elmore case, and it was the principal topic of conversation. Crippen must often have sat and listened to the passengers denouncing the murderer. How he managed to keep his countenance is a marvel; but one evening suspicion was aroused against him on the ship.

Captain Kendall, the master of the boat, was privately informed of these suspicions, and after a brief survey he ran the risk of communicating with land by means of wireless telegraphy. The message was to the effect that the captain believed he had "Dr" Crippen on board, and when it was handed

---

43   The song had been written by Harry Castling who claimed that Crippen had once approached him in a pub on the Westminster Bridge Road and asked him to write a song for Belle Elmore, which he did for a guinea. Castling said the song referred to here "was a very popular one and told of some gay young sparks who were out on the spree and sought shelter in several shops. For instance, seeing a milk shop with a sign displayed "Families supplied," they all walked in and demanded a family apiece. And so on.

This song was put on by an artiste on the ship and Crippen was one of the audience. He listened with a smile until the singer told of the visit to an ice cream shop as follows:–

We all walked into the shop,
To shelter from the rain,
We all had a lick at the raspberry stick,
Then we all walked out again.

When he heard that verse, Crippen lay back in his chair and roared so loudly that he revealed his fatal gold teeth. It was the one clue wanted." (*ETWN*, 13 January 1934). Captain Kendall claimed he told Crippen the following story which revealed the tell-tale teeth: "A certain provision merchant in a very big way was commissioned to supply a customer with a hundredweight of Limburger cheese. He endeavoured to get the railway company to deliver it, but each company refused to have anything to do with it. Limburger cheese is not a favourite with most people.

The grocer was in despair, because this meant that he would lose good business, so he went to an undertaker, induced him to put the Limburger cheese in a coffin, and to send it to its destination at a shilling a mile.

The grocer accompanied the coffin, dressed in deep mourning. At each of the stations at which the train stopped he strolled along the platform, looking the picture of woe. His object was to keep an eye on the old guard. The latter might easily throw the coffin containing the Limburger out of the window.

At each station the guard eyed the grocer without a word, but at the last station but one he called him over to him, and thus addressed him–

'If it's your relative, sir, you need not worry. Go back to your carriage, and sit there in peace. He ain't in no trance, sir; he's dead all right.'" (*The Sunday Post*, 13 April 1924).

to Chief-Inspector Dew he decided that Captain Kendall must be right. The Montrose was not a very fast boat, and after a study of the sailings the detective found a faster ship. On it he made the trip to Canada, and there he was waiting for Crippen when the Montrose berthed at Father Point.

A Dramatic Meeting.

The meeting between the notorious murderer and the famous detective must have been a most dramatic one, though Mr Dew is too unassuming to be fond of the sensational. Crippen realised the moment he set eyes on him that his doom was sealed.

It was remarked that Crippen tugged uneasily at his collar when he came face to face with the man from Scotland Yard. Perhaps he seemed to feel the rope round his neck. And yet when on his trial at the Old Bailey it was the subject of general comment that Crippen always looked out for the detective, and that he never settled down until he had received recognition, however curt, from him. Probably the hardened criminal had been touched by the officer's kindly attitude towards him on the voyage back to England. Mr Dew was, perhaps, the only person who looked upon him as a human being, and he treated him accordingly, though never forgetting that the scoundrel had committed a murder almost without parallel in its treacherous cruelty. Knowing that Crippen's punishment was coming Chief-Inspector Dew did not add to the horror of his position by broaching the subject of the poor, trusting woman whom he had done to death.

Mr Dew's Retirement from Scotland Yard.

The Crippen case over, Mr Dew announced his retirement from Scotland Yard. He had in fact decided to retire about the time when he was asked to inquire into Belle Elmore's death. When the case broadened out into one of the greatest of modern crimes he resolved to postpone his resignation until "Dr" Crippen had paid the penalty.

Because his retirement coincided with the Crippen affair it was rumoured that the great detective's decision had been caused by the worry and anxiety he had experienced whilst tracking down his man, but as a matter of fact it had nothing whatever to do with it. Having passed more than two-thirds of his life in the service of Scotland Yard and having been entitled to a pension for over three years he felt that he had earned a change. That is why he turned private detective, and he carried with him into retirement the best wishes of his comrades at "the Yard," for Walter Dew can be said to have never made an enemy, and, in the case of a successful detective, this is something of which he can be justly proud.

It has been mentioned that Mr Dew's elder son is following in his father's footsteps. His only other son, Stanley Dew, gave his life for his country at Givenchy last May. A bright, promising lad, he enlisted immediately war broke out, and his death was a heavy blow to his father.[44]

CRIPPEN WAS SUCH A NICE MAN-
APART FROM HIS ONE MURDER

"Daily Express" Special Correspondent.

WORTHING, Wednesday.

MR. WALTER DEW, retired Londoner, of The Wee Hoose, Beaumont-road, here, a white-haired old man who spends his days in his garden, was suddenly confronted yesterday by his former self of twenty-four years ago.

He saw a photograph in the "Daily Express" series, "These Exciting Years," which showed two men, one of them famous, the other infamous.

Chief Inspector Dew, of Scotland-yard, was leading Crippen, his prisoner, ashore after a man-hunt across the Atlantic which thrilled the world.

To-day, at The Wee Hoose, old Mr. Dew, the garden lover, talked about Chief Inspector Walter Dew, the detective who retired nearly a quarter of a century ago.

IDEAL PRISONER

"The 'Daily Express' picture set me thinking about Crippen," Mr. Dew said to me. "He gave me the greatest murder case of my career as a detective.

"Apart from the murder which he committed, I should describe Crippen as a kind-hearted, considerate little man. He was the ideal prisoner.

"His real anxiety all the time was not so much for himself, but for Miss Le Neve, who had accompanied him disguised as a boy.

"Crippen was a glutton for reading during the voyage home. He was locked in a state room on the Megantic. I used to bring him books from the ship's library. He always thanked me profusely. It seems strange, looking back on events, to think that this mild, benevolent-looking man was a fiend incarnate.

SUPREME MOMENTS

"The Crippen case, a strange medley of cold, calculated murder and great love and devotion, provided me with two of the most supreme moments of a detective's career.

"The first was when I dug into the cellar floor of Crippen's house in

---

44   *The Saturday Post*, 29 January 1916. Dew had oil paintings of Stanley and his father displayed at the Wee Hoose. (*Worthing and District Review*, January 1948).

Holloway and found Mrs. Crippen's remains–a total justification of my theory, based on the slightest of clues, that Crippen had murdered his wife.

"The second supreme moment was when I boarded the ship in the St. Lawrence, disguised as a pilot, and hailed the man I had hunted with the words, 'Good morning, Dr. Crippen.'

"I shall never forget how Crippen turned a greenish hue with surprise, and then collecting himself, replied, 'Good morning, Inspector Dew.'

"In my younger days as a detective I did C.I.D. work on a series of crimes much more terrible than the Crippen case. These were the unsolved murders of 'Jack the Ripper.'

"Compared with 'Jack the Ripper,' Crippen was an angel!"[45]

WHEN CRIPPEN WAS ARRESTED.

28 YEARS AGO THIS WEEK.

EX-SCOTLAND YARD INSPECTOR RECALLS EXCITING CHASE.

Twenty-eight years ago this week, perspiring in the heat of a Canadian summer, was a man who had just effected the most sensational criminal capture of the century.

He was Chief-Inspector Walter Dew, of Scotland Yard, who is now living in retirement at Worthing–at The Wee Hoose, 10, Beaumont-road,–and in talking this week to a *Worthing Gazette* representative Mr. Dew let his mind go back to that exciting summer of 1910 when he raced to Quebec to intercept Dr. Hawley Harvey Crippen, the murderer of his wife, Belle Elmore, before he could make his escape on Canadian soil.

"Twenty-eight years ago to-day," said Mr. Dew, "Crippen was already safe inside the gaol on the Heights of Abraham. As for myself, I was simply sweltering in the hot and humid atmosphere of the city.

"Much of my time was spent evading reporters and cameramen–who knew all about my arrival in spite of our efforts to keep it secret, and who frequently became personal when I did not give them a statement–visiting Crippen in gaol (he was continually asking for new books to read), and making arrangements for the return to England.

"As it happened, Crippen and his companion, Miss Le Neve, showed no desire to postpone our departure, and waived their extradition rights, which enabled us to make the return journey after being only three weeks in Canada.

"I had landed on July 29th by the liner 'Laurentic,' arriving two days before the 'Montrose,' which was already well out in the Atlantic when we first suspected that Crippen was aboard, but which was a much slower vessel than the mail-steamer 'Laurentic'."

On Sunday, July 31st, Inspector Dew, disguised as a pilot-officer, went on board the "Montrose' from a pilot vessel off Father Point, and, immediately recognising the murderer, made the arrest.

"Old Crippen took it quite well," he said. He was always a bit of a philosopher, though he could not have helped being astounded to see me on board the boat. . . . He was quite a likeable chap in his way."

Then followed the days of waiting while the formalities were gone into, until finally, on August 20th, the "Megantic" left Quebec with captor and captives on board, bound for the Old Bailey and the final episodes in the drama which is fully described by Inspector Dew in his recent book, "I Caught Crippen."

IN MEMORY OF THE VICTIM.

Worthing has another link to the Crippen case in addition to Mr. Dew's residence here.

The memorial stone which was placed over the remains of Mrs. Crippen–professionally known as Belle Elmore–in St. Pancras Cemetery was executed and erected by the late Councillor Francis Tate, the father of Mr. Francis Tate who now carries on the monumental mason's works in North-street.

It took the form of a headstone in Greek statuary marble, with a heavily moulded hood and a deeply sunk panel from which a Latin cross and bases stood out in high relief; and upon this was the simple inscription:

"In Memoriam, Cora Crippen (Belle Elmore), who passed away 1st Feb., 1910. Rest in peace."[46]

DEW, Walter. Author and Retired Chief Inspector, C.I.D. s. of Walter Dew Esq. Formerly Chief Inspector, Criminal Investigation Dept., New Scotland Yard. Queen Victoria Police Jubilee Medal, 1887, clasp, 1897; King Edward VII Coronation Medal. Is famous for the capture of Dr. Crippen in Canada (1910), for murder of his wife, Belle Elmore. *Author of* "I Caught Crippen; Memoirs of Ex-Chief Inspector Walter Dew, New Scotland Yard."– The Wee Hoose, 10, Beaumont Rd., Worthing.[47]

46   *Worthing Gazette*, 10 August 1938. Cora was buried in grave number 143 RC.7.
47   *Who's Who in Worthing and District 1938-1940*, p. 55.

MR. WALTER DEW

Mr. Walter Dew, formerly Chief Inspector, C.I.D., at Scotland Yard, died at Worthing yesterday at the age of 84.

The climax of his career was when, working on the slightest clues, he concluded that Dr. Crippen had murdered his wife, the music-hall artist Belle Elmore, and found the remains under the cellar floor of Crippen's house in Hilldrop Crescent, Holloway. His subsequent arrest of the disguised Crippen and his mistress on board ship in the mouth of the St. Lawrence River, which Dew carried out in his disguise as a pilot with the words: "Good morning, Dr. Crippen," was the first arrest of a criminal in which wireless telegraphy was used. When he had completed his last and most famous case Dew retired in 1910 to Worthing and published his reminiscences in 1938 under the title, "I caught Crippen."[48]

WALTER DEW, EX-AIDE OF SCOTLAND YARD, 84

LONDON, Dec. 16 (UP)–Walter Dew, retired chief inspector of Scotland Yard, who won fame for his 3,000-mile successful pursuit of one of England's most famous killers, Dr. Hawley Harvey Crippen, nearly forty years ago, died today. His age was 84.

Dr. Crippen poisoned his wife in 1910 and buried her body under the cellar of their house in London. He fled toward Canada aboard the liner Montrose with his mistress, Ethel Le Neve, who was disguised as a boy.

The master of the Montrose saw through Miss Le Neve's disguise and radioed Scotland Yard–believed to be the first radio message ever used in a man-hunt.

Mr. Dew boarded the liner Laurentic, which crossed the Atlantic at full speed while the Montrose slowed its pace. The liners came abreast near the Canadian shore and Mr. Dew boarded the Montrose, disguised as a pilot.

The greeting which he offered has become famous in criminology: "Good morning, Dr. Crippen."

He was one of the last links in Scotland Yard's search for the infamous Jack the Ripper, nearly sixty years ago. But in this manhunt he was foiled, never having seen the elusive Ripper. A patrolman had seen him racing away from the mutilated body of a woman, his green cloak flapping in the London fog. This was the only clue.[49]

---

48 *The Times*, 17 December 1947.
49 *The New York Times*, 17 December 1947.

"I CAUGHT CRIPPEN"

Detective Dies In Worthing

The death of Walter Dew, former Chief Inspector of the C.I.D. at Scotland Yard, who died at his home, 10, Beaumont-road, Worthing, yesterday, at the age of 84, recalls vividly his greatest and last triumph in the field of crime detection–the arrest of Dr. Crippen for wife murder in 1910, after a chase across the Atlantic.

In his book, "I Caught Crippen," published in 1938, the late Chief Inspector Dew emphasised the criminal's cleverness.

Chief Inspector Dew led the hunt and working on the first wireless message ever used to catch a criminal, from the Captain of the *Montrose*, pursued the doctor to Canada.

Arriving at Quebec before the *Montrose* he patiently waited the ship's arrival and then went aboard dressed as pilot and arrested the disguised Crippen, who surrendered calmly after greeting the Inspector.

Crippen was later sentenced to death at the trial which commenced on October 10th, 1910, at the Central Criminal Court, by Judge Lord Alverstone.

HIS CAREER

The late Chief Inspector Dew joined the Metropolitan Police at the age of nineteen, and was stationed at Paddington Green Police Station for the first three years of his career. He retired in 1910 shortly after the Crippen case and then came to live in Worthing.

The funeral service will take place on Friday at Durrington Chapel, and his remains are afterwards to be buried in the cemetery.

The Rev. B.C. Mowll will officiate.[50]

HE ARRESTED CRIPPEN

Mr Walter Dew dies

Ex-Chief Inspector Walter Dew, of Scotland Yard, the man who arrested Crippen, died at his home, 10, Beaumont-road, Worthing, on Tuesday. He was 84.

Although widely known for his writings on crime–he was the author of the book, *I Caught Crippen* and several articles–he seldom read detective

---

50   *Worthing Gazette*, 17 December 1947. Dew was buried in the same plot as his step-daughter Iris (plot 15-5-46). She had died on 10 February 1946. The funeral was attended by Dew's widow Florence, his daughters Ethel and Dorothy, his grandson Noel, representatives from Scotland Yard and the local police. (email from Kathleen Arthur to author, 28 August 2005).

stories, saying he had seen too much of the real thing.[51]

He retired from the police force in 1910, the year he brought Crippen to trial, and came to Worthing with his wife in 1928.[52]

Here, in his compact little bungalow, The Wee Hoose, he devoted himself to his hobby of gardening. About a year ago he became ill and was nursed by Mrs Dew until his death.

Mr Dew joined the Metropolitan Police in 1882 when he was 19. Then, the pay for a uniformed constable was 24s. a week, but he soon attracted the attention of his superiors and became a permanent member of the C.I.D. in 1887.

He investigated the "Jack the Ripper" terror that gripped Whitechapel during the following year, but the Crippen case was the culmination of his career. In after years, Mr Dew would tell how his Atlantic chase finished in Canada, when he boarded the ship on which Crippen was making his escape and confronted him.

"Even though I believed him to be a murderer, and a brutal murderer at that," he wrote many years later, "it was impossible at that moment not to feel for him a pang of pity. He had been caught on the threshold of freedom. Only 12 hours more and he would have been safely at Quebec."[53]

The funeral takes place at Durrington this afternoon (Friday).[54]

51   Dew described crime fiction as "tosh, nothing like the real thing." (*Worthing and District Review*, January 1948). His former colleague Frank Froest might have disagreed, having written several such books in his retirement.

52   Dew's first wife Kate died on 12 July 1927 in Croydon. He married Florence Idle (née Beadle), on 10 December 1928. They were both recorded as living at the Wee Hoose at the time of the marriage. After the death of Kate Dew, Walter fell out with his daughter Ethel and they did not speak again until 1931, when she visited him in Worthing with her son Noel. Ethel told Noel the woman living with Dew was his housekeeper, Mrs. Idle. Before the visit Dew sent Ethel a box of roses and sweet peas from his garden.

      Around 1946 Florence fell ill and had to spend a couple of weeks in hospital. Ethel went to Worthing to look after her father and was surprised when shopkeepers asked her how "Mrs. Dew" was. Dew confessed that he had married Florence without telling the family because his youngest daughter Dorothy would not have approved. (email Kathleen Arthur to author, 28 August 2005).

53   A quote from *ICC*, p. 44.

54   *The Worthing Herald*, 19 December 1947.

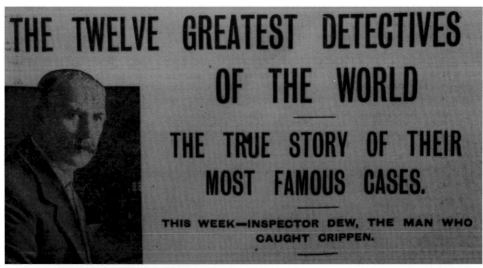

THE TWELVE GREATEST DETECTIVES
OF THE WORLD

THE TRUE STORY OF THEIR MOST FAMOUS CASES.

THIS WEEK—INSPECTOR DEW, THE MAN WHO CAUGHT CRIPPEN.

The Wee Hoose, now renamed "Dew Cottage."
(Lindsay Siviter)

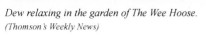

Dew relaxing in the garden of The Wee Hoose.
(Thomson's Weekly News)

The murder of P.C. Gutteridge in 1927.
(The National Archives)

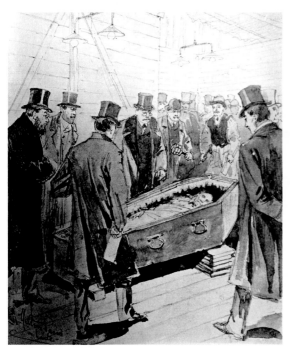

The exhumation of Thomas Druce in 1908.
(The Sketch)

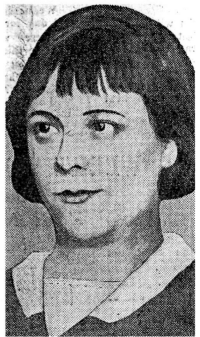

Constance Hind,
one of the Soho murder victims.
(Thomson's Weekly News)

Actor John Arnatt portraying Dew in the 1962 film Dr. Crippen.
(Author's collection)

BIBLIOGRAPHY

Begg, Paul, Fido, Martin, Skinner, Keith, *The Complete Jack the Ripper A to Z* (London: John Blake Publishing Ltd., 2010).

Berrett, James, *When I Was at Scotland Yard* (London: Sampson Low, Marston & Co. Ltd., 1932).

Bishop, Cecil, *From Information Received* (London: Hutchinson & Co., 1932).

Bloom, Ursula, *The Girl Who Loved Crippen* (London: Hutchinson & Co., 1955).

Browne, Douglas G. & Tullett, E.V., *Bernard Spilsbury His Life and Cases* (London: George G. Harrap & Co. Ltd., 1951).

Connell, Nicholas, *Walter Dew: the Man Who Caught Crippen* (Stroud: Sutton Publishing, 2006).

Connell, Nicholas, *Doctor Crippen: The Infamous London Cellar Murder of 1910* (Stroud: Amberley Publishing, 2014).

Cullen, Tom, *Crippen: The Mild Murderer* (London: The Bodley Head, 1977).

Dew, Walter, *I Caught Crippen* (London & Glasgow: Blackie & Son Ltd., 1938).

Dilnot, George, *Great Detectives and Their Methods* (London: Geoffrey Bles, 1927).

Eatwell, Piu Marie, *The Dead Duke, His Secret Wife and the Missing Corpse* (London: Head of Zeus, 2015).

Evans, Stewart P., Skinner, Keith, *The Ultimate Jack the Ripper Sourcebook* (London: Constable & Robinson, 2000).

Goodman, Jonathan, *The Crippen File* (London: Allison & Busby Ltd.,1985).

Gower, Henry Leveson, *Off and On the Field* (London: Stanley Paul & Co. Ltd., 1953).

Grant, Bernard, *To the Four Corners*, (London: Hutchinson & Co., 1933).

Hamilton, Duncan, *The Unreliable Life of Harry the Valet* (London: Century, 2011).

Humphreys, Travers, *Criminal Days* (London: Hodder and Stoughton Ltd., 1946).

Humphreys, Travers, *A Book of Trials* (London: William Heinemann Ltd., 1953).

Macnaghten, Melville, *Days of My Years* (London: Edward Arnold, 1914).

McKenzie, F.A., *The Mystery of The Daily Mail* 1896-1921 (London: Associated Newspapers Ltd., 1921).

The Newspaper Press Directory (London: Mitchell & Co. Ltd., 1935).

Oxford Dictionary of National Biography (Oxford: Oxford University Press).

Royal Commission on the Duties of the Metropolitan Police, 1906 (London: HMSO, 1908).

Smith, David James, *Supper With the Crippens* (London: Orion, 2005).

Wightwick, Dudley (ed.), *Who's Who in Worthing and District 1938-1940* (Worthing: Ludovic Grant & Co. Ltd., 1938).

Yates, Dornford, *As Berry and I Were Saying* (London: Ward, Lock & Co. Ltd., 1952).

Young, Filson (ed.), *The Trial of Hawley Harvey Crippen* (Edinburgh and London: William Hodge & Co. Ltd., 1920).

INDEX